From The Women's Press Ltd
124 Shoreditch High Street, London E1

The Women's Press is a feminist publishing house. We aim to publish books by women which reflect the goals of the women's liberation movement, which are stimulating, well produced and always readable.

Anthologies published by The Women's Press include *No Turning Back*: Writings from the Women's Liberation Movement 1975-80; *Learning to Lose*: Sexism and Education; and *Why Children*?

We would welcome suggestions for future collections of writings from the women's movement. Please send editorial suggestions to The Women's Press, 124 Shoreditch High Street, London E1 6JE, from which our complete catalogue can also be obtained. Send SAE.

SCARLET FRIEDMAN
AND ELIZABETH SARAH
EDITORS

On the Problem of Men

Two Feminist Conferences

The Women's Press

First published by The Women's Press Limited 1982
A member of the Namara Group
124 Shoreditch High Street, London E1 6JE

British Library Cataloguing in Publication Data

On the problem of men.
1. Feminists – Congresses
2. Interpersonal relations – Congresses
3. Men – Congresses
I. Friedman, Scarlet II. Sarah, Elizabeth
305. 4'2 (expanded) HQ1106

ISBN 0-7043-3887-4

Typeset by Red Lion Setters, London WC1
Printed in Great Britain by
King's English Bookprinters Limited
Leeds, Yorkshire

Contents

ACKNOWLEDGEMENTS

We would like first to thank the women who were involved in organising the conferences for which the papers in this collection were written.

Our thanks to all the women who engaged in the Summer School discussions, and to those in the Women's Liberation Movement who have debated with us and shared in the development of feminist ideas and practice. To the women of the WRRC Summer School Collective who made it possible – Sheila Allen, Liane Aukin, Gail Chester, Julia Dick, Scarlet Friedman, Eva Gamarnikov, Hilary Graham, Judy Hale, Jalna Hanmer, Sheila Jeffreys, Elizabeth Lebas, Diana Leonard, Sylvia Mann, Audrey Middleton, Renate Prince, Helen Roberts, Hilary Rose, Dale Spender, Jo Sutton, Margaret Versluysen – our special thanks.

The one-day conference on The Women's Liberation Movement and Men was a much smaller venture, but nevertheless required a lot of work. Thanks to all the participants – for their written and their verbal contributions – and to the facilitators who took registrations, provided refreshments, cleaned up afterwards . . . Above all thanks are due to Jan Bradshaw and Dale Spender, without whose sustained efforts the day would never have taken place.

It was hoped from the beginning that the papers would be published. Thanks to the women of the WRRC Publications Collective who prepared the pieces for publication – Renate Duelli-Klein, Diana Leonard, Elizabeth Sarah and Dale Spender; to the women of the The Women's Press for publishing them, and sharing the commitment of all concerned that the papers of two crucial feminist gatherings be made available to a wider audience of women; and finally to Jo and Jane for their patience and their love.

The editors acknowledge with thanks

Random House, New York, for permission to quote from *Feminist Revolution* by The Redstockings, 1978;

Diana Press, California, for permission to quote from *Womenslaughter* by Pat Parker, 1978;

Off Our Backs, Washington DC, for permission to quote from the article by Martha Thompson published in December 1979;

The Morning Star, London, for permission to quote from Vic Allen's article published in November 1979;

and Christine Delphy for permission to quote from her article in *Questions Féministes* in November 1977.

PREFACE

In this collection of papers men are put under the microscope. Their power, their privileges and their rights in a man-made world are dissected and examined – and the problems diagnosed.

The problems are divided into two sections. In the first, the focus is upon key patriarchal institutions which confine and control women. The questions these pose for feminist theory and practice are analysed.

The second section takes feminist political activity as its starting point. Feminists address the difficulties they face in dealing with men and boys. The problem of men's resistance to the transformation of male supremacy, and of their attempts to undermine the autonomy of the Women's Liberation Movement, is explored.

These critical exchanges on the problem of men took place at two conferences organised by the Women's Research and Resources Centre. 'Heterosexuality, Couples and Parenthood' formed one of the central themes at the Feminist Summer School in Bradford, September 1979; and 'The Women's Liberation Movement and Men' was a one-day conference in London, March 1980. Each set of conference papers provides the context for the other, and the issues which emerge can best be understood when viewed from both angles. In bringing the two sets of papers together, we hope to provide in this book a valuable addition to feminist debates.

SCARLET FRIEDMAN AND ELIZABETH SARAH

FOREWORD

The papers brought together in this collection are part of a continuing discussion within the Women's Liberation Movement: the issues of 'men' and 'heterosexuality' confront our feminist practice daily.

Because we all inhabit a world in which male power and institutionalised heterosexuality (and also racism and classism) impinge on our lives in one way or another, whether we choose to live as lesbian, celibate or heterosexual, the WRRC Publication's Collective thinks that it is important that these papers are available to as many women as possible.

Originally intended as contributions to our self-publishing activities which have been ongoing since 1977, the present WRRC Publication's Collective welcomes the opportunity of publishing the conference papers with the Women's Press.

Renate Duelli-Klein, Diana Leonard, Elizabeth Sarah, Dale Spender

Part One
Heterosexuality, Couples and Parenthood

Edited by Scarlet Friedman

SCARLET FRIEDMAN

Introduction

The political significance of what might appear to be the most individual and private part of interpersonal activity – sexual relationships – has been brought to light through the women's liberation movement. For over a decade feminists have discussed, written, shared and argued their views, and it has become clear that understanding the power invested in heterosexuality is essential to the analysis of the position of women in patriarchal society. Feminist research has revealed many of the misogynist myths and practices which promote the sexual subordination of women to men, and which deny women's attempts to achieve equality.

The family, too, has been recognised in the women's liberation movement to be a social institution which confines women, denies them opportunity for independence; while at the same time it holds women responsible for 'successful family life'. The behaviour of husbands and children, and the relations between them, are seen to be the woman's domain, particularly when they go wrong. Self-sacrifice is the rule of thumb in her repair manual.

The opportunity for women to spend four days together exploring these ideas was a rare one. Family responsibilities, and female types of employment, do not encourage and are unlikely even to allow women such possibilities for intellectual and political exchange. Despite these difficulties over 250 women joined in the debates of the WRRC Summer School in Bradford in September 1979. 'Heterosexuality, Couples and Parenthood' was one of the several themes which ran throughout the School.

The length of time we had enabled us to begin to analyse the links between heterosexuality, couples and parenthood rather than view them as separate aspects of women's lives. The problems associated with each gradually merged into one – the problem of men. So, too, in this collection of the papers we discussed, it is the total picture that emerges which is more revealing than any individual piece.

The emphasis in the papers and in the discussions which followed was placed upon developing our understanding of *how* male domination works in oppressing us. This meant that we limited ourselves to analysing some of the key features of patriarchy as they bear upon women's lives. Topics of interest to us all, such as lesbian sexuality, communal living, alternative forms of child care and other ways and means of surviving under patriarchy and creating change, had therefore to be excluded, except as they arose in the discussions. Although we regretted not having an even longer time together, so that we could explore alternatives for survival and change, the division turned out to be a very useful one. It helped us to clarify the differences between the source of our oppression and the frustration we may sometimes feel in fighting alongside other women for change.

Our experience of the Summer School was a very exciting and rewarding one. Ideas were sparked off by the initial presentations, and the discussions which followed encouraged us to develop our politics. We were asked by other women at the school, and by many others who were unable to attend, to share some of our experience of those four days. One way to do this was to publish this set of papers. Each of the women presenting the sessions on the theme agreed to have her work included. In some cases the papers are as originally presented; in others they have been revised in light of the discussion which followed.

SCARLET FRIEDMAN

Heterosexuality, Couples and Parenthood: a 'Natural' Cycle?

The present women's liberation movement has created, amongst other things, a wealth of literature documenting the experience of women and the conditions of oppression in which we live, and die. In our descriptions of women's lives, as well as in our analyses of our oppression, we employ concepts which have been derived from established theoretical frameworks, or views of the world. Whether we intend to imply that we agree with these theories or not, the terms we use often reflect assumptions which are integral to one or other of these views; in turn our own thinking is influenced and restricted when we employ these assumptions. Further, we frequently use a range of concepts, deriving from different theoretical frameworks, which may be incompatible with each other. This problem is, of course, not restricted to the work of feminists, but, as in other theorizing, the result is apt to be confusion rather than clarity. Whilst disagreement with part of a theoretical framework does not imply that all of the other concepts and assumptions it rests upon are of no use to us in developing our own theory, the concepts that we do use which are based in other theories need to be recognised for those assumptions which they do or do not imply.

Heterosexuality, couples and parenthood, for example, are frequently assumed to be natural, and further to reflect some kind of natural progression. In our own experience it seems somehow obvious that one thing tends to lead to another. Concepts such as the complementarity of men and women, and the mutual interest they have in rearing their children, are generally used without question. The naturalness of these social relations are so taken-for-granted that the concepts are rarely defined, or seen to be in need of definition, even where what is meant by natural is used in different and conflicting ways – as in what is biologically natural versus what is natural if social order is to be maintained and chaos avoided.

In this paper I will be exploring the theme of heterosexuality, couples and parenthood in terms of the perspectives of three established theoretical frameworks – biological (or sociobiological), functionalist and marxist – focussing upon the fundamental assumptions which inform the view of each theory, and contrasting these with those of the other two. Since this discussion must necessarily be brief, I shall concentrate attention on two questions: first, how does each view of the world describe the relations between men and women? and second, how adequately does each theory explain why these relations occur and are maintained? Finally, I shall question the usefulness of the search for an original cause of the oppression of women outside of the direct benefit men derive from it, and contend that the attempt to meet the demand for such a determining factor prevents the development of feminist theory.

Biological theory

All social behaviour, according to this approach, is derived ultimately from biology. The biological goal which is deemed to be the most important determining force affecting each and every man and woman – and the social relations between them – is the reproduction of young. It is success in producing offspring, rather than the characteristics of physical size or strength, which distinguishes the 'fittest' and, thereby, the genetic material which will survive through future generations. Social relations, then, are seen to be predominantly instinctual with environmental factors remaining relatively unimportant.

The instincts and interests of females and males are assumed to be different on the basis of their differing relations to biological reproduction. Because the female knows that the young she bears are biologically 'hers', her heterosexual concerns are presumed to be to do with the quality of a male's genes and his reliability in helping her to rear her young. The male, since he can never be certain which offspring are biologically related to his sperm, is presumed to be concerned to use his reproductive capacity towards producing as many young as possible; his interests, genetically speaking, are in mating with the maximum number of females while assuming a minimum of parental responsibilities. Heterosexuality is thus based primarily upon the 'survival of the fittest', a relationship characterised by conflict and antagonism (see Janson-Smith, 1980, for a more detailed discussion).

Political and economic relations are seen to be the other side of the coin to heterosexuality and parenthood, being derived from the competition to propagate. The motivating force for all social behaviour is self-interest in perpetuating one's genes, and any social structure is presumed to have resulted from this competition, indicating the most successful survival mechanisms which have evolved. Theoretically, men and women are considered biologically-driven equals. However it is sometimes argued that cooperation between males has developed in order to subordinate women and impose upon them an inferior status. In this way, their chances of gaining sexual access to women, and thereby perpetuating their own genes, are increased.

While social cohesiveness with regard to the mother-child bond is considered to be biologically natural, the male-female bond is viewed as an adaptive system of protection for the mother-child bond, and as not necessarily monogamous, long-lasting, nor solvent of the antagonisms of heterosexual relations. Behaviour in the female continues to evolve from her need to lure and keep the male for assistance in rearing her young; the male continues to fight other males for dominance over females and the maximum exercise of his reproductive potential. Marriage, for example, is viewed as a social mechanism adapted primarily to secure the interests of women, whilst men are more inclined towards multiple sexual relationships with minimal responsibilities to any partner or resulting offspring.

To opt for a theory of 'naturalness' based on biological necessity, then, is *not* to view the family, the relations of heterosexuality, couples and parenthood as based on a harmony of interests or on expressions of love, trust, security and mutual enjoyment. Rather, it is to recognise the present family system as an evolved form of antagonistic self-interest, of tenuous connection and temporary duration.

A major inadequacy of theories of this kind, whether biological or psychological, is that in locating the motivating force of social behaviour within the make-up of each individual, there is no way to explain variations. Whether variations occur between individuals in the same culture, or in different cultures or historical periods, there is no possibility of exploring the influence of different forms of social organisation, cultural distinctions or historical contexts – except as more or less successful adaptations of the organism. Women who do not conform to their assumed biological fate, for example, can only be seen, according to this approach, as biological failures, and their behaviour as a consequence of some hormone imbalance, genetic mutation or some other unfortunate lack in their make-up. Social relations are seen to require no wider analysis than as the sum total of individual instinctual expressions, consequences and adaptations; indeed, no other explanation is possible. Male domination of women, rape, and other forms of violence are explained as no more than biologically-driven activities for producing young. A moral stance would appear to be irrelevant; such activities are likely to be inevitable, and perhaps even necessary. The results of these aggressive instincts and behaviour comprise the societal power relations; if some people benefit at the expense of others, this is simply part of the 'natural' processes of selection. Thus questions which might indicate a need or desire for social change are explained away, conveniently (for those who enjoy the benefits of the *status quo*) avoiding even beginning to look at the social construction of such events, and at who holds responsibility for what consequences.

As all social behaviour is ultimately derived from biological instincts according to this view, there remains little possibility for change. For example, the fight for improved education and career opportunities for women is at best pointless and irrelevant, and at worst harmful in interfering with natural instincts (not the least concern being male impotence). As women we are left with the problem of male domination as a mere 'fact of life' – and by implication, we must learn how to cope with it as best we can; our concern with women's liberation is simply 'making everyone miserable' over something which admittedly exists, but cannot be changed.

Functionalist Theory

The advantage of a functionalist approach over a biological one lies in the recognition of social organisation – that people living together in societies involves more than the sum total of individual instincts and consequent behaviour. However, the functionalist view of social organisation is based upon a biological model, with its concepts of all the parts fitting together and performing activities which are necessary to the smooth functioning of the whole unit. Rather than being determined by biological drives, social relations and organisation are assumed to derive from the need for a stable social system in order that the biological reproduction and the social reproduction of the 'social body' may occur.

One major problem with posing social relations as analogous to a biological organism is that of assumed consensus. While an individual body could not exist without its parts working together in harmony, a social order could, and does. In assuming harmony to be necessary to the existence of any society, a functionalist approach excludes the possibility of recognising conflict between individuals and/or groups as based on antagonistic interests. Assuming a harmony of interest, conflict can be seen only in terms of confusion of roles, misguided judgements, or improper adaptation to changes in environmental (ultimately economic) conditions.

It is assumed, then, that people now combine into units of heterosexual couples and their biological offspring – 'nuclear families' – because this is functional (necessary) for meeting their own individual needs and for the stability of the whole societal body of which they are a part. If all of one's needs or desires (for example, sexual desires) are not able to be met within such an arrangement, this is seen to be because it is important for the stability of the social order that such activities be controlled (or repressed, as Freud would say). The particular form of the family and the functions which it is seen to perform is described as an evolutionary process of adaptation to economic progress. Parsons (1956), for example, contends that with increasing industrialisation, the family lost its productive economic function and became focussed on two major functions: the socialisation of children and the provision of emotional support for adults. In this way activities presumed necessary to ensure the survival of a stable social order can be seen to be subject to historical development, whilst a perfect fit between reproduction of young and economic production is maintained through a continuous process of social adaptation of the family unit to increasing industrialisation.

According to this view, men and women are different but equal. They are presumed to have roles to play which are not interchangeable with each other, since they are based on biological suitability; however, both are deemed to be equally necessary for the proper socialisation of children. The role itself, in each case, is considered to be a set of norms and expectations which governs a person's actions. Masculine and feminine roles are derived from the positions which men and women hold within the family – most importantly, those of husband/wife and father/mother. The relationship between these roles is seen to be one of mutual dependence and harmony of interests; the purpose of the activities governed by these roles is the provision of emotional support for each other, and the socialisation of the children into their appropriate sex roles so that the existing social order is reproduced.

This image of the perfect heterosexual couple whose members engage in mutual care of each other and their biological offspring is the romantic dream of love and security which appears so 'natural' and yet so difficult to attain in practice. In assuming that the family must have arisen because of the need for the social organisation of biological reproduction and the maintenance of social order, and that it continues because it is the best adapted system for achieving these needs, functionalists have allowed no space to question whether this romantic image is a reality – i.e. whether the family system works. Given evidence of the high percentage of the population which does not live in family units, of increasing divorce rates, of wife-battering, of child abuse, of juvenile delinquency, of rape, of 'break-downs' and 'break-ups' of families, they can suggest only poor adaptation, a strain in roles, inadequate socialisation or a cycle of deprivation in proper family life. Since it is assumed that the family works, evidence to the contrary must be explained in some other way.

Nor is it possible to question whether the role itself is achievable, especially in the case of the woman whose role it is to keep the family together, to smooth out any tensions between family members, and to make the family system work (despite the possibility of its impossibility, as suggested above). Rather than informing the theory, evidence is taken to indicate, and by implication to blame, those whose responsibility it is to make the family work – women. Almost anything which goes wrong with the way the system is supposed to work can be, and frequently is, put down to the problem of the inadequate wife/mother, the dominant wife/mother, the passive wife/mother, the overprotective wife/mother, the rejecting wife/mother, the castrating wife/mother, the permissive wife/mother, and on and on. It becomes increasingly difficult to imagine what it would take to manoeuvre one's way around this maze of the wife/mother role avoiding all these pitfalls. In short, rather than question whether the role is possible, and/or whether the family system as described by functionalist theory works, women are blamed for their inadequacy in fulfilling their role of making it work.

In assuming that men and women have different but complementary roles to play, and that these roles are equally necessary to the whole, it is suggested, by a sleight of hand or by omission, that the positions of men and women in occupying these roles are equally powerful. However, as with the roles of 'master' and 'slave', albeit they are complementary and equally necessary in the overall system, it is clear that this need not be the case. When one looks more closely at what is entailed in male and female roles in the family unit, the inequality of their positions becomes evident. Likewise the question of who benefits – and at whose expense – from the existence and perpetuation of this family unit, i.e. from heterosexuality, couples and parenthood, comes into view.

For example, although it is presented that the family is concerned with the emotional support of its adult members, it is in fact only the female role which is oriented towards providing for the emotional needs of the other members. The male role is, conversely, concerned with bringing into the family an income, with maintaining ties with the 'wider' society characterised by male occupations and status (although women work in industry as well as at home, they are considered to be primarily oriented towards their role in the family), and with introducing male children into this world of men. This would suggest that emotional servicing flows in one direction primarily – from women to men. Men, on the other hand, because of their access to the world of industry and occupational status (and money), are in a position to be able to afford to 'provide for' (in effect, to buy) the services included in the role of wife/mother. The division of these family roles according to sex are derived, we remember, from biological suitability; hence, the question of inequality and who benefits from these relations is not posited nor an answer seen to be required.

A concern for the position of men is the implicit, although generally unstated, basis for the functionalist view of the world. The starting point of the theory is the biological problem for men that they can never be certain that their biological offspring are 'theirs', in the way that women can. Why this should be considered a problem at all is not explored. It is presumed, nevertheless, to provide a necessary and sufficient reason for the formation of the social institution of the family. The particular form the family takes varies historically according to economic development in the 'wider' society – the world of men. It is considered the man's role (indeed, his prerogative) to ensure that the link between this 'wider' world of men and the more private world of the family is maintained, by virtue of his masculine authority, status and breadwinning capacity. Within the family itself the presence of a man is seen to ensure the social reproduction of the existing social order by ensuring, via his monopoly as 'authority figure', that sex roles are maintained between husband/wife and reproduced in the socialisation of the children. His presence is particularly seen to be important to provide male children with protection from being dominated by their mother, and to integrate boys into their appropriate dominant role in relation to women and their place in the 'wider' world of men outside the family.

Neither the concern of functionalist theory with the interests of men, nor the presentation of the 'natural' harmony of the family as a social institution as being in the interests of men, can be recognised from a functionalist vantage point; nor can the costs to women. So long as this is ignored, there may be a possibility of change, but there is no need for it. Any fundamental change is seen as likely to lead to chaos and disorder and hence be against everyone's interests. Should any costs to the woman begin to appear, they must either be minimised – so that it appears obvious that her concerns (or she herself) should be 'sacrificed for the sake of the family' – or else they must be seen to derive from her own inadequacies and difficulties in 'coping'. Once these costs are acknowledged as real, as important, and possibly as indicating a conflict of interests, the theory falls. It can no longer be maintained that there is a harmony of interests and, therefore, no need for change.

Marxist Theory

The very great advantage of marxist theory over functionalist theory lies in its recognition of the conflict of power between social groups throughout history. The social order is seen to be divided into antagonistic social classes – the ruling class deriving its power and benefits through its exploitation of the oppressed class. However, in assuming economic development to be the ultimate determining force in history, from which the relations of class conflict are derived, a marxist approach does not allow for the possibility of acknowledging any conflict of ruling class/oppressed class which is not derived from the economic class division. As such, the possibility of recognising men occupy a class position in relation to women, that they are a ruling class deriving their power and benefits through the exploitation of an oppressed class, is within the marxist concept of history (as the exploitation of some social groups by others) but denied by the marxist premise of economic reductionism (where all social relations are ultimately seen to be derived from the economic mode of production).

Marx and Engels maintained that until the development of surplus production and the antagonistic class divisions which resulted, the structure of society was based on 'an extension of the family; patriarchal chieftains, below them members of the tribe, finally slaves' (*The German Ideology* 1970, p 44). The 'slaves' are the wives and children of the men, and this slavery is the first property. The sexual division of labour is the first form of the division of labour, and is considered to be the reverse side of the coin to private property: 'in the one the same thing is affirmed with reference to activity as is affirmed in the other with reference to the product of the activity' (ibid., p 53). This is the basis upon which, later, more developed divisions of labour and property evolved. Sexual division and exploitation can thus be seen to be at the root of marxist theory.

It is important to note, however, that this sex-divided exploitation, where women were the slaves and property of men, is assumed to be a 'natural' state of relations between women and men. Such a conception of what is 'natural' contains both biological reductionist and functionalist assumptions. Heterosexuality is assumed to be a biological fact, a given from which the social relations between the sexes are said to have come about. 'The sexual act' is posed as the origin of the division of labour, which then develops 'spontaneously or naturally by virtue of natural predisposition', until there exists a division between material and mental labour. This mature phase of the division of labour implies that 'enjoyment and labour, production and consumption – devolve on different individuals, and that the only possibility of their not coming into contradiction lies in the negation in its turn of the division of labour' (ibid., pp 51-52). This negation, then, is a negation of biological predisposition. It is only by overcoming this 'natural' phenomenon, this biological fact, that it becomes possible to engage in voluntary activity and, thereby to bring the division of labour within our control.

The functionalist assumption implied in Marx's and Engels' conception of the 'natural' is that the patriarchal family spontaneously came into existence because of the need for men (sic) socially to organise the propagation of the species. The family, 'which to begin with is the only social relationship', is seen as the necessary circumstance in the historical formation of any society (ibid., p 49). Why this first social relationship is seen to necessitate men as masters over women and children is not explained, nor is any explanation indicated to be necessary. As with the functionalist approach, this framework presumes biological reproduction to provide a necessary and sufficient reason for the formation of the social institution of the family.

So, too, the functionalist concern with the position of men and the interests of men is incorporated into marxist theory at the level of its most fundamental premises. Once again we find this male orientation exists to the exclusion, trivialisation or assumed similarity, or at least harmony, of women's position and interests – despite formally acknowledging their slavery to men. The ambiguity in the use of the terms 'man' and 'men' to varyingly include and exclude 'woman' and 'women' enables both the denial and justification of the myopia to be maintained. Thus, for example, the premise referred to above – that from the outset of history 'men, who daily remake their own life, begin to make other men, to propagate their own kind: the relation between man and woman, parents and children, the *family*' (ibid., p 49) – is used both to imply the similarity and harmony of men and women as historical beings, and to explain their dissimilarity and disharmony in the family master/slave social relations as 'natural' (mutually necessary) for the propagation of human society. The former suggests that 'men' implies men and women in the premise; the latter is logically coherent only if men alone are implied by 'men'. The implicit concern with the position and interests of men is denied in the first case, justified in the second.

Whilst prior to the production of surplus with the domestication of animals, the social structure is said to be an extension of the patriarchal family system of the tribe (or gens), once this economic change occurs, the family is seen to become subordinate to a more developed form of private property. This transformation of the family from being the basis of the social structure to becoming the consequence of economic development, and functional (necessary) for its perpetuation, hinges on Marx's assertion that 'property differences in a gens changes the community of interest into antagonism between members of a gens' (Marx, quoted by Engels, *Selected Works* 1968, p 582). Although never explicitly stated, this assertion only makes sense where 'members of a gens' implies *men alone*. That is to say, in the early patriarchal tribe, or gens, the women and children constituted a pool of slaves, the communal property of the men. With the development of surplus production, property differences between men in a gens arise. The family system is transformed; the relations of men to women are adjusted such that they become functional for the continuation and further development of this economic class antagonism amongst men.

Engels suggests in *The origin of the family, private property and the state* that this transformation of the family was the consequence of the establishment of father-right to children. Father-right is deemed to have replaced matrilineal groupings when the establishment of private male property enabled the men of the gens to overthrow the mother-right, by virtue of their economically strengthened position relative to the women. At the same time, father-right to children was seen to be required by this economic development; in order to maintain this form of male ownership and control through inheritance, Engels argues, the men needed to know which boys were their biological sons. Monogamy is therefore required on the part of the woman, and the man is enabled to enforce it because of the exclusive rights of men to private property.

In this account of the development of the family, Engels contradicts his earlier joint writings with Marx, claiming that it was only with establishment of private property that male domination of women came into being. Previously, as outlined above, they had maintained that until the development of class society, the social structure was based on an extension of a 'natural' patriarchal division of labour, where women and children were slaves to the men. Whilst Engels' later position would more closely support the thesis that the social relations between men and women are derived from economic production, and change as a consequence of change in economic development, it is, however, an untenable argument.

The argument is logically inconsistent: Engels proposes that the conditions for male domination of women arose with the development of a 'hitherto unsuspected source of wealth' from the domestication of animals. Until this stage, property was communally owned and used, and no wealth greater than the subsistence requirements of the gens was produced. Suddenly the excess wealth was owned by the men. This is not considered a theoretical problem by Engels: 'according to the division of labour then prevailing in the family . . . (the new wealth) fell to the man' (*Selected Works*, 1968, p 494). But to suppose that this new wealth belonged to the men is already to presume them to be in a privileged and dominant position relative to the women. Whether or not they performed different tasks, to suppose that an event of such import, the first production of surplus wealth, simply 'fell' to the men by custom, rather than the new produce being shared by everyone, is either to presume that women are by biological predisposition extremely passive and/or stupid, or that this sexual division of labour, as the earlier work of Marx and Engels suggests, already comprises patriarchal master/slave relations.

Either way, the thesis is biologically reductionist. Whether male domination of women is seen to arise from 'the sexual act', or with the production of surplus wealth because of the need for men to know who their biological sons are, biology is presented as the determining factor. Why this heterosexual activity is assumed to be a biological given, why it is presumed to give rise spontaneously to a sexual division of labour, and why inheritance is presumed to need to pass along biological lines – these are not recognised to be questions which demand further explanation; nor is it seen that they question the validity of the theory itself.

Change, on the other hand, is presumed to depend upon and somehow follow from the overthrow of private property. I say presumed, since it does not follow from the accounts presented by Marx and Engels how this might come about. Indeed, a wide range of confusions and assertions arise in their work as a result of these inconsistencies, including, for example, that there is no basis for male domination in the proletarian family since there is not property to pass on; that if women are private property, then the first stage of the abolition of this property includes the community of women being owned by men (despite assertions to the contrary); that the family will be abolished; that the family will be secured with male monogamy as well as female, and so on.

Marxist theory, like functionalist theory, is protective of men. In presupposing heterosexuality to be a biologically natural phenomenon, and presenting couples and heterosexual parenthood as having arisen because they were functional for economic class-based societies, this approach conveniently (for men) averts its eyes from questioning how these social relations can be seen to benefit all men at the expense of all women. Men are excused from the oppression of women – in the first case, because it is 'biologically natural' and in the second, because it is 'necessary for the economic system'. And just as the direct interest of men in the exploitation of women is rendered invisible and legitimised in this view of the world, so any fundamental future problems in the achievement of the liberation of women remain unseen.

It is not surprising that marxist-feminists have run into major difficulties in attempting to 'extend' marxist theory to explain male dominant/female subordinate relations. This is not to deny the considerable and invaluable insights into the conditions of women's lives which have been highlighted in the work of feminists who use a marxist perspective. However, as an explanatory framework for understanding why these conditions exist for *women* and not for *men* – i.e. why they are not the same for anyone who labours in a particular job or task, whatever it might be – marxism is weak, contradictory and I would contend, precludes the possibility of creating a new theory which may provide an adequate explanation. As long as the framework which we use to understand male dominant/female subordinate relations denies the possibility of theorising that men directly benefit from the exploitation of women, that men as a group or class actively maintain, perpetuate and protect their privileges over and against women (whether they are aware of it or not), then, of course, such a theoretical perspective can never be developed. Again, it must be asked: in whose interests is it to deny the possibility of developing the theory of male supremacy?

Original Cause

In attempting to provide an alternative description as well as analysis of male/female relations, we are often confronted by the question:

what is the original cause – the conditions which determine that such relations exist? When we find it difficult to answer, it is proposed that even our description of the world as characterised by antagonistic power relations between men and women is unsound. That is, if there can be seen to be no cause outside of the relations of power described, then indeed, no such relations exist. However, it may be that the fault lies with the question, rather than in the lack of an answer.

The demand for an original cause of why men should oppress women is premised on the determinist assumption that there is such a thing. For marxists, antagonistic class relations are created by the economic development of private property, which itself arises out of the technological possibility of surplus production. The supposition is that the oppression of one group of people by another is predated and ultimately caused by the mode of production. Since, according to this view, antagonistic social classes did not and do not exist outside of the need for them in terms of the division of labour necessitated by the economic mode of production, then either (a) the division between men and women is false (we're all in this together; the oppression of women by men doesn't exist), or (b) the oppression of women is derived from the division of labour based on private property and is primarily in the interests of the maintenance of that economic system. The fact that men of whatever economic class benefit from the exploitation of women of whatever economic class (women being assumed to be of the same class as their fathers or husbands) is considered a mere by-product, a secondary consequence of economic class antagonism.

The inadequacies of the marxist economic reductionist approach have led many feminists to seek the cause of male domination of women in some determining factor other than the economic system. The intention is to indicate some causal factor which predates the development of private property and is founded upon a division of labour which is sex-linked. Generally, the solutions have been sought in terms of biological differences; these are said to have caused the conditions which provided for the establishment of patriarchal relations – through the physiological weakness or defencelessness associated with pregnancy and lactation causing women to be dependent upon men (see, for example, the now classic thesis of Firestone, 1971). Apart from the questionability of the assumptions about women's defencelessness, which seem to presuppose a continual state of childbearing for each and every woman, and that women are dependent only upon men rather than upon each other or upon the rest of the men and women in the society, the major difficulty with this approach is its reductionism. Such reductionism implies that the physiological differences between men and women in some determinate way cause the class of men to exploit the class of women for their own benefit. It fails to recognise that while biological differences may provide possibilities and limitations for heterosexual relations, the ways in which these biological factors bear social significance is the product of social relations, not the cause of them.

The untenability of claiming the cause of the power relations between men and women to be inherent in biology *per se* is widely recognised. What is less generally recognised is that this approach is modelled upon the marxist method of economic reductionism (except for Firestone, who identifies the method she uses as marxist). There is no more reason to support the proposition that the ultimate cause of power relations is the technological possibility of surplus production (economic development) than there is in biological possibilities *per se*. As with biology, the ways in which these economic factors bear social significance is the product of social relations, not the cause of them. Economics, as biology, may more fruitfully be viewed as one of the avenues through which those with power will try to maintain and perpetuate that power at the expense of those subordinate to them.

The demand for an original cause of why men oppress women, then, needs to be answered with the question: why does any group or class of people oppress any other group? That is to say, why is history a history of the domination and subordination of social groups? Why does any ruling class exploit the subordinate class to its own ends? It is not an easy question to answer, but we must not assume the answer is to be found in biology, economics, psychology, or sexuality *per se*. Social relations are based on actions taken by people; social structures are set up and maintained by people. The oppression of women is the consequence of men creating and perpetuating their position as the ruling class (knowingly or unknowingly, but benefitting all the same).

An easier question to answer might have been: how did it come about? I say might have, rather than is, since the recorded history we have of anything other than patriarchal relations, existing in one form or another, is severely limited. The history that we do have has primarily been recorded by men and shows not an overzealous concern with the conditions of women's lives nor a sympathetic bias towards their struggles for liberation from the rule of men. More recent history and our own experience of women's struggles do however make clear the tenacity with which men protect their position of power over women.

The question that we cannot avoid asking, since it confronts us daily in our lives and our politics is: why does it continue now? However it developed (and we can only speculate), what we need to know is how to overcome this structure of power relations, how to change it. We need to look at the structures and institutions of our society, including the economic, but not exclusively the economic, and question whether, and how, these can be seen to benefit men at the expense of women. Which are the key institutions through which men maintain their domination of women? How are patriarchal power relations perpetuated and protected against women's struggles for equality? In what ways are women divided against each other, and who benefits from these divisions? How have the particular forms these patriarchal relations have taken varied historically and cross-culturally? How have women organised to struggle against their oppression: where have they succeeded and failed? Where are the weakest links – where can the chains be broken?

References

Adlam, Diana, 'The case against capitalist patriarchy'. *m/f*, no 3. 1979.

Beechey, Veronica, 'On patriarchy'. *Feminist Review*, no 3. 1979.

Dawkins, Richard. *The Selfish Gene*. Oxford University Press. 1976.

Delphy, Christine. 'A Materialist Feminism is possible'. *Feminist Review*, no 4. 1980.

Engels, Frederick. 'The origin of the family, private property and the state', In Marx, K. and Engels, F. *Selected Works*. International, New York. 1968.

Firestone, Shulamith. *The Dialectic of Sex*. Jonathan Cape, London. 1971; The Women's Press, London. 1980.

Fletcher, Ronald. *The Family and Marriage in Britain*. second edn. Penguin, Harmondsworth. 1966.

Goldberg, Steven. *The Inevitability of Patriarchy*. Morrow, New York. 1973.

Harris, C.C. *The Family*. George Allen and Unwin, London. 1969.

Hartmann, Heidi. 'The unhappy marriage of marxism and feminism: towards a more progressive union'. *Capital and Class*, no 8, Summer. 1979.

Janson-Smith, Deirdre. 'Sociobiology: so what?' In Brighton Women and Science Group (ed) *Alice Through the Microscope: The Power of Science Over Women's Lives*. Virago, London. 1980.

Marx, Karl and Engels, Frederick. *The German Ideology*. Lawrence and Wishart, London. 1970.

Morgan, David. *Social Theory and the Family*. Routledge and Kegan Paul, London. 1975.

Murdock, George Peter. *Social Structure*. Macmillan, London. 1949.

Parson, Talcott and Bales, Robert F. *Family, Socialisation and Interaction Process*. Routledge and Kegan Paul, London. 1956.

Roche, Sheila. Sociobiology. Unpublished paper. 1979.

Tiger, Lionel and Fox, Robin. *The Imperial Animal*. Dell, New York. 1972.

Wilson, Edward O. *On Human Nature*. Harvard University Press, Cambridge, Mass. 1978.

STEVI JACKSON

Femininity, Masculinity and Sexuality

My intention in this paper is to look at some aspects of the ideology of femininity and masculinity as it is manifested in the sexual sphere. I will concentrate on two areas: first, the organisation and distribution of sexual knowledge, and second, ideas about the 'differentness' of women and men. I am not so much concerned with the process whereby men and women come to express their sexuality in different ways as with the ideology surrounding these differences. I will however, say a little about the ways in which these ideologies affect our sexual learning, especially the part they play in gaining women's approval of male domination. I apologise in advance for my failure to confront the issue of where these ideologies come from.

To some extent I will make use of rather extreme, polarised notions of femininity and masculinity which may make some of what I have to say seem rather outdated and more relevant to the Victorian era. This strategy, however, helps to bring certain issues into sharper focus. In any case, the ghosts of Victorian times are still haunting us. One further qualification must be made. This paper does not constitute a coherent, reasoned argument. Instead it represents a series of ideas, some only half formed, which I think are worth discussing.

The Organisation of Sexual Knowledge

I have come to believe that the organisation and distribution of sexual knowledge is of crucial importance to our sexuality. There are two reasons for this:

1 It serves to define sexuality in masculine terms and has denied women and girls access to vital information concerning their sexuality.

2 It disguises ideology as fact. All knowledge is socially constructed, produced within a given society under particular historical conditions

and it reflects the interests and priorities of dominant groups within that society (in this context, men). But knowledge tends to appear as objective 'fact' – hence statements which are really about what ought to be, come disguised as what *is*.

Now what sex *is* in conventional terms, is heterosexual intercourse. Equating sex with one particular type of sexual act means that any other form of sexual activity is automatically defined as a perversion, as second best, or as leading up to the 'real thing'. These labels then assume the appearance of factual descriptions rather than reflections of values or preferences. In these supposedly 'enlightened' times, women's sexual functioning is given some recognition and some concessions are made to it. But take a look at the average sex manual and you will find that everything intended to turn *us* on is called 'foreplay'. The 'real thing' is still copulation, even if we are now expected to have orgasms and are entitled to get on top once in a while and to have a little clitoral stimulation thrown in as an optional extra.

All the evidence confirms what we know from our own experience and that of our sisters: that many women find sexual intercourse emotionally or psychologically satisfying, but few of us find it totally physically satisfying. Part of the reason we enjoy it, if and when we do, is because men do – a kind of vicarious pleasure. While not denying that enjoyment of turning on your partner is part of what sexual relationships are all about, we need to question the way in which sexual intercourse is seen as the end point, the final and culminating act in any sexual encounter.

Sexuality is defined in these masculine terms partly because it is defined in reproductive terms. This is how we learn about it: as the 'facts of life'. In learning this way, the average boy cannot help but notice that the penis is his chief sexual organ, whereas amid all the information about penises and vaginas, eggs and sperm, or in the more vague versions of 'where babies come from', it is unlikely that girls will even hear the clitoris mentioned, let alone learn of its function. What passes as sex education is, in fact, education about reproduction rather than sex and rarely about sexuality in its broader sense.

Most of us learn, either at the same time as we are assimilating these facts about reproduction or later, that sex is supposed to be pleasurable. Since sex has been pre-defined for us as coition, it is assumed that the ultimate in pleasure must derive from this act. How many of us during adolescence enjoyed petting, expected the 'real thing' to be even better and were disappointed when it was not?

Of course, it may be just coincidence that the emphasis on

reproduction leads us to view as the 'real thing' something that is more pleasurable for men then for women – but I doubt it. If men happened to have separate sexual and reproductive organs, I'm sure we would *all* know about it. The present structuring of sexual knowledge is, after all, the product of a male-dominated society. Often in the past this has been legitimated by equating women's sexual desire with a sort of reproductive urge, and it is no coincidence that the link between this form of sexual activity and reproduction is part of a system that denies us control over our own bodies.

Another aspect of the way in which sexual knowledge is organised is the language used to depict the 'sexual act'. Terms such as *penetration* or the *insertion* of the penis into the vagina give the impression of male activity and female passivity. Hence 'factual' descriptions contain within them ideological assumptions.

When interviewing teenage girls as part of my research I was struck by the way in which they discussed sexual encounters in terms of what was done to them. They talked of themselves as passive objects (except insofar as they referred to what they 'let' boys do) and I recalled that I and my friends had once done the same.

It is sometimes suggested that this way of talking about sexuality has little to do with the way people really think and act, that it is 'just a manner of speaking'. But language is not merely a tool we use to express ourselves, it also shapes the way we think, which in turn affects our actions.

The ideology of male dominance, then, is expressed in the organisation of sexual knowledge through the selection of a particular set of 'facts' which constitute what is taken to be sexual knowledge, and by the language through which these 'facts' are made available. What emerges from this could be summed up by the following equation: sex = coition = something men do to women. This definition of what sex is illustrates the extent to which coercion is an inbuilt element of current sexual arrangements.

This definition of sex conditions what we learn about sexuality, and how we learn it. Most of us first encounter sexual knowledge in a male-defined, reproductively-focussed form. This has two consequences, one relatively short-term and one longer-term or even permanent. First, learning of sex as a means to an end may in part explain why so many of the girls I talked to reacted negatively to their first awareness of the sexual, expressing shock and revulsion – feelings that might be heightened if they were also being given the impression that this was something that would be done to them. Somehow most girls eventually overcome these negative attitudes.

This change, however, by no means implies a move towards self-defined sexuality, but rather an accommodation to conventional sexuality involving the assumption that sexual intercourse is the key to erotic pleasure. This leads on to the second consequence of learning about sexuality in this way: that it makes it difficult for girls and women to gain access to information about their own sexuality. Almost all of the girls I interviewed were totally ignorant of the existence of the clitoris and the nature of the female orgasm – most did not even know it was possible for women to have orgasms.

Although knowledge of our own sexuality is important if we are to control our own bodies and be self-determining in our sexual relationships, knowledge alone is not enough. The women whose experiences are recorded in *The Hite Report* were, on the whole, well informed about female sexuality and knew how to gain pleasure from their own bodies. Most, however, found it difficult to put such knowledge into practice in their relationships with men. Even given knowledge of our own sexuality, we do not enter heterosexual relationships on equal terms with our partners. Men's definitions of what sex entails are the conventional and accepted ones, so if we attempt to restructure the sequence of events in a sexual encounter, to give precedence to acts other than sexual intercourse, we are challenging not just ideas of how sex ought to be, but how it *is*. This makes us vulnerable to a variety of derogatory labels; we may be called perverted, frigid, or be categorised as cock-teasers. If we have come to accept (for whatever reason) that we ought to be deferential towards men, that we should minister to their fragile egos, then our difficulties are compounded.

Traditional ideas about the 'differentness' of men and women come into play here. This also plays a large part in our sexual learning: along with the facts we learn that men 'need' sex more, that they are more easily aroused and less in control of themselves than women are, and that they are more easily satisfied. However much women *know* that these ideas are myths, they still seem to affect the ability of many of us to make demands on male sexual partners.

The idea of differentness also acts as a barrier to those women who remain in ignorance of the 'mechanics' of female sexuality, preventing them from asking what is wrong and working towards discovering their sexual potential. The idea that women's orgasm is more 'diffuse' than that of men is still around. It would not be surprising if many women do not know whether or not they experience orgasm since what we are supposed to feel is often explained in romantic rather than physical terms. If sex as coition turns out not to be as great as we expected, we can always fall back on the idea that it is not the same for us, that we've always 'known' that men enjoy it more – without thinking that if it was organised differently we might enjoy it too.

Maybe we should also try to challenge the whole notion of goal-oriented, orgasm-as-end-point sexuality – but it is not easy to persuade the average man that love-making doesn't have to involve genitals and orgasms.

The Ideology of Differentness

Ideas about the differentness of women and men are not only incorporated into what counts as sexual knowledge, but form part of a more explicit ideology. In the sexual sphere this ideology provides a major means of justifying sexual apartheid: the *'vive la difference'* lobby, the notion that sexual attraction itself depends on women and men behaving as two separate species. The ways in which boundaries are drawn between feminine and masculine attributes serve to illustrate both the fact of women's subordination and the manner in which it is legitimated.

One aspect of this ideology is the parallel that may be drawn between stereotypes of women and stereotypes of children (which are oppressive to both). Stereotypes tend to polarise into dichotomies, viz. masculine/feminine, adult/childlike. What is adult is often equated with what is masculine, and that which is childlike with that which is feminine. An example of this is provided by a study of American clinicians' assessment of indicators of mental health (Broverman et al., 1970). Their depiction of the 'normal healthy adult' proved to be almost identical with that of the 'normal healthy man' while the characteristics of the 'normal healthy woman' were virtually the opposite. Women, in order to be characterised as 'healthy', should be dependent, emotional, vulnerable, child-like creatures.

If normal, adult humanness is by definition male, then, given our cultural tendency to think in opposites, the female of the species is not quite normal, not quite adult, and not quite human. Conceptions of maturity are gender-bound: there is a contradiction between the requirements of maturity *per se* and those of mature womanhood. The attainment of the latter would seem to be dependent upon retaining certain child-like attributes in order to progress from being a girl child to become a feminine child-woman.

This is an obvious ideological reflection of women's material dependence in the form of a psychological dependence which we are supposed to share with that archetypal dependent: the child. Just as children are deemed to be in need of adult protection, so are we – where adult = male.

This may well be the basis for the commonplace observation that girls mature earlier than boys. Possibly girls have less to mature into, that maturity for them is little more than a superficial gloss on existing child-like attributes. This seems to be the implication of the upper-class myth of the finishing school, wherein the gawky schoolgirl is transformed almost overnight into a sophisticated 'young lady' by virtue of a few lessons in dress and deportment.

This superficial gloss on childishness has much to do with sexuality, or more specifically with what passes as sexual attractiveness. Signs that a girl is 'growing up' tend to be bound up with her interest in, and ability to attract, the opposite sex: not for her such characteristics as independence and self-determination which indicate 'normal' (male) maturity. In presenting herself as sexually desirable, a girl may well find that certain childlike attributes such as 'cuteness' are useful in gaining attention and approval. Of course only young women can play this game successfully, but the ideal of sexually attractive femininity is, in any case, ageist as well as sexist.

Other aspects of the feminine/masculine dichotomy are also bound up with notions of sexual attractiveness. I have said that the *'vive la difference'* idea rests on the assumption that heterosexual attraction depends on these oppositions. More specifically, it is believed that what makes women attractive is their differentness, their mysteriousness. This may be important in gaining women's support for the feminine ideal. If, for many women, both economic survival and a positive self-image depend on nailing your man, then this notion of femininity becomes an ideal to be aimed for, thus encouraging women to collude in maintaining false images of womanhood which are part of their oppression.

Those men who eulogise about femininity, the allure of its differentness and mystery, imply that women are somehow both less than human and more than human. This too may serve to legitimate male dominance. If in most spheres of life one is considered less than human, it helps if one male (or if you are successful, many) is prepared to put you on a pedestal and worship you as more than human. Shulamith Firestone, in discussing love (1972), argued that men have to put the woman they love on a pedestal in order to place her above the despised common herd of womankind. If this is the case, the idea of women as more than human may serve both to reinforce and legitimate male opinion of us as less then human. Many anti-feminist women assert that, although we may seem to be treated as inferior, really we have men just where we want them – provided, of course, that we are skilled in the use of 'feminine wiles'.

Part of the allure of femininity is sexual unattainability, which depends on women projecting themselves as attractive but not available. Here there may again be a connection between women and children. Both are seen as requiring protection from the sexual. Both, of course, are vulnerable to sexual coercion, but it is not this, but sex itself, which is seen as potentially damaging to them, as somehow degrading and defiling them.

In maturing to adulthood, men are expected to become sexually active, women to become sexually attractive. To be too active would destroy the allure and mystery of femininity and the childlike 'innocence' which is paradoxically a part of it. But while children are not supposed to be sexual, women are expected to express their sexuality only within certain boundaries. We are not supposed to own our sexuality: it is something detached from us with which we can bargain with men. Here there is another reflection of the material conditions of our lives: our sexuality is the only commodity with which we may bargain for economic, social and emotional security. The relationship between women and their sexuality is expressed very well by Lorenne Clark and Debra Lewis in this passage from *Rape: the Price of Coercive Sexuality.*

> Prior to marriage, a woman's sexuality is a commodity to be held in trust for its rightful owner. Making 'free' use of one's own sexuality is like making 'free' use of someone else's money. One can act autonomously only with things that belong to oneself. Things held in trust for others are surrounded with special duties which place the trustee under strict obligations for the care and maintenance of the assets in question . . . Women are not regarded as being entitled to use their sexuality according to their own desires because their sexuality is not theirs for the use of such purposes. Their duty is to preserve it in the best possible condition for the ultimate use and disposition of its rightful owner. (1977, p 122)

Part of the allure of femininity involves a detachment from our own sexuality, conveying the impression that it is something precious which we might offer to some man who is willing to pay the appropriate price.

This was another common theme emerging from my interviews with teenage girls. Not only did they tend to describe sexual acts in terms of what was done to them, but also referred to sex itself as something they 'gave' in exchange for something else. The girl who expressed this trustee relationship most strongly said, when describing her relationships with boys:

> They can have some of this (indicating her breasts) but not that down here – that's for the man I marry.

Later, when I talked to her about masturbation she said indignantly:

> I wouldn't touch myself down there!

No one, it seems, had the right to do so except her future husband.

This girl's conformity to the ideal is, no doubt, extreme but the end point of the feminine-masculine dichotomy is our alienation and detachment from our own sexuality.

References

Broverman, I.K. et al. 'Sex-role stereotypes and clinical judgements of mental health', *Journal of Consulting and Clinical Psychology,* vol 34. 1970.

Clark, Lorenne and Lewis, Debra. *Rape: The Price of Coercive Sexuality*. The Women's Press, Toronto. 1977.

Firestone, Shulamith, *The Dialectic of Sex*, Jonathan Cape, London. 1971; The Women's Press, London, 1980.

Hite, Shere, *The Hite Report*. Dell, New York, 1976.

ANNABEL FARADAY

'On the Other Side of the Billboard . . . ': Pornography, Male Fantasies and the Objectification of Women

The term 'pornography' is generally applied to visual or written depctions of explicitly 'sexual' scenes or encounters, presented in the form of movies, magazines or novels, which are specifically designed to arouse 'sexual' excitement in their audience. According to the estimation of the Williams Committee, pornographic magazines alone are used by a 'gross (sic) audience' of eight million in this country. That audience is male. Men create porn and it is they who defend it. When sixteen women were arrested in Soho in the October 1978 Reclaim the Night march, what was being protected was big business (in the States the annual turnover in the porn industry is four *billion* dollars). But what was also being defended was the construction and maintenance of a form of male power that requires the domination, intimidation, humiliation and violation of women in both the physical and psychological world – the power wielded through the construction of male sexuality. This construction relies not only on so-called 'erotic' images, but on every written or visual, commercial or 'artistic' image which portrays or suggests the (preferably involuntary) availability of women's bodies for men's use and 'pleasure'.

That 'pleasure' has boundless sources; it takes on, literally, fantastic dimensions. In the most public sphere, the images are ubiquitous in product advertising. Cars become 'seductresses', or, for those who prefer the less forward type, they cry out to get their bottoms pinched. That uppity-looking woman in her baggy overalls may not *look* too available, but she is really 'lovable' underneath. Give her a pair of Pretty Polly tights and she will be lovable a.m. and p.m., or slap a map of the London Underground across her breasts and she'll be lovable 'anywhere, any time'. For those who prefer less resistance, there are always the children: in thigh-high Elliot boots, they transform into little Lolitas.

So-called 'soft' pornography, used to promote consumer goods and in which women themselves are portrayed as consumer goods, also functions as a permanent symbol, 'everywhere, all the time' – a public form of flag-waving from billboards, 'pin-ups', and page three onwards – to remind women that our bodies are supposed to be men's territory. What would seem to be defined as 'soft' porn are those static images of women, clothed, semi-clothed or naked, which only *hint* at the innumerable possibilities to which our bodies may be put. Such images are deemed to be acceptable because the suggestions remain implicit; it is on the other side of the billboards, in the realm of so-called 'hardcore', that the game is really given away.

'Hard-core' pornography is almost by definition masturbatory material, used by men to conjure up and reinforce their sexual self-images as omnipotent. Here we can see that male sexual 'pleasure' can be derived from anything between a quick impersonal fuck in any setting and circumstance the imagination can summon up, and involving women of any age, through to torture, rape and murder. The depictions in such magazines as *Whitehouse* or *Hustler* are not of 'playthings' or pawns, so much as the enactment of the game of war itself. A magazine available on pavement newstands and entitled *New M.S.* (the pornographer's reaction to Women's Liberation?) contains a photo-story of a woman picked up at a bus-stop by a passing man in a car. Inevitably she ends up in his flat and is gradually unclothed, fingered and exhibited, whilst the captions tell us she is feeling mildly bored and a trifle blasé, but if that's what he wants . . . The final frame, presumably designed to precipitate the wanking audience to orgasm, is entirely filled by an almost life-size vulva, anonymous and disembodied, and occupied by the man's fingers. The caption is written in the first person from the woman's point of view and tells us that another 'conquest' has been made:

> I'm glad there's nobody behind me right now' [i.e. 'the joke's on you, babe'] – 'they'd be able to see just about everything I've got' [i.e. 'vulva = woman']. 'I'd really hate that – which reminds me of my recurring nightmare: some porno pictures of my most private parts are published in a girlie magazine and millions of men masturbate over them. Phew, I'm so glad that's only a dream. [i.e. 'you've lost by over a million to one'].

We can see how male sexual arousal and hatred of women are closely intertwined. The written part of pornography is very often posed from the woman's viewpoint. This has two major effects: men imagine they know what we are thinking, and we are more likely to identify with it. It leaves men feeling omnipotent – after all, they do not read what they themselves are supposed to be thinking or feeling; they fill that gap in for themselves. They are 'reading the mind' of the woman portrayed.

Men gain, then, a sense of total control through the use of such material. But the thrill, it seems, is in the battle for control, in the sense of opposition. The more opposition, the more that 'manhood' is proved. Research by Judith Reisman in the States has shown how the steady increase in page-three-type images in the more public sphere has led to a decrease in the sales of 'soft' full-frontal-type porn, and to a growth in demand and acceptance of depictions involving paedophilia, incest and more overt sexual violence. The familiar becomes predictable, the forbidden becomes permissible, and the sense of battle and 'manhood' is lost.

It is not surprising that sex between women has always featured highly and widely on the porn menu. Laboratory research has shown, in a very convoluted way and what lesbians knew all along, that lesbianism poses one of the ultimate threats to the heterosexual sense of 'manhood'. Porn provides the necessary mechanism for diffusing that threat to the male psyche. Mavissakalian et al (1975) showed that, when exposed to various forms of erotic stimuli, men were overwhelmingly 'turned on' (i.e. got erections) by images of lesbian sex, in contrast to those of hetero sex or of women alone. Within the 'action mags', the lesbian depictions are never completed without the inevitable male entering the scene wielding what (he would like to think) they 'really need' – his 'angry' prick. It seems probable that as lesbians and the women's liberation movement become stronger and more visible, so such porn depictions will escalate.

The search for widening forbidden frontiers to cross extends now to older women and children and to horrendous extremes of torture and violence. Reisman's study shows how the 'softer' porn magazines, such as *Forum*, constantly encourage readers to overcome their repugnance at new methods of 'getting it off'. Once desensitised, they are then ready to encounter the 'harder' stuff both in thought and in practice. A recent copy of *Forum* contained an article on 'Passionate Grandmothers', and the avid enthusiast can find specialist magazines with pictures of older women in shiny boots and black knickers. There is still a big market for photos of women in gym slips, but how long before the thrill gives way to the 'need' for (already available) photos or eight-or-nine-year-old children poised in the act of fucking, whilst grinning at the cameraman for approval? *Screw*, a widely available magazine in the States, carried a photo of a mastectomy patient in one of its S/M features, suggesting breast mutilation as a form of 'sexual excitement'. And, of course, at the most extreme, there are the 'snuff' movies emerging from South America, in which women are sexually assaulted, mutilated and finally butchered.

Meantime, for those men who want the necrophiliac's thrill of the conquest without any of the battle or mess, there is always the logical extension of masturbating to a two-dimensional image – doing it into a life-size rubber doll, widely advertised in even the so-called 'softest' magazines.

If the fantasies which feed and are fed by pornographic images provide a key to our understanding of the nature of male sexual supremacy, the arguments used in support of porn help to show how that power is constantly rebuilt and maintained. The current debates about pornography are confined to discussion of its effects on men. As men create and use pornography, so they defend it, and the major lines of defence are constructed as follows. (Each of these arguments was found in a volume by G.L. Simons entitled *Pornography Without Prejudice*, 1972).

First, pornography is enjoyable. 'Only in a sexually neurotic society could a tool for heightening sexual enjoyment be regarded as reprehensible and such as to warrant suppression by law' (Simons, 1972, p 87). This kind of defence is another example of the now well known line of 'blaming the victim'; to object to being humiliated is to be 'sexually neurotic'. The message is clear: whatever men enjoy, whether it is a straightforward gang bang or the somewhat more 'wasteful' forms of torture, it cannot really be anything other than the exercise of a healthy, lusty sexual drive.

G.L. Simon's concern with 'sexual neurosis' seems to be shared by the researchers Gagnon and Simon. They see all objections to pornography as the result of muddled thinking, misguided fears, and guilt-ridden sexual learning, whilst the porn dealer, cast as the central villain, deserves our sympathy rather than our hostility.

> Thought of as a public nuisance, he appears in somewhat more realistic hues. Here we find not a sinister villain, but a grubby businessman producing a minor commodity for which there is a limited market and a marginal profit and which requires that he live in a marginal world. Here, our collective displeasure may be derived from

> his association with a still greater obscenity – economic failure. He is one of the few in our society whose public role is overtly sexual, and that is perhaps reason enough to abandon any expectations of rationality in public discussion of the role. (Gagnon and Simon, 1967, p 43)

Whilst this may have been an acceptable dismissal for those who share those authors' economic aspirations above all else, it is in fact grossly untrue. Since when were Hugh Heffner or Paul Raymond forced to join the dole queue? During the course of a research project about male sexual variations, I had the dubious pleasure of interviewing one of the less financially successful variety of porn dealers. He operated from an office-cum-bed-sitter on the outskirts of London, where he compiled a contact magazine. He showed me the hooks on the ceiling where he tied up the women who had offered themselves as models for his publication. The photographs taken between bouts of fucking and whipping would then be sold through the magazine. The creation, distribution and use of pornography are inextricably linked.

Secondly, it is argued that pornography aids the 'normal' sexual development in males. It shapes the content of adolescent masturbatory fantasy, nurturing and reinforcing feelings of omnipotence. Since males learn their sexual meanings through masturbation prior to learning how to fuck, pornography provides the necessary scenario and props with which to practise. Too true. But 'normal'? 'Normal' in this sense is both a prescriptive and descriptive term; sadistic male sexuality is not only acceptable, but expected. As Gagnon and Simon explain it, most pornography 'is not sadistic beyond the general levels of violence common in contemporary kitsch' (1974, p 268). Here, the message seems to be that violent images abound in society; what is common must therefore be acceptable.

For those men who do not react in the 'normal' way, pornography is used in sex therapy as a means of overcoming impotence or 'premature' ejaculation. One of the leading sex therapists in this country, Patricia Gillan, explains how porn was used as an integral part in the behaviour therapy of single men with 'sexual problems':

> All these (ten) men were encouraged to masturbate to fantasy and if they had difficulty with this I suggested some suitable books or magazines. Many men who are shy and lonely through social diffidence are also unadventurous in their thinking. I tried to stimulate their attitudes towards sexuality as much as possible by giving them new ideas of where to go and what to do. For all of them I pushed pornography,

> as books, tapes and films, in order to increase their sexual enthusiasm. Nine out of ten of the group made progress in dating and had a clearly more positive and hopeful attitude towards their sexuality. These nine all managed to get a girlfriend. (Gillan, 1977, p 23)

Whilst this line of defence, in terms of 'therapeutic value', is used as a justification, it also provides evidence of the power of porn to mould sexuality.

Fourth, it is stressed that pornography provides 'sex by proxy' for men who are too inhibited to achieve orgasm in company, or whose fantasies are too way out to enact. We have seen what those fantasies may involve. Research by Kutschinsky (1970) in Denmark, since the legalisation of pictorial porn in 1969, suggests that free availability of porn results in a decrease of the incidence of sex crimes. If this is true, then it is hardly reassuring – help is available for the shyer rapist while the rest are given food for thought. ('Feel like a good rape? Why not buy a copy of *Butcher*? All the fun without the fine'). It is called the 'catharsis effect'.

It is further argued that regular access to pornography actually protects young people from developing a morbid fascination with, and distorted attitudes to sex. The more you see of it, the less exciting it is. Reisman's research corroborates this latter argument, but also points to its logical extension: it is the forbidden element in porn which men find exciting and so when saturation is reached and excitement wears thin, more and more 'forbidden' types of activity are sought.

The justifications are probably endless. A final gem is the one about the need for exploitative porn in order to increase our awareness of the importance of romantic love – an updated version of the old virgin/whore dichotomy?

Which brings us back to the importance of breaking down categories and examining definitions. The concepts of 'sexuality', 'obscenity' and 'pornography' are commonly used unquestioningly. After all, 'everybody knows' that men have innate sexual 'needs', often beyond their control, to which women, like it or not, have to cater. It's much easier, of course, if we are persuaded that we do like it, which is what the sexual 'liberation' of the sixties was about. Alternatively, if women's minds cannot be changed, why not start at the other end and change the body to fit the 'need'? This is variously known as 'plastic surgery', 'clitoridectomy', 'foot binding' etc., depending on where or when you happen to live. Failing these methods, there are always more overt forms of violence . . .

Likewise, 'everybody knows' what is 'offensive'. The recently submitted government report of the Williams Committee, whose recommendations include the free availability, within licenced premises rather than in local newsagents, of all pornography except that which involves extremes of violence, is built on the notion of consensus. If the Williams recommendations were enacted, most types of porn would be *more* easily available under restricted circumstances, whilst the so-called 'softest' material, such as *Forum* and *Playboy*, would remain public. 'Consensus' dictates that we shall no longer be offended. The flag waving will continue.

The Festival of Light prefers the term 'obscene' to the word 'offensive'. Whilst the Williams Committee aims to protect only the susceptibilities of the public, the Festival of Light would protect the private world of the nuclear family. They assert:

> All obscenity and pornography is an assault on the family. Much of it today is a deliberate unconcealed incitement to promiscuity and to homosexual and other vice. Its disruptive effect on married life must be obvious to all who have not entirely abrogated the use of common sense. Sex in marriage is not just the use of bodies but the natural coming together of two who share their lives. Pornography provides a counter attraction. The soft kind leads to promiscuity of the sex-object kind, the hard to perversion. We agree that there is a certain degree of licence available in regard to entertainment. There always has been. A delight in what is beautiful, whether in the human form or elsewhere, is not to be forbidden. Where, however, it becomes a real and unnatural threat to the stability of family life, it constitutes a threat to the security of the state and to the happiness of its citizens. The gigantic circulation of pornographic magazines constitutes, we maintain, just such a threat at present. (N.F.of L., 1978, p 15)

If the Festival of Light had their way, then, women would be shackled to the kitchen sink rather than be constricted in more patent forms of bondage. Any material suggesting women's autonomous sexuality, such as Betty Dodson's *Liberating Masturbation*, a pamphlet written to help women regain their sexuality through masturbation and self-examination, would presumably be banned, together with any other information which tells us how we define our sexuality (e.g. Nancy Friday's *My Secret Garden* and *Forbidden Flowers*, the Women's Health Handbook *Our Bodies, Ourselves*, etc.).

The Festival of Light are mistaken, however, if they think that to remove porn from public display will help to strengthen the institution of the family. Marriage *depends* on the double standard of the virgin/whore dichotomy which pornography exploits and perpetuates. The porn dealer I met went home to his wife and family every night after his day's sweat.

There *is* a war going on, but the assaults are not on the family; they are on *all* women, whether married or not, young or old, lesbian or heterosexual. We must fight back in whatever ways we can. Looking collectively at porn is probably one of the most immediate methods of consciousness-raising – but we also need to act. We are not fighting 'images', but male supremacy. Attacks on such images, on men who create and use them, whether on posters or in porn shops, is part of that battle. We must Reclaim the Night *and* the Day.

Bibliography on Pornography

Barnes, Clive (intro). *Report of the Commission on Obscenity and Pornography*. Bantam Books/New York Times, New York. 1970.

Blachford, Gregg. 'Looking at pornography: erotica and the socialist morality'. *Gay Left* 6, Summer. 1978.

Clark, Lorenne. 'Sexual equality and the problem of an adequate moral theory: the poverty of liberalism'. In Shirley, M. and Vigier, R (eds) *In Search of the Feminist Perspective*. Resources for Feminist Research, 252 Bloor Street West, Toronto, Ontario, M55 1V6. 1979.

Clor, Harry M. *Obscenity and Public Morality – Censorship in a Liberal Society*. University of Chicago Press. 1969.

Dodson, Betty. *Liberating Masturbation: A Meditation on Self Love*. Betty Dodson, Box 1933, New York, NY 10001. 1974.

Dworkin, Andrea. *Woman Hating*. Dutton, New York (esp. chaps 3-5). 1974.

Freeman, Gillian. *The Undergrowth of Liberature*. Panther, London. 1969.

Friday, Nancy. *My Secret Garden;* 1977. *Forbidden Flowers*. Trident, New York. 1976.

Gagnon, J. 'Erotic Environment'. Chapter 17 in *Human Sexualities*. Scott, Foreman & Co., Glenview, Illinois. 1977.

Gagnon, J.H. and Simon, W.S. 'Pornography – raging menace or paper tiger?' *Transaction*, July-August. 1967.

Gagnon, J.H. and Simon, W.S. *Sexual Conduct: The Social Sources of Human Sexuality*. Hutchinson, London. (esp. chap 9). 1974.

Gillan, Patricia. 'Sex therapy for single people'. *Psychology Today*, August. 1977.

Goldstein, M.J. and Kant, H.S. *Pornography and Sexual Deviance – A Report of the Legal and Behavioral Institute*, Beverly Hills, California. University of California Press. 1973.

Hyde, H. Montgomery. *A History of Pornography*. Four Square, Cambridge, Mass. 1966.

Kutschinsky, Berl. *Studies in Pornography and Sex Crimes in Denmark*. New Social Science Monographs, Copenhagen. 1970.

Longford Committee. *Pornography: The Longford Report*. Coronet, London. 1972.

Mavissakalin, M. et al. 'Responses to complex erotic stimuli in homosexual and heterosexual males'. *British Journal of Psychiatry*, vol 126. 1975.

Michael, Richard. (ed.) *The ABZ of Pornography*. Panther, London. 1972.

Morgan, Robin. 'Theory and practice: pornography and rape'. In *Going Too Far: The Personal Chronicle of a Feminist*. Random House, New York. 1978.

Nationwide Festival of Light. *Obscenity, Indecency and Violence in Publications, and Film Censorship:* Submission to the Home Office Committee under Professor Bernard Williams, January. (available from N.F.o.L., 21A Down St, London W1). 1978.

Owen, Lyn. 'Taboo or not taboo?' Article on the work of Judith Reisman and on her paper given at the Swansea Conference on Love and Attraction (5th-9th September, 1977), in *The Guardian*, 16th September, 1977. (Reisman's paper, which included a historical survey of porn, was titled: 'Pornography and female identity'. Reisman is at Case Western Reserve University, Ohio. 1977.

Phillips, Angela and Rakusen, Jill. (eds.) *Our Bodies, Ourselves*. (Boston Women's Health Handbook) Penguin, Harmondsworth. 1978.

Russell, D.E.H. and Van de Ven, N. (eds.) *Crimes Against Women: Proceedings of the International Tribunal*, Les Femmes, California. (see chap 13). 1976.

Shear, Marie. 'Free Meat talks back'. *Journal of Communication,* vol 26, no 1, Winter. 1976.

Simons, G.L. *Pornography Without Prejudice: A Reply to Objectors*. Abelard-Schuman, New York. 1972.

Wallsgrove, Ruth. 'Pornography'. *Spare Rib*, 65. 1978.

Williams, Bernard et al. *Report of the Committee on Obscenity and Film Censorship*. Bernard Williams (Chairman). HMSO. Cmnd. 7772. London. 1979.

LONDON RAPE ACTION GROUP

Towards a Revolutionary Feminist Analysis of Rape

This paper was originally written for the Bristol Women's Liberation conference on rape in 1978.

We are three women who have been working together in a rape group for more than a year. We think it is vital for women who are fighting rape to discuss and understand the nature of rape, its purpose as a weapon of the patriarchy, its history, as well as the myths which surround it, and the politics of law reform. We have tried to bring up these issues in this paper.

It is essential for the women's liberation movement fully to develop a feminist theory of rape: to expose rape for what it is – 'a conscious process of intimidation by which *all men* keep *all women* in a state of fear' (Brownmiller, 1976, p 5). The fear of rape is always with us. It affects our day-to-day lives in countless ways – not only in that we are afraid to walk the streets late at night, but in all our dealings with men, however superficial these may be.

Men's images of our bodies are thrust upon us wherever we go – in magazines, on advertising hoardings, on the tube, in the newspapers, in films, etc., etc. This makes us self-conscious about our bodies, the way we sit and stand and walk – when was the last time you saw a woman sit sprawled across a bus seat the way men do all the time? We keep our knees together, our legs crossed, our faces neutral. Somewhere in our minds we are always aware that any man – every man – can, if he wants to, use the weapon of rape against us.

And men know it too. The man who utters obscenities at us in the street knows it, the local greengrocer who insists on calling us love (although we have objected) knows it, the wolf-whistling building workers know it, the man on the tube reading page three and grinning at us knows it. At one point on a Reclaim the Night march in Soho, we were confronted by a large crowd of men shouting: 'We're on the rapist's side – we're with the rapist'. They did not really need to tell us. We already knew.

Rape has nothing to do with uncontrollable sex urge – rape is an expression of power and hate. Men rape to cause fear and pain and to prove their superiority. Read any woman's account of being raped.

Male myths about rape abound, naturally, for in a society controlled by men they have the power to spread their propaganda effectively. Many women are confused by these lies – it is really important that we work on understanding what rape actually is and that we share our ideas and experiences with each other.

Rapes have been documented from very early times, but until the end of the thirteenth century, in Britain at any rate, they were not treated in law as crimes against women, but as violations of male property. In early Hebrew law virgins were sold into marriage by their fathers for fifty pieces of silver. A man who raped a virgin outside the walls of the city had to pay the bride-price to her father, and they were commanded to marry. If, however, the rape took place within the city walls, both rapist and victim were stoned to death, the argument being that if the woman had screamed she would have been heard and rescued. Under Assyrian law, the father of a raped virgin was allowed in return to violate the rapist's wife.

During the Middle Ages in England, the rape of an heiress became a common method for men of power to extend their wealth and property. On the Continent, meanwhile, a manorial lord had the right to take the virginity of the bride of any of his serfs (the *jus primae noctis*), unless the bride and groom paid a certain fee.

From the time of Potiphar's wife, men have perpetrated the myth that women are prone to making false accusations of rape. This myth has been so thoroughly absorbed by male culture that warnings of women's tendencies to lie are handed out regularly at police colleges, and sometimes even in instructions to juries.

Men usually deny their responsibility for rape, and disassociate themselves from rapists, either by blaming the victim for her provocative behaviour, or, when that is impossible, by placing the rapists in some special category: pervert, lunatic, etc. However, in war, men admit that rape is an act of power when committed by the enemy (the rape of the Hun), but the result of an uncontrollable sex urge when committed by themselves:

> That's an everyday affair . . . The guys are human, man. (American squad leader in Vietnam, quoted in Brownmiller, 1976, p 108)

The threat of rape is a weapon which men use to perpetuate their dominance over women. The ways in which it is used in western, 'civilised' society are less obvious than in some of the primitive cultures studied by anthropologists, where rape was customarily a punishment for women who were sexually demanding, disobedient to their husbands, quarrelsome, or simply without a male protector. There is no law in Britain which forbids women to be independent, to live alone or with other women, to go out alone at night, to refuse to relate to men sexually or emotionally; yet in so many reported cases of rapes the behaviour of the victim is cited as provocation. She was hitch-hiking (she asked for it). She was wearing a low-cut dress (she asked for it). She left her door open (she asked for it). She seemed friendly in the pub. She came up for coffee. I only wanted to talk to her and she told me to fuck off. She's a lesbian. She's a prostitute. She's had two abortions. *She had to be punished*. Feminists: bitter, frigid, man-haters: what you need is a good fuck. The whole point being to keep each woman isolated from her sisters, the protected property of one man, who has exclusive sexual rights over her body. It is not a crime for a man to rape his wife.

A man can force sexual intercourse upon a woman without the fact of his forcing her spoiling his enjoyment. Obviously, in most cases of rape what the man is getting off on is the woman's fear, pain and humiliation, so we may say that rape is not a sexual crime. This is true in that rape is about male power and therefore political. But it is important also to recognise that the willingness and pleasure of women is very often, and very generally, unnecessary and irrelevant to men in sexual interactions. Many women say that they have never, ever, enjoyed sex with their husbands, but they have existed through years of married life 'letting' their husbands 'exercise their marital rights' when they could not put them off with one of the excuses women have been using over the centuries to deter their spouses from raping them.

Since in patriarchal society man is considered to be the hunter/doer/seducer/instigator, the one-that-goes-out-and . . . it is considered quite OK and normal for a man to try and persuade a woman to have sexual intercourse. He asks her to dance, she accepts. (She wants to, or she doesn't want to, but she's afraid of hurting his feelings, she's afraid of making him angry, and wants a man to dance with). He asks her out, she accepts. (She wants to, or she doesn't want to, but all her friends have got blokes, she's afraid of making him angry, he might feel hurt and she can't go out if she's on her own.) He kisses her. He puts his hand on her leg, her breast, her cunt. He wants to see how far he can go. She lets him. (She wants to, or she doesn't want to, but he's taken her out after all, and spent money on her, she needs a lift home, she doesn't want to seem a prude, and he might be angry.) He asks her to sleep with him. She accepts. (She wants to, or she doesn't want to but she thinks she might as well, she can't back off now, it might be OK, she's flattered that he wants her, and he might be angry.)

Or she refuses. He tries to persuade her. He tells her he loves her. He says she doesn't love him. He calls her a prude, immature, frigid. He says he 'needs' sex, so if she doesn't come across, he'll have to find a girl who will. Each time they meet he carries on a bit further, a bit further. ('Why not go all the way?') He buys Durex to demonstrate his sense of responsibility. Each time she finally tells him to stop and breaks away, he gets angry, he rages, he sulks; he tells her how bad it is for men to be left 'excited'. (Prick-teaser!) He teaches her to suck him off. He works towards his goal, which is her vagina. He means to have, to possess this woman.

This is not rape, this is normal everyday stuff. The magazines call it young love.

So if this is normal and acceptable, no wonder the rape law in this country is ambiguous. If a man believes, however erroneously, that the woman he is fucking has consented to being fucked, he is not guilty of rape. So if a woman shows any signs of reluctance, that is not to say she does not really want to. She needs talking around, she is playing hard to get, she needs turning on, she likes a rough time.

In heterosexual relationships it is the man's desires which come first and which are necessary. Then it is up to him to make the woman want sex as well. But if she does not, he can go ahead anyway. He has his penis. He has his erection. There is the woman, there is the vagina. So what is rape? And what, exactly, is 'consent'?

Some women would argue that a top priority must be the reform of the law on rape and a new legal definition of rape – one much broader than the current definition of forcible penetration, an act of sexual intercourse on the body of a woman not one's wife – and longer jail sentences for rapists, etc. While such reforms might have some good effects, we think that this perspective ignores a very important area – the *administration* of the law. Without radical change in the attitudes of the police, judges, juries, etc., any changes in the law will come as small comfort to rape victims. In general women who have been raped receive appalling treatment both by the police and by the courts – if indeed they get as far as the courts. The police accuse them of lying, of being prostitutes who did not get paid, etc. In court a woman's sexual history may be brought up at the discretion of the judge (the rapist's may *not*) – the result of this is that in many cases the *woman* ends up being on trial for 'promiscuity', the assumption being that if she has previously had an active sexual life, then she no longer has the right to refuse a man!

Whatever improvements may be made to the law on rape, so long as it is 'enforced' by misogynists (men), we can see no way it can be used to women's advantage.

So what is the answer? Shall we have a national campaign against rape, People Against Rape, the initials indicating the essential equality of sisters and brothers in this struggle, mixed marches, Men Against Rape groups, Trade Unions passing anti-rape resolutions, etc.? Or shall we fight every step of the way against the de-radicalisation of rape, against rape being amalgamated into the liberal consciousness along with abortion? In the same way that the radical meaning of 'a woman's right to choose', a woman's right to control her own body, has been watered down and lost, shall we sit back and let hordes of self-congratulatory men say 'Of course, I'm against rape'? For many men will flock to disassociate themselves from those those awful men who rape women.

We must be clear – *all* men are potential rapists.

References

Brownmiller. Susan. *Against Our Will: Men, Women and Rape*. Bantam, New York. 1976.

TINA HILL

Rape and Marital Violence in the Maintenance of Male Power

Male violence towards women works in two distinct, but inter-related and, I will argue, mutually dependent, ways in the maintenance of the subordination of women within patriarchal society.

Firstly, in a direct way, the use of physical and/or sexual violence by a man (or by men) on a woman is an exertion of male power over individual women. It is becoming clear that the incidence of such male coercion of women is widespread. Smart and Smart (1978) note a 20 percent increase in cases of rape reported to the police in England and Wales between 1969 and 1975. In the United States, reported rape and attempted rape increased by 62 percent between 1969 and 1973 (Edwards, 1976). Whilst Wilson says in his study of unreported rapes in Brisbane that during the course of his study

> it became obvious that sexual assault in one form or another is a common experience in the lives of most women (1978, p 24).

The literature on marital violence, like that on rape, reports only 'the tip of the iceberg'. However, findings indicate that the use of physical violence as a means of men maintaining their power position within the family is very widespread. In one survey of the adult population of the United States, one-fifth approved of a husband 'slapping' his wife on 'appropriate' occasions. (Stark and McEvoy, 1970).

We live in a society which has a long history of men having complete authority over women. A woman passed from the authority and control of her father, upon marriage, to that of her husband. The husband was given the legal and moral rights to manage and control her behaviour. As Dobash et al write:

> Men were charged with the responsibility of controlling women

> individually and within the privacy of the home and the use of physical coercion was merely one of the 'legitimate' means which was used to achieve such control. The subordinate position of women in the family and in other social institutions made them the legitimate victims of such domestic chastisement (1977, p 8).

This was legally recognised as late as 1915 when a London police magistrate ruled that:

> the husband of a nagging wife could beat her at home provided that the stick was no thicker than a man's thumb (ibid.).

These legal and moral sanctions given to men are examples of the second way in which male violence functions in the maintenance of women's position in society. It is neither so direct nor so obvious, yet in its many forms it pervades society. Its form and functioning are many and it feeds directly from violence at the interpersonal level, whilst feeding into this level by the tacit sanctioning of such violence, or, at the very least by the overt approval of the male aggressive/female passive stereotypes of which rape and battering are simply the extremes. It is the social control of women by the 'male state', i.e. the historical, cultural and social context, which sanctions and promotes the differing power relationships between men and women. This means that acts of physical and sexual violence by individual men can be seen not as deviant, but as an over-zealous use of power vested in them by being members of the male 'class' with all that this implies. Further, this over-zealous use of power by a few serves to maintain the power position of all men.

The most interpersonal events have their roots and correlates in the cultural and historical basis of society's norms and values. The institutional, social, interpersonal and personal cannot be divorced from each other. The wider context of prevailing and past ideologies must be seen as an integral part of interpersonal events.

The mutual interdependence of these two levels of male power in the interpersonal and social control of women should become clear by looking at rape and the battering of women in more detail.

Rape

In recent years we have seen a change in the approach to the study of rape. The widely held belief that rape was solely the act of the psychologically unbalanced male or social deviant is no longer the picture which emerges from the current literature on the subject. Despite this, the sex-crazed madman is still the rapist of widespread media coverage and of popular fiction. However, research has shown that the rapist is more likely to be the man from next door or round the corner, or even a member of your family or a friend. Also, contrary to the popular image, the attack is likely to have been planned.

In 1961 Manachem Amir conducted a detailed study of 'rapes known to the police', gathering all information on police files for the years 1958 to 1960 in Philadelphia City (Amir, 1971). This was the first full study to attempt to get away from the individual pathology model and the extrapolation of theories from a few clinical case studies. Amir advocates a situational approach:

> In cases of rape, one must consider the existing notions about male and female sex roles when they encounter a situation charged with sexuality. Another element is the opportune situation and its definition by the offenders who may already have anti-social and sexual aggressive attitudes which make the act possible. Such a situational approach allows gaining insight into the problem of differential behaviour of predisposed persons or of those who are pulled into committing the crime by circumstances of the situation (p 340).

Whilst not believing that rape is an either/or event as Amir suggests above (i.e. either 'personality' or 'situational'), nor being convinced by his 'lure of the situation, approach (and his own data does not bear this out as he found that 71 percent of rapes were planned), I nevertheless find Amir's empirical study revealing. Time, place, circumstance, and the social characteristics of the individuals, as well as the characteristics of both victim and offender and the relationship between them, are all examined. Amir found that in 48 percent of rapes, the victim knew her offender(s) and that these men, neighbours and acquaintances

> were found to be the most dangerous people so far as brutal rape was concerned (ibid.).

Further in 48 percent of the cases he studied, the initial contact was made in the streets and 26 percent in the victim's home, but rape took place in 56 percent of cases in either the victim's or the offender's home. As Amir's study is of cases of rape reported to the police, it is likely that women who have had even closer relationships with the rapist are less likely to report the rape, e.g. rape within the family or date rapes.

Pauline Bart, in an article called 'Rape doesn't end with a kiss', based on over a thousand questionnaires of rape victims, found that 5 percent of rape victims in the sample were raped by relatives, .4 percent by husbands, 1 percent by lovers, and 3 percent by ex-lovers. A total of 8.4 percent of women were therefore raped by men they had had a close relationship with, whilst a further 12 percent were raped by dates, and 23 percent by acquaintances, and 41 percent by total strangers (Bart, 1975). Curtis (1974) also found that of 250 victims under 18 years of age, 58 percent were raped by a relative or acquaintance. Wilson's (1978) study on unreported rapes in Brisbane found that the proportion of rapes involving relatives, friends, or acquaintances was higher than that in the rape studies based on official reported rape figures. His study reveals that nearly 70 percent of the unreported rapes were of this type. He goes on to say that,

> Family rape is probably one of the most unreported forms of rape that there is (p 40).

The most unreported of all forms of rape is that where the woman's relationship with the rapist is closest, that is rape within marriage. It is not recognised within the law and therefore never shown in any official statistics, but it is likely to be the most widespread of all forms of rape as it is both legally and socially sanctioned.

Rape, then, cannot be understood in terms of random attacks by sex-crazed psychopaths. Rather rape emerges from these studies as a product of the situational and social differences in the power relationships between men and women. At the interpersonal level, rape is an exercise in male power over specific women. At the level of the male/female class or caste system, it is a form of social control of all women. It is the exercise of dominance and power of the male rapist over the female victim which seems to be of prime importance in the relationship of male offender and female victim.

Wilson (1978) found that rape was often accompanied by extreme verbal and physical abuse. There was, he says, an 'aggressive anti-woman element'. Wilson also found that amongst a group of fifty men from all social classes, the fantasy of the master-slave relationship was extremely common. He reports that,

> A vision of titillating sexuality often reported by men was of a scantily-clad girl, quivering with terror, submitting herself to sexual intercourse through fear of physical humiliation. These fantasies were not accompanied by a desire to inflict physical violence on the girl but more by the satisfaction of seeing the girl shake in fear at the anticipation of violence (p 86).

Wilson goes on to say,

> Clearly, the enjoyment of the rape was increased by the ability to control and dominate another person' (p 86).

It is not surprising that, in summarising some of the findings of his Brisbane unreported rape study, Wilson should state,

> In short, rape becomes the epitomy of the supreme act of domination by one human being over another (p 92).

for many other studies have reached a similar conclusion, e.g. Bart writes,

> Rape is a power trip not a passion trip (1975).

and Gelles says,

> Rape is less a sexual act and more an act of power in the relation between men and women (1976, p 6).

while Brownmiller states that,

> All rape is an excercise in power (1976, p 256).

This exercise of power is seen most clearly and in its most brutal form within the context of group rape. War is a prime example of male physical aggression and men in war tend to rape in groups. Brownmiller gives a detailed account of this throughout history and most recently in the first and second world war, Bangladesh, and Vietnam. She says that,

> War provides men with a tacit license to rape, (it) reveals the male psyche, without the veneer of 'chivalry' or civilization (p 33).

Her view is not quite the same as one soldier's at the My Lai enquiry:

> (rape) that's an everyday affair. You can nail just about everybody on that – at least once. The guys are human, man (p 105).

However, his words echo Brownmiller's.

Amir, in his Philadelphia study, found that 43 percent of rapes were committed by two or more assailants. He briefly skates over the power relationships by saying that the assailants have to possess 'certain attitudes towards women and hence (to be) prepared to participate in group rape (1971, p 181). His basic tenet is that there is a subculture of violence, of male physical aggression, of what he terms the 'machismo factor', and of which sexual aggression is a major part.

Rape is set firmly within the context of male aggression and violence, and the control and subordination of women. It is a natural extension of existing values in our culture: of male aggressiveness and female passivity. If rape is not just a function of the different power relationships that occur within individual interpersonal situations, but a function of these power relations being structurally determined by the social definitions of masculine and feminine, then one would expect that in societies where male control of women is strongest, the incidence of rape would be highest.

Barbara Toner (1977) in presenting 'the cultural background of rape' states,

> To rape is not a fundamental instinct. It flourishes where the culture encourages it. This hypothesis is supported by comparison of the Arapesh, among whom rape is virtually unknown, and the Gusii, among whom this is a major problem. The cultural background of these two tribes offers some insight into the way sexual behaviour is learnt (p 39).

The studies of the Arapesh by Mead (1932, 1972) and the Gusii by Levine (1959) show that these two groups contrast markedly in the ways in which their societies are organised, their attitudes to men and women, and their incidence of, and attitudes towards, rape. The Arapesh have a non-competitive, non-aggressive social organisation. There is little or no difference between the behaviour of men and women. The men do not exercise control over women – the Arapesh society does not contain rape (Toner, 1977). In the Gusii culture, men and women are traditionally antagonistic toward one another. Marriages take place between men and women of hostile tribes. Men traditionally exercise control over women – and the incidence of rape is very high amongst the Gusii, to the extent that sexual intercourse within marriage is an enactment of rape and sexual violence.

> The husband is determined to force his wife into a position of subordination by repeated attacks of intercourse, preferably to hurt her so much that she is unable to walk the next day. The bride is

> determined to resist to the utmost, to bring shame on the husband. The act of intercourse is seen as an act of subjugation of the female and as such it continues to be important in the marital relationship (Toner, 1977, p 42).

Thus it can be argued that the sex role differentiations and differential power relations between men and women they imply, make rape inevitable in our culture and make women the perfect victims. As Josephson and Colwill write,

> It could be that rape is the inevitable crime of a misogynous society, one that has historically devalued women and exalted men. Coupled with this philosophy is a sex role prescription for male aggressivity and female passivity, male dominance, and female compliance (1978, p 197).

Not all men have to rape all women for rape and its threat to be an effective form of controlling women. As Brownmiller states,

> (Rape) is nothing more or less than a conscious process of intimidation whereby all men keep all women in a state of fear (1976, p 15).

The social control of women is achieved not just by the act of rape or the threat of rape, but by the power and control men gain from their protector role. Brownmiller suggests that,

> The historic price of women's protection by man against man was the imposition of chastity and monogamy. A crime committed against her body became a crime against the male estate (p 17).

The social control of women in this form, i.e. as men's property, also works to control women in a further way: as Wilson found, it was one of the main reasons why married women did not report rapes.

> Our responses give considerable support to the view that many women perceived their husbands as relating to them in a landlord-property type situation. In effect, the husband will consider his property as being damaged and assume as well that his property (his wife) contributed towards the violation (1978, p 61).

The mere fact that rape is so under-reported shows its effectiveness as a form of social control. What is more, it is a dual form of social control, as pointed out by Smart and Smart (1978):

> First, inasmuch as it is a form of physical coercion and violence, and second, insofar as the fear or threat of rape as communicated by the media, in literature, on film and in the press, serves to socialise women into tacitly constraining and limiting their own forms of behaviour and social activity (p 102).

Not only is it social control in a dual sense, but it serves two sets of interests: that of individual males, and that of the male state. Both sets of interests are served by women being kept in 'their place'. And both sets of interests are dependent upon each other to keep women in that place.

Marital Violence

In domestic violence what we see is not just the socially sanctioned dominance (and its maintenance) of male over female, but also of husband over wife. The ways in which violence, or its threat, functions as an effective form of social control of an individual woman, and, in turn, of women in general, are very much the same as we have seen through rape. It shares the same dualistic forms and serves male interests at both the micro and macro levels. Its effectiveness as a form of social control is again reflected in its vast underreporting. The available facts and statistics on the extent of marital violence tend to come from reported incidents, and these represent only a tiny proportion due to the feeling of shame and the threat of retribution. Dobash and Dobash (1977) in their study found among those women who did eventually report an assault, that they had only reported two in every ninety-eight to the police.

Research conducted by McClintock (1963) in England and Wales for the years 1950 and 1960, revealed that 30 percent of all violent offences were 'domestic disputes', and 90 percent of these attacks were husband on wife. The Dobashes analysed 33,724 police charges in 1974 for Edinburgh and one district of Glasgow, and found that violence accounted for only 11 percent of these charges. However, of these violent offences, the most numerous category was violence inflicted by husbands on wives – 26 percent. They found that in the home, women were victims in 95 percent of all cases. They conclude,

> The home is simply not a dangerous setting for men, but it is for women. Females, whether they be sisters, mothers, wives or daughters, are more likely to be subject to control through the use of physical force than are their male counterparts – and it is in their capacity as wives that the risk is highest and the danger the greatest (p 20).

Again we can see the workings of the two levels: women are encouraged into 'the home' by all levels of the male state and its ideology, and once there, the social control of them is reinforced through the potential of socially sanctioned male violence. Both (social and individual) levels of male interests are served. As Hanmer (1978) points out,

> The pervasive fear of violence, and violence itself, has the effect of driving women to seek protection from men, the very people who commit violence against them. Husbands and boyfriends are seen as protectors of women from the potential violence of unknown men. Women often feel safer in the company of men in public and the home, and marriage is portrayed, and often feels, the safest place of all, even though statistically speaking women are more likely to be violently assaulted in marriage and from men known to them (p 229).

Dobash and Dobash (1976) attempt in their study to focus on the inter-personal variables and to place these within the context of society's norms and expectations of male/female relationships. They argue strongly throughout their work that interpersonal violence is only meaningfully studied when the social context is specified. They state that 'Violence is not generated solely in the process of interaction', but is a combination of the historical, learned behaviour, and the interactive processes between husbands and wives.

> Although the institution of the family, as historically and socially given, is characterised by physical control of wives, not all husbands strike or beat their wives. It is necessary to examine the context of the family more closely in order to account for this differential use of violence. The potential for the use of violence resides within the institution of the family; the actual emergence . . . and continuation of marital violence is a dynamic interpersonal process. The probability that violence will occur between particular husbands and wives is associated with their individual biographies prior to marriage and their interactive relationships within marriage (pp 8-9).

They identify several interactional factors, including relative role expectations, the relative status of the wife vis à vis the husband, the relative abilities of the partners in problem-solving techniques, and their individual and familial experiences of violence (Dobash &

Dobash, 1974). In a sample of 100 women they found four major sources of conflict leading to violence: sexual jealousy 45 percent, role expectations 16 percent, money 17 percent, and drink 7 percent. A further major variable that they identify is that of marriage itself and its implied power relationships. In indepth interviews of 109 women, they found that 23 percent were hit during courtship, but that violence occurred mostly soon after marriage: 59 percent by the end of the first year, and 92 percent within the first five years (Dobash & Dobash, 1977).

Work by Hill (1978) in an exploratory survey of 146 battered women found only 6.5 percent had been hit during courtship. Similar results to those of the Dobashes were found regarding the first year of marriage, in that 53 percent of women experienced the onset of violence within this period. What is more revealing in Hill's study is that the first year was broken down into three time spans: within the first month, one month to six months, and six months to twelve months. It was found that 45 percent of the women had experienced the onset of violence within the first month of marriage. This lends even more support to the Dobashes' statement that,

> After marriage, the authority relationships between men and women become more explicit, husbands came to feel that their wives should meet their demands immediately and without question no matter how reasonable or unreasonable. The major source of contention centred on what might be called 'wifely obligations' and husbands' authority.
>
> In our research, it was the real or perceived challenges to his possession, authority and control which most often resulted in the use of violence. A late meal, an unironed shirt, a conversation with any man, no matter how old or young, all served as 'justification' for beatings (1977, p 24).

What seems to be important is the perceived change in the power relationship between a man and a woman when that woman becomes that man's wife. He not only feels that he has the right to expect his wife to obey him but that he is expected to make sure that she does. The role of wife carries with it implicit expectations of control, or at least the legacy of ownership by the husband. He in turn has an implicit licence to keep her within the wifely role. Thereby he exercises both interpersonal and social control over her. It is therefore not surprising that Dobash and Dobash in 1975 reported,

> A man seen beating and kicking his wife on the street, when confronted by the police told them, 'I can do what I like to her, she's my wife'. (Quoted in Sutton, 1979, p 14)

Nor is it surprising that the police rarely intervene in 'domestic disputes' (Select Committee on Violence in Marriage, 1975), given that they serve the male state.

What I have attempted to argue is that violence and its threat towards women is a form of social control as well as interpersonal control. Such violence in part at least is the product of the differing social roles of men and women and the unequal power relationships that these sex roles imply. Both are, in part, the legacy of our culturally ascribed female 'passive'/male 'aggressive' roles. And, as such, men have a vested interest in maintaining sex role socialisation in that they derive power at both the interpersonal and social levels. Physical and sexual violence or its threat is just one of the methods used to maintain their power, their social dominance, and women's social subordination.

Any analysis of male violence towards women must look at the ways in which male power is maintained through violence in interpersonal relations, and, further, the ways in which this use of violence collectively serves to maintain male control of women at the social level. In turn, such social control sanctions and encourages the use of violence at the interpersonal level, and so the cycle continues.

References

Amir, Menachem. *Patterns in Forcible Rape*. University of Chicago Press. 1971.

Bart, Pauline B. 'Rape doesn't end with a kiss'. Reported in Gelles, R.J. 1976. 1975.

Brownmiller, Susan. *Against Our Will: Men, Women and Rape*, Penguin, Harmondsworth. 1976.

Curtis, Lindsay. 'For Women Only'. *Denver Post*, December 1974. Reported in Gelles, R.J. 1976.

Dobash, R. and Dobash, R.E. 'Battered women: the importance of existing perspectives'. University of Stirling. 1974.

Dobash, R. and Dobash, R.E. 'The importance of historical and contemporary contexts in understanding marital violence'. Paper presented at the Annual Meeting of the American Sociological Association, New York. 1976.

Dobash, R.E. and Dobash, R. 'Wives: the "appropriate" victims of marital violence'. *Victimology*, Vol. 2. 1977.

Dobash, R.E., Wilson, M. and Cavanagh, K. 'Violence against wives: the legislation of the 1960s and the politics of indifference'. Paper presented at the National Deviancy Conference, Sheffield. 1977.

Edwards, M.L. 'Rape – at a time of social change'. Unpublished paper. 1976.

Gelles, R.J. 'Power, sex and violence: the case of marital rape'. Department of Sociology and Anthropology, University of Rhode Island. 1976.

Hanmer, Jalna. 'Violence and the social control of women'. In Littlejohn, G. et a. (eds.) *Power and the State*. Croom Helm, London. 1978.

Hill, Tina. 'Battered women: an exploratory survey'. Unpublished paper. 1978.

Josephson, Wendy L. and Colwill, Nina L. 'Males, females and aggression'. In Lips, H. and Colwill, N.L. (eds.) *The Psychology of Sex Differences*. Spectrum, Englewood Cliffs, N.J. 1978.

Levine, Robert A. 'Gusii sex offences: a study in social control'. *American Anthropologist*, vol. 61. 1959.

McClintock, F. *Crimes of Violence*. St. Martin's Press, New York. Reported in Dobash, R.E. and Dobash, R. 1977. 1963.

Mead, Margaret. *The Mountain Arapesh*. 3 vols. Muller and American Museum Science Books 1932; and *Sex and Temperament in Three Primitive Societies*. London. 1972.

Report from the Select Committee on Violence in Marriage Together with the Proceedings of the Committee, Vol. 2, Report, Minutes of Evidence and Appendices. HMSO, London. 1975.

Smart, Carol and Smart, Barry. *Women, Sexuality and Social Control*. Routledge and Kegan Paul, London. 1978.

Stark, R. and McEvoy III, J. 'Middle-class violence'. *Psychology Today*, vol. 4, no. 6, November. 1970

Sutton, Jo. 'Modern and Victorian battered women: a look at an old pattern'. In *Battered Women and Abused Children*. Issues Occasional Paper No. 4, University of Bradford. 1979.

Toner, Barbara. *The Facts of Rape*. Arrow, London. 1977.

Wilson, P.R. *The Other Side of Rape*. University of Queensland Press. 1978.

SHEILA JEFFREYS

The Sexual Abuse of Children in the Home

The sexual abuse of children is overwhelmingly a crime of adult men against female children. Nine out of ten of the victims of reported cases are female, and the offenders are male with almost no exceptions. This is not the way it appears from the literature on the subject, which talks of adults, not men; parents, not fathers; and victims, not young girls. Sexual abuse covers everything from indecent exposure and genital manipulation to child rape. The great majority of offenders, except in the case of indecent exposure, are known to the victims and come from the same neighbourhood, street or home. As in the case of rape, only a tiny percentage of cases get reported to parents, or the police, or lead to court proceedings.

In this paper I will concentrate on sexual abuse in the home. It is misleading to call such offences incest because that word can mean the sexual activity of consenting adults. The sexual abuse of children in the home takes the form of the rape and assault of largely female children by male adults. Three quarters of all reported cases are of the father/daughter type, and of the rest the vast majority are brother/sister, usually older brother/younger sister. Only about one percent of cases involves mothers and sons.

The number of cases which come to the courts in Britain each year is between 250 and 300. This in no way indicates the true size of the problem. The American Humane Association study of 1968 suggests that sexual abuse might actually be more common than other physical abuses of children. There is a taboo surrounding the subject which prevents it being thought about, let alone talked about. Professionals in jobs where they might be in a good position to discover it, e.g. social workers, psychologists, doctors and teachers, are unwilling to recognise the problem when they come across it. For instance, doctors in the US are prepared to attribute VD in little girls of four and six years old to contact with dirty sheets, an explanation which was long ago rejected as being a possible cause of VD in adults, rather than accept that a father has used the mouth, vagina or anus of his tiny daughter to masturbate in (Sgroi, 1975).

Reporting

There are many reasons why sexual abuse in the home goes unrecognised and unreported. To begin with, it usually leaves less obvious marks on the child than other types of physical abuse, except in cases where a careless father rapes a daughter who is very young and causes massive internal injuries. Often the victims do not know what is happening to them and their fathers tell them that every daddy does this to his daughters. By the time the daughters realise that it should not be happening, they often feel so guilty about having taken part in any way that they dare not report it. Who should they report it to? One of those who is supposed to be protecting them from harm, father or father substitute, is actually responsible. How do you tell your mother that your father has tried to rape you or has been doing so since you were eight years old? It is especially difficult when the child knows that it may mean the break-up of the family, the loss of the breadwinner and the father being sent to prison. Many of the fathers are physically violent to both children and mother, and the child will simply be very afraid.

If the mother does suspect or is told of the assaults there is good reason for her to be afraid to report it to the police. Her husband may be removed and sent to prison, which will seriously affect the family's finances, or the daughter may be taken into care, which will break up her family anyway and mean that the daughter is effectively punished for the father's offence.

Some Experiences of Sexual Abuse

To show how sexual abuse in the home begins and what it involves, I will quote from some of the letters I received in response to an appeal for information on the subject. None of the women concerned used their real names or wished to be identified.

One woman in a very brief note which gave no details wrote:

> It happened to me as a child and nobody knows what hell I went through because nobody cared but it has ruined me. Nobody knows, I'd no one to turn to. It has ruined my marriage. I'll never get it off my mind. Nobody knows what I went through.
>
> Please don't let any other child go through what I went through.

> There should be somewhere a child could go to for help. It only needs someone like you to help.

Another wrote:

> My father was a very violent man and all our family was terrified of him including me. It started when I was about thirteen years old. He did it so cleverly and very convincing that I didn't realise until it was too late. At first it was a goodnight kiss that lasted a little too long, or a friendly tickle in the wrong place, then eventually touching, exposing himself and finally intercourse, although it was quite a while before things got so far . . . We saw mum punched, kicked, beaten and generally knocked about continuously but I knew I could stop some of these beatings by 'being a good girl' as dad would say. I couldn't do anything about what was happening because dad would say if I didn't do it, he would start on my mum, and he would beat her up to prove it. This went on until I was nearly eighteen . . .

One woman wrote about her uncle:

> He used to call me in from playing, lock the door and subject me to all kinds of what I now know was sexual abuse. If I objected or cried I was punched in between my legs. He was very clever, not to mark me where it showed . . . He said if I told anyone he would kill me, if only I dared have told my mother, she would have killed him.

Another woman wrote in great detail about her experience with her father:

> Because my mum worked on evening shifts he was able to do things to me when we were alone. Every night he would take me up to bed and after undressing me he had to go all over me. He told me this was to make sure I was growing up properly and I believed him, I really did.
>
> Quite often he would get into bed with me and I would masturbate him. To be honest I much preferred doing this to being smacked which was the alternative. Almost every night he would masturbate me and from about that time on he began inserting his fingers.
>
> About three or four times a year he would strap me and I was

absolutely terrified of this and would do anything rather than have it. Once because I mentioned something of what was happening to my friend at school he strapped me so hard I was kept off school for a week because of the marks on my legs and body. Afterwards I never said a word to anybody right up till I was eighteen and I left home to become a student nurse. Even then nobody believed me.

From about eleven or twelve years old he was having me do fellatio. I was still only twelve when one night he made me get astride him and I was horribly frightened when it just slipped inside me . . . It hurt me terribly and made me feel sick but even so he made me do it that way about once a month or so.

Soon after that he found that if I lay on my face with my legs straight and together and with him on top of me he could get into me from the back. Not into my anus, and perhaps the penetration was not so deep and so it did not hurt so much. He did it this way to me about once or twice a week until I left home.

The Literature

Most of the literature is from the United States and has been written by psychologists and social workers; little has been written on the subject in Britain. Very little has a feminist perspective (except Rush, 1974). The literature makes every possible attempt to explain and excuse the behaviour of the male offender by blaming it on the victims or the mothers and wives of the offenders. The effects of sexual abuse, particularly on the female victims, are usually minimised.

The commonest form of sexual abuse in the home is father/daughter. But this is not considered the most serious form by writers on the subject. Masters and Johnson, for example, view the most serious kind as mother/son, a form which is extremely rare. They suggest that the forms of sexual abuse may be arranged according to the seriousness of their effects in the following order; the most serious is mother/son, then father/daughter, older sister/younger brother, older brother/younger sister.

> The most traumatic of incestuous relationships is that between mother and son. A mother destroys her son socially when she brings him to her bed, for inevitably she is overprotective and over-demanding. While isolating him as much as possible from peer-group influence, she renders him insecure and extremely self-conscious; usually he becomes a loner. The harder he tries to withdraw from her influence, the tighter she holds the reins. (Masters and Johnson, 1976).

They go on to say that cases of actual coitus in mother/son incest are so rare that they are unable to comment on them. They describe two basic forms. One is that the mother may go on washing her son in the bath long after he is capable of washing himself, during which she stimulates him sexually and may go on to masturbate him when he reaches puberty. The other is that a mother who has been widowed, or left without a husband for some other reason, might take her son into her bed, where they may lie side by side without clothes on but having no sexual contact. These then are the experiences which prove so traumatic for the son, whereas rape by fathers of their daughters is considered less serious. Of the very few cases of mother/son coitus actually reported in the literature, all but one that I have come across have taken the form of rape of the mother by her son.

The Kempes, considered to be 'experts' on child abuse, also, in their book published in 1978, state that boys suffer more serious effects than girls from incest, whether with their mothers, fathers or grandmothers. Boys are left with

> such severe emotional shock as to block normal emotional growth. They tend to be severely restricted and may be unable to handle any stress without becoming psychotic. Incest may be overcome – with or without help – by many girls, but it is ruinous for boys. (Kempe and Kempe, 1978).

What are we to make of the fact that the 'experts' consider the rarest form of incest, that in which rape of the child cannot occur and in which little physical contact occurs at all, the most serious in its effects? One simple explanation seems to fit. It is that father/daughter abuse and that of older brother/younger sister are expected to be less traumatic for victims than cases where the older participant is female because they do not upset the pattern of male dominance. Women are brought up to submit passively to sexual activity with older men who are in positions of authority over them. Their experience of sexual abuse with older, more powerful males in youth is but a premature encounter with what they may expect in adulthood. It is small wonder that the idea of boys being exposed to sexual activity with older, and in some ways more powerful, females in childhood sends the 'experts' into a tizzy. How will a man who has experienced this be able to exert his destined dominance over women in adulthood? The seriousness of childhood sexual experience is assessed according to whether it reinforces or undermines the training of children into the normal system of power relationships under male supremacy.

Explanations in the Literature

The explanations for sexual abuse in the home which are given in the literature have one thing in common. They attribute no responsibility to the adult male offender and put the blame on women – either on (a) the wives and mothers of the offenders or on (b) the female victims. Such explanations are based on an uncritical acceptance of the way in which male sexuality is constructed. It is assumed that men have uncontrollable urges which they will direct towards their children at any possible opportunity. Sexual self control is not expected of men. Women and children are expected to take responsibility for the way an adult male acts.

Blaming wives and mothers

One study suggests that the wives of rapists and incest offenders are not only responsible for their husbands' assaults, but that they gain positive advantages from them (Garrett and Wright, 1975). The study was carried out through interviews with the wives at an American hospital. It concluded, 'for this sample, rape and incest by husbands served as a particularly useful lever by which the wives can further build positions of moral and social dominance.' The authors found that the wives had, on average, more years of schooling than their husbands, and suggest that they deliberately married men to whom they could feel superior. The men were then driven to their assaults, they say, by a feeling of inferiority. Educational advantage on the part of wives has also been used to explain wife-battering in a study which Garrett and Wright mention (O'Brien, 1974). They also mention, in passing, that the wives of the rapists and incest offenders were also battered by their husbands. The explanation reveals the naked reality of male supremacist thinking. It assumes the naturalness and desirability of male dominance. A husband's educational advantage would never be used to explain his wife's misdemeanours since almost all husbands have such an advantage.

Many other writers give reasons for sexual abuse by the husband which clearly blame the wives. The wife may be rejecting and threatening; she may indulge the daughter and encourage her to a maturity beyond her years, she may be disenchanted with her husband and her marital role, turning outside the home for a job and other interests; she may 'arrange' situations that allow privacy between husband and daughter, such as getting work outside the home; she may fail to service her husband sexually. Mothers may also, apparently, precipitate sexual abuse by complaining about aspects of their husbands' behaviour such as his alcoholism, infidelity or his paedophilic exploits with other neighbourhood children (Cavallin, 1966; Shelton, 1975; Summit and Kryso, 1978; Kempes, 1978; Maisch, 1973; Henderson, 1972). The only way a woman can escape blame for her husband's assaults on her children, it seems, is to be a submissive, passive and uncomplaining wife, who fulfills her husband's sexual demands whether she wants to or not.

Some writers go so far as to describe the mother as the 'cornerstone of the pathological family system', saying that she is totally responsible for any breakdown of family relationships. Some even accuse her of deliberately pushing the daughter into bed with the father to compensate for her own infidelity, because she wants to give the husband a sexual substitute or because she has a voyeuristic interest (Machotka et al, 1978; Schechter and Roberge, 1976). Many others accuse the mother of being 'collusive', of knowing about the sexual abuse but deliberately not reporting it. The Kempes reject the claims of mothers that they had not known and say such claims 'can generally be discounted – we have simply not seen an innocent mother in long-standing incest, although the mother escapes the punishment that her husband is likely to suffer.' (Kempe and Kempe, 1978).

Such books as Louise Armstrong's *Kiss Daddy Goodnight*, which recounts the stories of sexual abuse victims in their own words, suggest that the mothers rarely have any idea what is happening (Armstrong, 1978). But victims and mothers are not believed by the professionals. When mothers *are* aware, they are hardly in a position to make an unrestricted choice of what to do. Incestuous fathers are often violent so that wives would be afraid of their wrath. Mothers must risk the break-up of their families and loss of the breadwinner if they take any action. They risk more than that: they face all the problems that any woman who seeks to live independently of men must face, including loss of status, lack of protection against male sexual violence and harassment, the suspicion of the social services, the indifference of building societies, repair men, shops and the gas board, difficulties in walking into pubs or on the streets at night. There is no consideration in the literature of the enforced dependency of women on men which is created under male supremacy, so that somehow the Kempes, who never speak of the molesting father as being 'guilty', can accuse the mother of not being 'innocent'.

The responsibility of the mother to prevent the husband from making sexual advances to the daughter is a common theme of the literature. Writers stress that the mother must be alert and on the lookout for incest and must guard against it. Such statements assume an equality of power between husbands and wives which simply does not exist. They also assume a knowledge on the part of the wife which has in fact been carefully concealed from her. Sex education lessons at school do not instruct girls that the men they marry are likely to make sexual assaults on their children. Such candidness might, after all, discourage women from entering marriage and heterosexual relationships where their children will be in such danger.

The most popular current form of explanation for sexual abuse in the home is the 'psychodynamic' approach. It looks at the whole family and the relationships within it to see how the abuse arises. The abuse is seen as a symptom of the tensions within the family or as a method of relieving them. In fact the 'psychodynamic' approach is just another woman-blaming strategy. Writers concentrate on the mother and her relationship with her daughter. The mother often, they say, forces the eldest daughter to assume many of what should be her own responsibilities. This means that the daughter performs household tasks such as dusting and helping with cooking (Browning and Boatman, 1977; Summit and Kryso, 1978). They say that this leads to role confusion and hence to sexual abuse. The implication is that the husband gets confused because he is used to imposing his sexual demands on whoever does the housework and he does not really notice who it is.

Victim blaming

Another line of explanation is to blame the victim. Victim blaming has become a popular approach to the explanation of crime in the last thirty years. A new discipline called 'Victimology' has been invented with its own journal and institutes, to stand alongside criminology. The victimologists claim to study the victim in the same way as criminologists study the criminal. Victimology has been applied to rape from its inception. It has been a particularly popular approach to child sexual abuse because of the Freudian assumptions behind much work in the area, i.e. that children really want sexual relations with their parents and are likely to initiate them. Many studies adopt this approach and divide victims into participant or non-participant, precipitating or non-precipitating groups. The evidence used to prove participation or even precipitation involves such things as accepting sweets or talking to strangers (Virkkunen, 1975). The greater power, authority and influence of male adults combined with the fear, lack of understanding of adult male sexuality and the desire for approval of the child, are never mentioned, or taken into consideration.

In the case of incest, the victims are often described as being unusually attractive or even seductive. One example of this kind of study is

Lindy Burton's *Vulnerable Children* in which she reports on the study of three types of child victims: those who suffer from road accidents, those who suffer from childhood asthma and those who experience sexual assault. She sets out to prove that there is something about the personalities of these children that accounts for them becoming victims in these different ways. She finds that the victims of road accidents are more likely to be adventurous children who will cross roads, and that sexual abuse victims are more likely to be attention-seeking children who will be friendly and affectionate to adults (Burton, 1968). Does this explain their victimisation? It may explain why some children are in more danger than others and why it is that it is necessary to destroy a child's trust and interest in male adults. It does not explain why the adult male offenders make sexual advances to children in the first place.

The beauty of the victimological approach is that it accounts for the occurrence of crime without any necessity to consider the deficiencies of the society in which the crime became possible. So rape and sexual abuse can be explained without criticising the system of male domination under which women and female children live.

The Effects of Sexual Abuse

The effects of the sexual abuse on children are precisely those likely to escape the scrutiny of researchers intent on upholding the *status quo* between men and women. It is because such abuse in the home reinforces rather than disrupts male authority that its effects are considered minimal. It is probable that all father/daughter relationships contain some element of sexual pressure which is merely part of the normal training programme for young girls. We learn to flirt, to please and to win affection from older males in a position of authority by 'being a good girl for daddy'. Some fathers cause distress to their daughters by watching them undress or giving prolonged goodnight kisses. The point at which being 'daddy's little girl' shades into what can be called sexual abuse is not as clearly defined as writers on the subject would have us believe.

Those who proclaim that there is nothing wrong with a healthy reciprocal sexual interest between parents and children, such as the Rene Guyon society in the US (an organisation of 200 parents whose motto is 'sex before eight or else it's too late'), overlook one crucial point. We live in a society in which adult males have power over all women and children. The nuclear family is not the 'natural' way to bring up children, but an institution which maintains male control. It facilitates the exercise of male authority and the exploitation of women, and trains children into the dominant or subordinate positions considered appropriate for men and women in the system of power relationships that is male supremacy. A female child is not permitted to develop a self-defined sexuality in her own time and according to her inclinations. We must assert her right to grow up free from the sexual attentions of her father or father substitute.

What Is To Be Done?

Recommendations for treatment in the literature concentrate on 'family therapy', a logical extension of the idea that paternal abuse is a 'family problem' rather than the abuse of daughters by their fathers. Central to this approach is the idea that maintenance of the family is all important, more important than the welfare of women and children. Child sexual abuse treatment centres have been set up in the US. In such centres, the child, the mother and the father are all persuaded that they are in some way responsible for what has happened so that they can all apologise to each other and relate to each other in future without any repetition of the offence. Such programmes claim great success. Women and children are forced to acknowledge responsibility for a situation in which they had no power or control and their experience of reality is brutally distorted.

We must work towards solutions which validate the experience of women and children, which give us the strength to make real decisions and work out what is in our interests. Such solutions may involve setting up sexual abuse phone-lines for children and their mothers, publicity around what is currently a taboo topic, instruction to children in schools about the behaviour they should be alert to, and have the right to object to, in fathers and husbands. The ultimate solution is the destruction of the political system of male supremacy, but meanwhile we must work out how best to help and support the women and children who are suffering at the hands of sexually abusive men.

References

Armstrong, Louise. *Kiss Daddy Goodnight*. Hawthorn, New York. 1978.

Browning, Diane and Boatman, Bonny. 'Incest: children at risk'. *American Journal of Psychiatry*, vol. 123, no. 1, January. 1977.

Burton, Lindy. *Vulnerable Children*. Routledge and Kegan Paul, London. 1968.

Cavallin, Hector. 'Incestuous fathers: a clinical report'. *American Journal of Psychiatry*, vol. 122, no. 4, April. 1966.

De Francis, Vincent. *Protecting the Child Victims of Sex Crimes Committed by Adults*. American Humane Association, Children's Division, Denver. 1969.

Garrett, T.B. and Wright, R. 'Wives of rapists and incest offenders'. *Journal of Sex Research*, vol. 11, no. 2. 1975

Henderson, D.J. 'Incest: a synthesis of data'. *Canadian Psychiatric Association Journal*, vol. 17. 1972.

Kempe, Ruth S. and Kempe, C. Henry. *Child Abuse*. Fontana, London. 1978.

Machotka, Paul et al. 'Incest as a family affair'. *Family Process*, vol. 6, no. 1. 1967.

Maisch, H. *Incest*. Andre Deutsch, London. 1973.

Masters, William H. and Johnson, Virginia E. 'Incest: the ultimate sexual taboo'. *Redbook Magazine*, April. 1976.

O'Brien, John E. 'Violence in divorce-prone families'. In Steinmetz, S.K. and Straus, M.A. (eds.) *Violence in the Family*. Dodd, Mead, New York. 1974.

Rush, Florence. 'The sexual abuse of children: a feminist point of view?' in Radical Therapist Collective. (ed.) *The Radical Therapist*. Penguin, Harmondsworth. 1974.

Schechter, Marshall D. and Roberge, Leo. 'Sexual exploitation'. in Helfer, R.E. and Kempe, C.H. (eds.) *Child Abuse and Neglect*. Ballinger, Cambridge, Mass. 1976.

Sgroi, Suzanne M. 'Sexual molestation of children: the last frontier in child abuse'. *Children Today*, vol. 4, no. 3, May-June. 1975.

Shelton, William R. 'A study of incest'. *International Journal of Offender Therapy and Comparative Criminology*, vol. 19, no. 2. 1975.

Summit, Roland and Kryso, JoAnn. 'Sexual abuse of children: a clinical spectrum'. *American Journal of Orthopsychiatry*, vol. 48, no. 2, April. 1978.

Virkkunen, Matti. 'Victim-precipitated pedophilia offences'. *British Journal of Criminology*, vol. 15, no. 2, April. 1975.

KATHY OVERFIELD

The Packaging of Women: Science and our Sexuality

Women have always been defined in terms of their biological functions. This definition has usually been negative, male-orientated, and restricting, so women are forced into seeing themselves, and being seen, exclusively in terms of biology which in its cruder form turns into biological determinism. Biological determinism is expressed in explanations of human or social behaviour solely in terms of biology. For instance, biologically based ideas about hormones have been used to 'explain' the existence of homosexuality, and arguments been put forward about the biological 'inferiority' of blacks and other non-white races. Used in this way, social structures are completely ignored and the biology is thoroughly spurious – but it sounds good. 'Sociobiology', as advanced by Morris, Tiger, Fox, Wilson and Ardrey is the most recent version of this kind of determinism (Janson-Smith, 1980).

The baseline for scientific definitions of women has been relative to definitions of men: the male (white, middle class, heterosexual) is taken as the norm against which everything else is measured (Wallsgrove, 1980). As anthropologists and others have observed (Horney, 1978; Zilboorg, 1978), whatever men do in any patriarchal society is revered and respected – from digging potatoes to wearing make-up and masks; whatever women do – even if it is exactly the same activity – is denigrated and accorded little respect. If the male, or masculine, is the baseline from which everything is measured, anything else tends automatically to be defined as deviant, prohibited, or an expression of 'otherness' (de Beauvoir, 1976; Mathieu, 1978). Conversely, it is seen as an achievement to *reach* male standards, to become *equal* on male terms, to attain accredited status.

It is tempting to speculate *why* definitions in these terms have stuck, to the exclusion of all others. Some feminists (de Beauvoir, 1976;

Daly, 1973) have traced this phenomenon to an inherent pattern of male thought which, in naming itself subject, must create in opposition, object. Dichotomy and division is part and parcel of all the concepts of Western, so-called 'rationalist' thought – and has come to be the dominant mode, eliminating or ridiculing any ideas or cultures in any way at variance. I do not have time to go into philosophical speculations about this, but will concentrate instead on the fact that science and technology are represented as the 'good' side of the dichotomy. There is a strict hierarchy of scientific importance – that is, physics stands much higher in esteem than engineering and chemistry. The social sciences (the debate still rages) have blatantly *not* fitted into a 'scientific' framework pure and simple, for science as it now is has to be in terms of dichotomy – proven/unproven; good/bad; male/female; light/dark; positive/negative. This has something specifically to do with capitalism and the development of the sciences (BWSG, 1980; Rose and Rose, 1976) in the West, but now science and technology have both been the means to, and appropriated the rewards of, 'progress'. After the event, science declares itself to be good, based only on impartial observation and rational deduction: it has nothing to do with emotions and diaphanous fancies. All *objects* of study tend to be classed as either good or bad, light or dark – and, most importantly, male or female. The female side is always the emotional, feeling, irrational (to feel is to be irrational according to this ethic) and, therefore, so easily, bad. (Lesbianism – female/female; negative/negative – is obviously almost as pernicious as is conceivable!)

My concern, specifically, is what happens to women when defined according to these rigid classifications. Female sexuality, in fact, provides a particularly important – and stubborn – example of how things female have been forced into categories which they do not, and cannot, fit. The result tends to be not that the categories – or the assumptions around which they are built – are ever questioned, but that the *objects* of study are 'blamed' for not fitting, and are expected then to sort themselves out.

From Aristotle and Pythagoras, from St. Augustine and St. Paul, through to Tolstoy, Freud, Stokely Carmichael and Margaret Thatcher, hatred and fear of women has been normal and accepted, the old myths perpetuated generation after generation (Morgan, 1970). Whereas in the Old World definitions came from the Church and the philosophers, now this function has been largely assumed by the new religious order – science and the scientists – and their spokespeople – the medical profession, the psychiatrists, and others. Some feminists (Firestone, 1972) have tried to trace the historical takeover or submersion of female power. There is little we can be sure of in the past, but it does seem that societies where women held power were based more on harmony than domination; on cooperation than destruction. Mary Daly extends this argument to say, '"On top" thinking, imagining and acting is essentially patriarchal' (1973, p 94). Certainly, the definitions are now formed and expressed largely by men. While Daly links this to patriarchal religion ('to be human is to be male is to be the Son of God', p 139), which totally excludes women from a positive identity of our humanity and womanfulness (BWSG, 1980, introduction) – de Beauvoir refers to the distinction between Self and Other. Woman, inevitably, is Other, the object.

Two fundamental things happen as a result: (1) women are defined not on their own terms, not even from their own point of view, but in relation to the male – to men's wants, prejudices and fears; (2) the male/female distinction is the first in a long line of divisions: masculine/feminine; subject/object; good/bad; logical/emotional – and the whole point of having categories means that entire populations are placed according to certain features. In our case, the genetic fact that we are born with an XX chromosome combination, rather than XY, more or less determines what is expected of us, how we will be brought up, how we will acquire and express our personal identity (Sayers, 1980; Jackson, 1978). Throughout centuries of total ignorance of genetics, woman was assumed to be a 'misbegotten male', a deviation, whereas modern research now tells us that the basic, chromosomal formation is female, XX, and 'it would be far more accurate to designate the male (produced by a Y chromosome, which is an incomplete X chromosome) as a misbegotten female' (Daly, 1973, p 95).

Nevertheless, women have been, and are, seen only in terms of their biological – or rather, reproductive – functions; and generally negatively. Menstruation, for instance, is generally regarded as unclean and defiling (especially to men). Menstrual taboos are usually interpreted as a way of protecting men from 'polluting fluids'. In fact such taboos might equally have been another form of control of women's sexuality, since a peak in sexual desire is felt by some women during menstruation (Faulkner, 1980). Such explanations of taboo are not generally considered by male anthropologists.

In talking about sex, too, the negative definition of woman becomes very clear. Our function has been, and is (supposed) to be, only defined in terms of male hopes and fears. The widely-accepted view until very recently was neatly summed up in the early twentieth century:

> If the feminine abilities were developed to the same degree as those of the male, [woman's] maternal organs would suffer and we should have before us a repulsive and useless hybrid (Quoted in Morgan, 1970, p 37).

In other words, no energy should be diverted from reproduction into intellectual or other interests. Such arguments have (most flexibly) been used to prevent women having the vote, being educated, entering male-dominated fields such as the physical sciences or electronics, and rounded off with an ideology which makes us feel guilty for wanting the freedom to choose anything other than what we are allowed.

The spread of psychological ideas – and particularly Freudian psychoanalysis – perpetuated many mistaken opinions of female sexuality and personality. Freud's own work was based entirely on sessions with some of his patients, at a time when little was known in the West, scientifically or physiologically, about women. Freud's work has taken something of a bashing recently, but it is rarely questioned as being misogynist. And, as Naomi Weisstein has said: 'consider Freud. What he thought constituted evidence violated the most minimal conditions of scientific rigour . . . years of clinical experience is not the same thing as empirical evidence' (Weisstein, 1973, p 182). However, this did not prevent women being burdened and conned with the 'mythical vaginal orgasm', and their seemingly inexplicable failure to achieve mature, vaginal sexuality.

I will try to explore the ideas about female sexuality which have come from that supposedly most objective, rational, experimental – male above all – of disciplines, namely, science. In order to understand why some questions were asked and not others, how they were asked, and which answers met with approval and dissemination, we must first of all explode some of the myths around the concept of 'science'.

The Scientific Ethic

The development of science and scientific knowledge as we know it today was very closely bound up with the history of Western, rationalist thought, and the growth of capitalism and industrialisation. The way in which scientific knowledge was taken over and used for certain ends – generally for the benefit of the elite rather than the good of society as a whole – was an indication of the powerfulness of the new knowledge and, therefore, those who had access to it (Barnes, 1972; Kuhn, 1970). As patriarchal religion before it, science came to be used to control and manipulate, rather than to work in harmony with nature. The label 'science' now means to most people simply a great deal of information that they do not understand. This image is manipulated in everything from television advertisements about painkillers, to round-the-bed discussions among in-the-know consultants. The mystification and jargon which surround much science, and the alienation which is built into an elitist form of knowledge, serve effectively to keep the powerless (those who do not have the expertise) out (BWSG, 1980); and to discourage us from finding out, participating and believing in our own effectiveness against the privileged few, whether they be heads of multinational corporations or individuals. This only further convinces people in power that the masses are stupid and can be manipulated.

Science is a social activity and it – as well as the workers within it – is inevitably affected and guided according to the values of the society in which it takes place. In our society, science has been used to justify the *status quo*. In the case of women, it has been further used to create and sustain an image of the helpless, hopeless, passive woman, biologically suited to do only certain things (housework, servicing the 'real' workers'). This is no doubt partly because science is a nearly-all-male activity – most women involved are likely to be in subordinate, supportive roles and not in the forefront of decision-making and policy execution. It is also because science embodies the dichotomies of Western thought – it is supposedly the good half of the good versus bad; experimental versus intuitive; masculine versus feminine categories. As well as *practically* excluding women from the activity of science, the image is everything women are not supposed, or thought, to be: objective, rational, steady, active, intellectual. (I am not saying it *is*, or that women never are, but trying to point out the falseness implied in rigid dichotomies). However, some people, those in the Radical Science movement and others, have already made similar observations (Rose and Rose, 1976), though not from the feminist viewpoint (this was an added incentive to the writing of BWSG, 1980 from a female and feminist point of view). I will go on, however, to discuss science and sexuality – specifically, female sexuality.

Science and Sex

Nowadays, nothing can be certain or really accepted without the scientific stamp of approval. The label 'science' – or, better still, 'laboratory experiments' – implies that good, rational, unemotional experiments have taken place, and the results are not just a product of, say, chance or good weather. Sex, too, has succumbed. This might be laughable, except for the fact that the first researches into sex and sexuality were needed for the physiological details they gave. Sex, of course, was a very touchy subject and the auspices of scientific respectability promised something new, 'the last word'.

Scientific research on sexuality falls loosely into three categories: studies of animal sexual behaviour; direct physiological measurements of human sexual experiences; and cross-cultural studies of human sexual behaviour (Faulkner, 1980). Definitions of animal sexuality (generally in terms of posture, penetration and male ejaculation) are about as limited as are concepts of human sexuality, and revolve almost exclusively around reproductive, heterosexual intercourse (Birke, 1980). These studies are often used, rather dubiously, as direct analogies with human behaviour, sexual or otherwise. This approach is fraught with problems, not least of which is that generalisations from animals should be made with great caution, as we know very little yet about what determines and influences human behaviour. Neither the original ideas for research, nor the eventual results, are 'objective' or 'neutral'.

> Many of the ideas . . . reflect particular social values concerning women. These in turn provide legitimation of particular beliefs about 'appropriate' sexual behaviour. The concept of female sexuality seen through the pages of animal studies is essentially a passive one . . . (Birke, 1979).

The old myths about women, and what is natural to a 'normal' woman, dictated that female sexuality was totally disparaged, except insofar as it was reproductive, and centred around male satisfaction (Whiting, 1972). Even reproduction was turned against women – an uncontrollable function for which we were blamed and penalised. Knowledge of, and control over, the reproductive functions has never fully been ours.

Until very recently, women were not considered to have, or allowed to enjoy, a self-defined sexuality; any practice not presupposing male penetration/satisfaction has never been openly approved. If we look a little more closely at what research has been done on 'sex', we find not only that it was based on totally male-defined and delimited ideas of heterosexual penetration; but also that women were (obviously) found wanting according to these criteria and labelled generally in need of treatment in order to reach our 'true being'.

There were only two choices: to be sexual in the narrowest sense of the word, for the purpose only of reproduction and/or male satisfaction; or to be completely non-sexual (the Virgin mother, the nun) (Whiting, 1972). Any other form or expression of sexuality was repressed, denied, condemned or – literally – chopped and changed. Szasz points out (1971) that for centuries no distinction was made between religious unorthodoxy and sexual misbehaviour; for centuries, too, both were condemned and punished.

Direct, brutal, physical methods to control and repress female sexuality have been around for a long time: there are an estimated (probably underestimated) ten million women alive today who have undergone some form of sexual mutilation (Hosken, 1976). They suffer long- and short-term complications such as haemorrhage, pelvic sepsis, and infertility – and of course it becomes impossible for these women to realise their sexuality.

In eighteenth and nineteenth century England and the US ovariectomy/ovariotomy (removal of the ovaries) and clitoridectomy (removal of the clitoris) – without anaesthesia or asepsis – were advocated for anything from masturbation to 'inordinate passion'. The last recorded clitoridectomy in the US took place in 1948 on a child of five (Ehrenreich and English, 1976). (There are reports of more recent mutilations well into the 1970s – see, for example, *Spare Rib* 92 and 95, 1980). Most of these 'cures' for female sexuality happen at times and in societies where nothing whatsoever is known of hormonal influences, the menstrual cycle, or of female sexuality as a physiological phenomenon. No explanation need be offered: the age-old fear and hatred of the mysterious unbiddable womb, and female sexuality, is sanction enough (Daly, 1978; Dworkin, 1974).

Where direct physical mutilation is not so widely used to control female sexuality, the methods are no less far-reaching: the terms 'mother-fixation', the 'Oedipus complex' and 'repressed incestual feelings' are commonly, often ignorantly, bandied about. The labelling process is now so refined as, first, to accuse us of being maladjusted and/or deviant, and second, to blame us and/or our mothers for getting ourselves into this pickle, and for the lack of 'intelligence' and 'understanding' to get ourselves out. What is wrong, rather, is not millions of guilty and frustrated women, but the definitions, stereotypes and social structures which confine us to one form of sexual expression – a form which is innately unsatisfying to women. We are condemned both for accepting and for rejecting these forms, locked in a never ending double bind. Pills, psychiatry and surgery are put forward as the cure for all things.

The Puritan ethic – and all patriarchal religions before that – in saying that sex was only for reproduction made it very much less likely that women would have sexual satisfaction, while hardly interfering with male satisfaction. (Reproduction, after all, is ensured by male orgasm and ejaculation, and conception is perhaps less likely to take place if the woman has orgasms—Hite, 1977.) Just to make sure, women have also been encouraged to see reproductive sex *as* sexuality – and all of it, anyway, as sinful, dirty, and only a 'male need' – an attitude which is not so hard to find in most of us still. The dichotomy that sex equals sexuality still persists – and along with the idea that sex also equals or expresses the passive/active, submissive/dominant equations, still traps women into the 'lady or whore' circle. Sex, in being subjected to scientific study, has been mystified, surrounded with jargon, and dehumanised.

The Studies – Sexology in Progress

In fact the well publicised studies of Kinsey and Masters and Johnson were *not* the first and only well documented studies of female sexuality. In any case, those studies represented female sexuality as an adjunct to male sexuality. Sexuality was, once again, assumed to be male, and the female form merely a curious deviation. Such studies often represent what Naomi Weisstein calls the 'maiming and selective truncation of the evidence in the service of a plea for the maintenance of male privilege' (Weisstein, 1973, p 193).

There were at least two fairly detailed studies carried out by women on female sexuality at the turn of the century. That these are nearly unknown might perhaps have something to do with the fact they were done by women with the specific purpose not of accepting the male stereotypes of what women want and need, but of finding out and reporting what women themselves say and know.

The first was carried out between 1890 and 1920 by Dr. Clelia D. Mosher, a professor at Stanford Medical School, and was a personal survey of 45 women. (Her manuscripts were lost until very recently; I have been unable to obtain a copy in this country and am going on Shade's article in the *International Journal of Women's Studies*.) The second study – a major contribution to sex research – was conducted in the 'twenties by Katherine B. Davis. *Factors in the Sex Life of Twenty-two Hundred Women* included college women who ranged in age up to seventy (Davis, 1929). It is most important to realise that *nothing* on this scale was carried out again until *The Hite Report* of 1976 entirely by and for women. It is significant both that these findings are not general knowledge, and indeed were 'lost', and that none of them had the benefit of large-scale funding or backing, in total opposition to the Kinsey and other researches.

A great many things were happening around medicine and things loosely medical at the turn of the century – among others, the medical profession's increasingly technological takeover of birth and child-bearing (Ehrenreich and English, 1976; Ann Oakley, 1975), and the fight between male obstetricians and gynaecologists and female mid-wives (Donnison, 1977). In his paper on female sexuality in Victorian America, Shade argues that interest in and studies of female sexuality were connected to the blossoming of 'sisterly' feelings generated by the feminist upsurge at this time. This may be his euphemism for women's anger, which gave life to both feminist and lesbian consciousness. Other men, too, were observing the phenomenon, such as Denslow Lewis in his 1899 paper delivered to the American Medical Association:

> They embrace . . . with mutual satisfaction . . . They learn the pleasure of direct contact, and in the course of their fondling they *resort* to cunnilinguistic practices . . . after [which] the *normal* sex act fails to satisfy . . . ' (Shade, 1978, p 16, my italics).

Thousands of 'prophylactic' ovariectomies were performed between 1860 and 1890; and in 1872 a Dr. Robert Battey of Rome, Georgia advocated this operation as cure for 'troublesome, erotic tendencies, and dysmenorrhoea [extreme pain or dragging ache during menstruation]. Most apparent in the enormous variety of symptoms doctors took to indicate castration was a strong current of sexual [interest] on the part of women' (Ehrenreich and English, 1976, pp 39-40).

These operations were performed exclusively by male 'surgeons' on women; ovaries were 'handed around at medical society meetings on plates like trophies' (Barker-Benfield, 1972).

At the time of these researches, not only was sex still surrounded with myths and prohibitions, but women were the problem – and female sexuality was, obviously, a thorny issue. From these beginnings, it is hardly surprising that Freud's work gained so much currency (though revolutionary in that it accepted that women, too, had sexual feelings, it legitimated totally the passive, neurotic woman, satisfied only in heterosexual intercourse, and obviously abnormal if fixated on clitoral satisfaction). Second, female sexuality and sexuality in general were to become scientific objects – notably of the US National Council for Research into *Problems of Sex*. This Council was set up in the 1930s and was instrumental in 'transforming human sex into a scientific problem and making it an object for medical therapy' (Haraway, 1978). Problems it was empowered to study and 'solve' included homosexuality and unhappy marriages. A very large part of its research funding in the early years went on studies of other species – and, often, resulted in the simplistic analogies between animal and human sexual behaviour which I have mentioned.

If we bear in mind the time at which these studies were carried out, the ideas then in currency about women, the false comparisons made with animals' and other cultures' sexuality, and the false assumptions on which the whole research was based, it is hardly surprising that most of it merely validated the truism that, of course, women were lacking, and of course they couldn't help it, poor things – but for god's sake don't tell them or they'll all be too damn demanding . . .

As I do not think the Kinsey *et al* and Masters and Johnson researches told women much that they did not already know (though perhaps they eased the burden of guilt a little), I will merely skip over the main results of those studies, and then briefly discuss *The Hite Report*. Here, I will only say that *The Hite Report* (of 3,000 women) has been widely criticised as methodologically and scientifically inaccurate and dubious – ignoring totally what Hite herself says of her research methodology and aims.

The problem has not been a lack of knowledge, but that the details were presented in fairly obscure, medical langauge; and for the most part ignored by the popular media.

Kinsey, for example, in 1953 reported that the vagina 'like nearly all other internal body structures [is] poorly supplied with end organs of touch . . . [and is] similar in this respect to the rectum and other parts of the digestive tract' (Kinsey et al, 1953, pp 579-80). Kinsey goes on to say that 'it is difficult to understand what can be meant by a "vaginal orgasm" . . . that the vagina itself should be the centre of sensory stimulation . . . is a physical and physiologic impossibility for nearly all females' and that 'there are *no anatomic data* to indicate [that Freud's vaginal vs. clitoral orgasm distinction] has ever been observed or is possible' (Kinsey, 1953, p 582, my italics).

The clitoris, on the other hand, has no other function than that of sensual pleasure (Koedt, 1973, p 199 ff). Nonetheless

> some hundreds of the women in our own study and many thousands of the patients of certain clinicians have been much disturbed by their failure to accomplish this biologic impossibility (Kinsey, p 584).

As Koedt states, 'looking for a cure to a problem that has none can lead a woman on an endless path of self-hatred and insecurity' (1973, p 204).

Kinsey continues:

> Biologists and psychologists who have accepted the doctrine that the only natural function of sex is reproduction, have simply ignored the existence of sexual activity which is not reproductive. They have assumed that heterosexual responses are... innate, 'instinctive'. Such interpretations...do not originate in our knowledge of the physiology of sexual response' (1953, pp 447-8).

The Masters and Johnson research again reiterated the physiological facts; and their conclusions were as follows (Lydon, 1970, p 222): (1) that the vaginal/clitoral orgasm distinction thought up by Freud and propagated by many psychologists was totally false – all orgasms centre in and emanate from the clitoris; (2) that women are often multi-orgasmic; (3) that orgasm varies not in kind, but in intensity for women; (4) that orgasm is as real and necessary to women as it is to men and in fact (5) that there is an 'infinite variety of female sexual response'.

Such findings have been discovered and repeated *ad nauseam*. Shere Hite's study, however, for the first time reported women's feelings about their own sexuality, and their felt needs and desires. Many of the women wrote full details – anonymously, as the old ideas of women's sexuality prevented many of them openly acknowledging and avowing their needs, for fear of being told by their male partners they were abnormal and perverted.

The paperback Masters and Johnson studies were a bestseller in the US. Nevertheless, the male-oriented attitude that sex is only really a 'male need', that it is defined (teleologically) according to penile penetration and ejaculation, and that sexual fulfilment is somehow less important for women than men, still persists among women (Friedman, 1979). As Susan Lydon says, 'the mythology remains intact because a male dominated . . . culture has a vested interest in its continuance' (1970, p 223).

Some writers – 'feminists' among them – have even gone so far as to suggest, approvingly, that the modern, industrialised world could not have been without the repression and conversion of sexual energy (Sherfey, 1978). It always seems, though, that it is *female* sexuality which is bound, and turned to whatever particular ethos is in fashion. This is as much true of socialist revolutions to date (for example in Algeria and China) as for capitalist countries.

The supreme arrogance of the male standards – applied willy-nilly to all and sundry – is never seriously questioned and never likely to be. While science and technology remain male-controlled and the definitions male-orientated, women can only ever be 'other'. We can be nothing but deviant, abnormal, and ripe for 'cure' – physical, psychological or medical. In other words, we are either to be raped, or to rely on the rapists for our protection. While scientists and politicians, for example, see nothing at all wrong in a huge imbalance in the sexes – with more men of course (now an imminent possibility with researches into reproductive engineering – Hanmer and Allen, 1980); while doctors and theologians have control not only over the doctrines which are propagated to millions of women, but also of the rules and conditions under which we may have rights over our own bodies; while women's ignorance of and confusion about our sexuality and our biology remain – why should anything change?

Mary Daly speaks of 'raising up female pride, recovering female history, healing and bringing into the open, female presence' (1973, p 96). She calls the 'obsession with genital sexuality' a 'currently popular form of rape...the rape of mind and will that robs the female self of precious time, energy and self-esteem' (1973, p 123). In some ways, this seems to be forcing us back into the denial and repression of female sexuality at a time when, perhaps, we are just beginning to discover what it might be.

Individual change is not enough. If we ignore science and scientific research, or if we turn in anger and frustration against biology and science because of the undoubted harm that has already been done in their name (Seaman and Seaman, 1977; Weiss, 1975), we have, in a sense, accepted the arguments of our powerlessness and the inability of the oppressed to act. The whole of the scientific ethic and methodology, for starters, must be redefined and overturned before all humankind is overturned by dogmatism and mania. The scientific ethic allows and even encourages the rape and destruction of whole peoples and lands which do not 'fit'. There is as yet no woman-orientated science; and little awareness of the need for one.

I will end with two quotations – the first from a nineteenth-century American feminist, Harriet Tubman:

> There are two things I've got a right to, and these are death or liberty. One or the other I mean to have (Parker, 1974).

The second is an extract from a poem called 'Womanslaughter' by a black, lesbian feminist, Pat Parker:

I have gained many sisters.
And if one is beaten,
or raped, or killed,
I will not come in mourning black.
I will not pick the right flowers.
I will not celebrate her death
and it will matter not
if she's black or white –
if she loves women or men.
I will come with my many sisters
and decorate the streets
with the innards of those
brothers in womenslaughter.
No more, can I dull my rage
in alcohol and deference
to *men's* courts.
I will come to my sisters,
not dutiful,
I will come strong.
(Parker, 1978)

References

Barker-Benfield, Ben. 'The spermatic economy: a nineteenth century view of sexuality'. *Feminist Studies*, vol. 1 Summer 1972. *The Horrors of the Half-Known Life*. Harper and Row, New York, 1976.

Barnes, B. (ed.). *The Sociology of Science: Selected Readings*. Penguin, Harmondsworth 1972.

de Beauvoir, Simone. *The Second Sex*. Penguin, Harmondsworth 1976.

Birke, Lynda. 'From zero to infinity: scientific views of lesbians'. In BWSG (ed.) *Alice*. Virago, London. 1980; and Best, Sandy. 'The tyrannical womb: menstruation, menopause and science'. In BWSG (ed.) *Alice* 1980.

Brighton Women and Science Group. (ed.). *Alice Through the Microscope: The Power of Science Over Women's Lives*. Virago, London. (Referenced elsewhere as: BWSG (ed.) *Alice*) 1980.

Daly, Mary. *Beyond God the Father*. Beacon Press, Boston. 1973;

Gyn/Ecology: The Metaethics of Radical Feminism. Beacon Press, Boston. 1978; The Women's Press, London. 1979.

Davis, Katherine B. *Factors in the Sex Life of Twenty-two Hundred Women*. Harper and Row, New York. 1929.

Donnison, Jean. *Midwives and Medical Men*. Heinemann, London. 1977.

Dworkin, Andrea. *Woman Hating*. E.P. Dutton, New York. 1974.

Ehrenreich, Barbara and English, Deirdre. *Complaints and Disorders – the Sexual Politics of Sickness*. Writers and Readers Publishing Collective, London. 1976.

Faulkner, Wendy. 'The obsessive orgasm: science, sex and female sexuality'. in BWSG (ed.) *Alice*. 1980.

Firestone, Shulamith. *The Dialectic of Sex*; The Women's Press, London, 1980.

Friedman, Scarlet. 'Women, sexuality and contraception'. Unpublished paper. 1979.

Hanmer, Jalna and Allen, Pat. 'Reproductive engineering: the final solution?' in BWSG (ed.) *Alice*. 1980.

Haraway, Donna. 'Animal Sociology and a natural economy of the body politic, part I: a political physiology of dominance'. *Signs: Journal of Women in Culture and Society*, vol. 4, no. 1. 1978.

Hite, Shere. *The Hite Report*. Talmy Franklin, London. 1977.

Horney, Karen. 'The flight from womanhood'. In Miller, J.B. (ed.) *Psychoanalysis and Women*. Penguin, Harmondsworth. 1978.

Hosken, Fran. *The Hosken Report: Genital/Sexual Mutilation of Females*. WIN News, Lexington, Mass. 1976.

Jackson, Stevi. *On the Social Construction of Female Sexuality*. WRRC Explorations in Feminism no. 4, London. 1978.

Janson-Smith, Deirdre. 'Sociobiology: so what?' In BWSG (ed.) *Alice*. 1980.

Kinsey, A.C., Pomeroy, W.B., Martin, C.E., and Gebhard, P.H. *Sexual Behaviour in the Human Female*. W.B. Saunders, London. 1953.

Koedt, Anne. 'The myth of the vaginal orgasm'. In Koedt, A. et al (eds). *Radical Feminism*. Quadrangle, New York. 1973.

Kuhn, Thomas S. *The Structure of Scientific Revolutions*. University of Chicago Press, Chicago. 1970.

Lydon, Susan. 'The politics of orgasm'. In Morgan, R. (ed.) *Sisterhood is Powerful*. Vintage Books, New York. 1970.

Masters, William H. and Johnson, Virginia. *Human Sexual Response*. Little, Brown, Boston. 1966.

Mathieu, Nicole-Claude. *Ignored by Some, Denied by Others*. WRRC Explorations in Feminism no. 2, London. 1978.

Morgan, Robin. *Sisterhood is Powerful*. Vintage Books, New York. 1970.

Oakley, Ann. 'The trap of medicalised motherhood'. *New Society*, vol. 34, no. 69. 1975.

Parker, Pat. *Child of Myself*. Women's Press Collective, Oakland. 1974.

Parker, Pat. *Womanslaughter*. Diana Press, Oakland. 1978.

Rose, Hilary and Rose, Steven. (eds.) *The Radicalisation of Science* and *The Political Economy of Science*. Macmillan, London. 1976.

Sayers, Janet. 'Psychological sex differences'. in BWSG (ed.) *Alice*. 1980.

Seaman, Barbara and Seaman, Gideon. *Women and the Crisis in Sex Hormones*. Rawson, New York. 1977.

Shade, William G. '"A mental passion": female sexuality in Victorian America'. *International Journal of Women's Studies*, vol. 1, no. 1, January-February. 1978.

Sherfey, Mary Jane. 'On the nature of female sexuality'. In Miller, J.B. (ed.) *Psychoanalysis and Women*. Penguin, Harmondsworth. 1978.

Szasz, Thomas. *The Manufacture of Madness*. Routledge and Kegan Paul, London. 1971.

Wallsgrove, Ruth. 'Towards a radical feminist philosophy of science'. In BWSG (ed.) *Alice*. 1980.

Weiss, Kay. 'Vaginal cancer: an iatrogenic disease'. *International Journal of Health Services*, vol. 5, no. 2. 1975.

Weisstein, Naomi. 'Psychology constructs the female or the fantasy life of the male psychologist (with some attention to the fantasies of his friends, the male biologist and the male anthropologist)'. In Koedt, A. et al. (eds.) *Radical Feminism*. Quadrangle, New York. 1973.

Whiting, Pat. 'Female sexuality: its political implications'. In Wandor, M. (ed.) *The Body Politic*. Stage 1, London. 1972.

Zilboorg, Gregory. 'Masculine and feminine: some biological and cultural aspects'. In Miller, J.B. (ed.) *Psychoanalysis and Women*. Penguin, Harmondsworth. 1978.

SANDRA McNEILL

Transsexualism . . . Can Men Turn Men into Women?

Transsexualism is a difficult and complex issue. I do not pretend to have all the answers worked out, nor even to ask all the questions. But I hope the following will be a useful framework for discussion.

Most studies of transsexuals start by talking about hermaphrodites, whether they are trying to prove gender identity is conditioned or gender identity is innate. Focussing on hermaphrodites leads to focussing on transsexualism as if it were an isolated phenomenon; isolated from the power relations between the oppressor class, men, and the oppressed class, women. Hermaphrodites have problems, but so do those born with unmistakeable genitals and brought up to fit the stereotypes, as are nearly all women.

As women, we are conditioned to a feminine image. I am sure I do not need to go into what that means here. Many books have been written on it, and in consciousness-raising groups for years women have discussed how we have been and are affected by images of women produced by men, and how we can try to fight them to establish our own identity as women.

We are conditioned by our body experiences. Men and women are different sexually; we respond differently. The problem is that under male supremacy the finding of any difference has been used to justify and maintain the stereotypes. (We have the babies so we must have an innate capacity for washing nappies, and underpants while we are at it.) So here we are, women, products both of our conditioning by our culture from birth, and of our conditioning by our bodies. What is a woman? We do not know.

But some men say they do. These men say they are women, have always known they were women. They know what a woman is and they are that, even though they have men's bodies and were brought up as men. One way or another they get the 'transsexual operation', that is, massive doses of female hormones, removal of their beard, and, ultimately, removal of their penis and testicles and creation of a false vagina, kept open with a plastic 'form'. And then they come among us as women.

I suggest that the only definition of woman they can be using is that supplied by men. First of all, a physiological one: man = cock; so, no cock = woman; i.e. woman is just man without cock and balls. Secondly, a psychological one: the only image of woman they can be thinking they fit is that created by men – the stereotype we are fighting. So the acceptance of transsexual men as women (and probably vice-versa) is a reinforcing of the sex role stereotype, of the image of woman created by men. Rather, I believe that if such men are dissatisfied with their sex role, they should fight the system, not change their own bodies.

What the Experts Say

Robert Stoller, who runs a gender identity clinic in California, was one of the first doctors to develop transsexual counselling and he is still regarded as the greatest expert in that field. He began his experiments on hermaphrodites. He decided what sex the 'indeterminate' person was and they were operated on accordingly. As news of techniques developed, it reached those with no genital defect but who believed themselves to be of the opposite sex. Stoller found himself deciding – he does not accept patient self-diagnosis – who, out of the many who came, should get the operation. I suggest below, that in the future Stoller and his ilk will be so deciding even if the 'case' does not come of his/her own free will.

All gender identity clinics, as they are called (even the one at Charing Cross in London), have criteria for deciding who gets the operation. Note well, the doctors do not themselves believe the patients to be of the opposite sex, they just decide to do the operation if they think the person will fit better as the opposite sex. Stoller's criteria are acknowledged to be stricter than most. A man presenting himself must a) be homosexual currently, so the operation will make him 'straight', b) be pretty, c) never say he is 'better' than real women, d) have an interest in art – painting, music, appreciation of colour and texture, e) strike Stoller as 'profoundly feminine', and f) have a certain upbringing – which Stoller believes essential. Briefly, the upbringing is this: he must be the longed for son of a woman who herself was a latent transsexual, a mother who suffered penis envy (e.g. was good at games or had a relatively decent job before marriage), so she longed for a son to fulfil her. She must have loved him, doted on him, given in to him, his wishes must have come first. He must have been carried around a lot. (Stoller admits many African babies are also carried a lot, though this does not make them even homosexual; there must be something different in the way Western transsexuals are held, he muses.) She encourages his development as a person. So, on the son's side, he experiences no break with the mother, as all normal boys do.

Normal Boys

In Stoller's clinic, when really young boys are brought to him who are not developing normally, he first of all tries psychotherapy, to cure them. I am now going to describe three cases of little boys he 'successfully' treated (Stoller, 1975). These were successful in that they stopped thinking of themselves as women; Stoller thinks they will probably still become homosexual.

1.) One boy in the weeks following treatment was reported by his mother to have begun 'hitting his sister and calling her names for the first time in his life. He had also become angry and verbally abusive towards his mother for the first time . . . Aggression towards women increased in his drawings; for instance, he drew a man with a woman lying at his feet. He smiled as he said the woman had made the man angry, and he had then thrown her down in the mud and beaten her.' (p 101-2)

2.) During four years of treatment, another boy 'moved from a totally feminine orientation . . . towards a considerably more masculine existence . . . He now loves to tell the therapist "horror stories" in which violent themes are played out: for example, in a favourite game gleaned from movie ads and redrawn by the patient, beautiful women are tortured and raped by brutal men. The boy identifies himself as "one of the men who tie them up and abuse them".' (p 104)

3.) For the first year of the treatment a third boy 'showed no interest in guns, shooting, knives or fighting. (This is remarkable for an American boy.)' In fact he played with dolls. The therapist encourages the boy to express more hostile feelings and notes that gradually he becomes more aggressive and slams Barbie (a female doll) in the face with mud, shouting, 'Shut up' or 'Take this, Barbie' or some other girl's name . . . At the same time overt aggression to his mother appeared. (p 104-5)

All the above, please note, are regarded by the male therapists as good, positive signs. By the way, the therapists are always male. Stoller thinks this is important to encourage male identification. He

Stoller thinks this is important to encourage male identification. He talks of the boys 'slowly developing masculinity'. Elsewhere Stoller defines masculinity as 'preoccupation with being strong, independent, untender, cruel, polygamous, misogynous, perverse'.

Of course, if all this treatment fails to produce a normal male, there is always the operation. Stoller says that it is not that anatomy is destiny, but that one's anatomy must fit one's identity – an identity decided by Stoller. Nowhere does Stoller claim his patients are women. All his criteria, or tests, for the 'true' transsexual amount to, is a set of explanations for why some men consider they are not men – and therefore, are women. Basically it seems to come down to the fact that they do not hate women. Since male bonding against women is at the root of male society, they must have a tough time.

So do women. It is not in our interests if the few men who do not hate women try and cope by changing their anatomy. Instead they should launch a political attack on the gender stereotypes that uphold this political system based on the slave/master relation of women to men.

Is the Growth of Transsexualism Part of a Plan to Eliminate Women?

Finally I want to ask: why is research going on into how to perfect these operations? why are gender identity clinics mushrooming? Research does not take place by chance. Governments and foundations decide which projects to set up and fund. To get this into perspective we must consider some of the simultaneous developments of male medicine.

A recent BBC *Horizon* programme gave validation to an East German scientist's experiments which 'proved' homosexuality to be caused by hormone imbalance, and which suggest ways of treating/curing/preventing it. Dr Dorner believes that there are such things as male and female brains. Sometimes, he suggests, if the testes do not develop, a baby is born with a male brain in a female body; it will be homosexual. Dorner's solution to this is the detection of the event in the womb, followed by doses of androgen. (The idea that homosexuality needs curing is not new . . . Hitler was a fervent proponent.) Presumably, if hormones fail, corrective surgery can be performed. We know that sexuality is a social construct. But the pushing of such theories as Dorner's validates the use of male medicine to 'cure' such 'ills.'

Dr John Pollard of Manchester is currently testing sex choice gels on 200 'couples'. If they are 75 percent to 80 percent effective they will be marketed – 'by a cosmetics firm as it is not a drug'. These gels will enable you to choose the sex of your child. This could mean in Bangladesh ten males to one female in the next generation (this estimate was made at a workshop by two Bengali women), resulting in genocide as well as gynocide, and in Britain and the United States it is anticipated that this would lead to a slight preponderance of male, and male as first-born. Hanmer and Allen (1980) point out that although a potential imbalance is noted in recent US Sub-Committee Reports, it is implied to be 'either desirable (as population will be limited) or a matter of little concern'. There have always been slightly more women than men. This is about to change.

Other experiments in reproductive technology clearly aim for total control over reproduction, without the need for women's bodies. When they succeed, women will be needed only to supply ova, and so far fewer women will be needed, unlike currently when men are needed only to supply the sperm. Sex choice gels could be a way of reducing our numbers preparatory to almost wiping us out altogether.

Whenever I have suggested this women have reacted with incredulity: 'but men need women', they say, 'in so many ways'. Sure, the power class depends on having a slave class – the whole system is based on it. But it need not be biological woman. Particularly if the current generation are getting uppity and trying to upset the system. With the spread of gender identity clinics, parents can take children who are not developing the appropriate sex role characteristics, to the clinic. There (see above) psychotherapy will first be tried; if that fails the child will simply be given the appropriate set of genitals – remember, anatomy must fit identity, and the experts decide on identity not you. So in the future potential feminists, stroppy little girls, would be adjusted by counselling, or turned into 'men'.

And, as women are being phased out, our place will be taken by those men created to fit the 'female' role. The men turned into transsexuals, passing tests of femininity, are often closer to men's ideas of what 'real' women are, than you or I would be. The following is part of a letter from a male-to-constructed-female transsexual to *Sister* magazine, August-September 1977 (quoted in Raymond, 1980, p 117):

> Genetic women cannot possess the very special courage, brilliance, sensitivity and compassion – and overview – that derives from the transsexual experience. Free from the chains of menstruation and childbearing, transsexual women are obviously far superior to Gennys in many ways.

Genetic women are becoming quite obsolete, which is obvious, and the future belongs to transsexual women. We know this, and perhaps some of you suspect it. All you have left is your 'ability' to bear children, and in a world which will groan to feed six billion in the year 2000, that's a negative asset.

References

Hanmer, Jalna and Allen, Pat. 'Reproductive engineering – the final solution?' In Brighton Women and Science Group (eds.) *Alice Through The Microscope: The Power of Science over Women's Lives*. Virago, London. 1980.

Pollard, John. Interviewed by *The Sunday Mirror*. 23 September 1979.

Raymond, Janice G. *The Transsexual Empire*. The Women's Press, London. 1980.

Stoller, Robert. *The Transsexual Experiment*. Hogarth, London. 1975.

JILL LEWIS

The Politics of Monogamy

'Somewhere there is Someone who is Right for you.'
Dateline Ad
'You're the one that I want.'
Song from GREASE

I am not looking here into the anthropological or historical dimensions of the way monogamy developed or became institutionalised in different cultural and historical contexts. The particular ritualising of power, control and ownership which exists or existed as integrally connected to different cultural codings of monogamy does, in fact, need to be more challengingly explored and researched by feminists. But – without fetishising monogamy or investing it with determining or essentialist causality – I want to raise here what I see as pivotal questions and problems implicit in the monogamous forms of relationship we are now drawn towards and the cycles of power they embody and reproduce. In that, my aim is both to generate further questions about the historical, social, psychological and gendering systems in which our sexuality is shaped; as well as to attempt to find viable ways of thinking about monogamy as a *political* construct which is integrally connected to patriarchal modes of sexual oppression.

My premise is that monogamy *is* highly relevant in the institutionalising of male domination and hierarchies of sexual power between individuals (men and women) in our society. We are each of us concerned by the questions about sexuality, violence, autonomy and political commitment and potential within our social forms of patriarchal hegemony which monogamy invokes. Monogamy involves certain laws and consequences which the Women's Movement has designated – as we all know too well from our own rhetorical, stubborn, or defensive responses – as problematic. Yet beyond feminist assertions or indictments about monogamy, it has nonetheless been just as problematic to evolve, even within the Movement, an engaged political practice which does not just result in the isolated struggles (or failure) of our own 'personal' journeys, where the easily spoken political dictates wreak havoc or cause collapse: where our choice is polarised between the loss of a sustained relationship and a sustained relationship in patriarchal form. It is that old familiar gap between collectively shared ideas, the vertical pulls of individual relationships we actually engage in, and the socially and psychologically determined emotional investments we bring to them whatever our political thinking. And these contradictions and intolerable irreconcilables often lead us, too easily, to give up, opt out, or even find ways of rationalising and justifying these destructive structures to which the Women's Movement has vividly alerted us. Although, as with many issues in the initial stages of feminist critique, primitive feminist intuitions and onslaughts can often name oppressive structures, they do not 'instantly' provide the substantive understandings of the complexities which converge in and around these structures. And, of course, there are no instant solutions or turn-of-the-switch correct modes of behaviour or feeling: only the commitment to shadowy fabrics of struggle, intricate explorations of the political fabric of our lives – along with the momentum to want it all to be easier, to prioritise certain things and forget others, to fight formally over issues 'out there', as if the forms our lives embody and reproduce have no connection to the discriminatory allotment of powers which our society formalises.

Now, problematising monogamy has to be done in the context of the following qualifications, each of which is informative in that it touches on different tips of the iceberg in which the institution of monogamy as we know it is embedded.

First, the sixties and seventies are behind us now, with their certain forms of disruption of life-styles, experiments, sense of rapid change, and explosive possibilities – and you only have to glance at *Cosmopolitan, Playboy* or *The Observer* Colour Supplement to get a strong whiff of the way patriarchal capitalism capitalised on all this. We know how the 'double standard', that privilege of male sexuality, was made 'cool' and accessible. We have multifaceted evidence of the superficially and newly institutionalised exploitation resulting from that 'sexual revolution' which occurred in advanced capitalist societies when we look at the ideological and political *marginality* of the different forms of feminism within it. The variety of the sexual market may have proliferated, but the feminist intervention has as vast as ever a terrain to cover to build the material political and emotional revolutionary process necessary to confront the sexual oppressions capitalism thrives on. Our feminist engagement exists both within each of us and in the social realities in which we participate, affected by the patriarchal and bourgeois connotations which recurrently inhibit radical forms of transformation. Our anti-capitalist imperative has a high stake in a radical re-thinking of the institutionalising of every level of our subjective experience. The 'sexual revolution' and experimentation in lifestyle opened up by the sixties and seventies allowed new avenues of freedom and diversity to emerge on the horizon. Yet these, including anti-monogamy strategies, were constructed by gendered minds and bodies and out of patriarchal imaginings of what sexuality itself must be – which we feminists still have difficulty understanding, deconstructing and re-inventing. The complexity of sexual psychology and the gendered rituals they sustained are still – when we find the will or time to address them – sphinx-like on the agenda.

The next necessary preamble to thinking about monogamy is that there is no way in which we can underestimate the fact that the economic and social context of the lives of the vast majority of women in our society necessitates monogamy as their/our only option for survival. Monogamy is the taken-for-granted term of 'contracted' commitment from men: it is spontaneously 'normal'. As men or *women*, born of our own particular nuclear family structures, we are – whether heterosexual or lesbian – socially and psychologically prepared to assume monogamy as the 'meaningful' condition of our lives. Political questions need to be asked, not in order to articulate some polemical indictment of monogamous practice, but so as to begin to explore the terms and consequences of this 'normal' and 'spontaneous' structure: to examine the coercions dormant in the consents monogamy unquestioningly co-ordinates.

Thirdly, the institution of heterosexuality has played and plays a key role in determining and sustaining the laws of monogamy. Monogamy has to be discussed in the context of the history of marriage and the history of the control of reproduction and female fertility within the patriarchal traditions of western societies, where the institution of heterosexuality itself comes to connote gender divisions interwoven with male dominance. It must also be acknowledged that whatever choice or orientation we as men or women affirm in our own personal lives, we are all children of the father and mother whose social, gender and sexual identities were constructed from and within these patriarchal traditions.

There is a final parameter to thinking about monogamy – which interests me since my feminism is couched within the spokes of socialist feminist enquiries. In all the socialist countries where women's roles and lives have been profoundly revolutionised within the socialist imaginings of 'human equality', yet where there are still sustained *inequalities* in the patriarchal imaginings of sexual divisions and the organisation of gender, monogamy is affirmed and upheld by the socialist idea of *the family*. The formal socialist ideologies (which turn deaf ears to the enquiries of citizens such as Alexandra Kollontai, etc.) enshrine monogamy as being protective of women and an essential part of the formal sexual moralities. The monogamous organisation of, in particular, *women's* sexuality is not seen as problematic or as political.

Now monogamy is relevant for political analysis because sexuality and its organisation are central to the structuring of ourselves and our social identity. The personal is political since social relations comprise roles which are not simply imposed by a coercive State or some eternal male triumvirate, nor do they emerge for 'natural' or genetic reasons; rather they embody a complexity of 'values' which we adopt in continual processes of consent and identification at conscious and unconscious levels. We are *of* the production of those relations. Only by political analysis of the structures round sexuality, and questioning and understanding what is produced by them and in us, can we become enabled to transform them. Sexual politics are not diversionary to practices of class struggle, racial struggles, etc. Rather they can develop in us the material experience of engagement with *change*, with a questioning process. They can recurrently initiate us into the dismantling of the 'harmony' of normative subjective relations which are integral to the functioning of our society and its power relations. Sexual political analysis can relate dynamically to other practices of transformation and empowering to which political consciousness brings us.

Male domination is articulated in practices integral to patriarchal hegemony, which is comprised of 'normative' and 'natural' relationships, which in turn affirm, at each subjective moment, the plausibility and stability of the world they sustain by their strength and continuity. To begin to see society from the terrain of marxist exploration, or from sets of feminist questions, or from a point of view that gives integral priority to questions of race, has vast consequences in its disruption of our normative white, male, bourgeois assumptions. Our resistance to engaging in challenges raised by these perspectives is powerfully structured in the taken-for-granted terms we are used to and use.

Monogamy is a 'state' which is anticipated, socially legitimated, and powerfully amplified in our emotional imagination by the logics of 'romantic love' and by the emotional imperatives of the unconscious formed in the nuclear, heterosexual family long before we actually come to consolidate it. As a practice it involves, however, not some consistent extension of the terms of identity we have been developing within, but on the contrary a dramatic act of redefinition; a centring of practice around two people who name themselves in the context of each other. Hierarchy is consolidated, and a privileged private sphere inaugurated which is, by its celebrated definition, to rule out all others. For monogamy, by its very *rules*, produces and enacts sets of priorities that connote the power and control which capitalist relations (and those of all societies dependent on authoritarianism) demand.

It is within the privatised and privileged space of the monogamous relationship, echoing the emotional landscape of our nuclear childhood and our gendered unconscious, that the strongest confirmation of identity, security and intelligibility is sought. Here, more than anywhere else, is imagined the power to shape a world that will confirm us: one that is apparently shaped by autonomous choice. Once established (and, after all, what else should 'true' love lead to), it does however set up a 'segregated subworld with its own controls and closed conversation'. Through the privileged dialogue it ritualises, it becomes the site of normative corroboration, a dominant area in rewriting oneself and others. Now, on the one hand, there are many ways of justifying this redefinition, which after all is to do with 'love' and the 'deepening of a real commitment', but in a patriarchal society, with its specific gender divisions and gender allocations of power, economic and nurturant organisation, there seem to me to be political problems inherent in the construct of monogamy itself and the other political realities it connotes. I emphasise this, because one of the usual ways we have of dealing with relationships is to accuse and resent subjective failures, to say 'it *was* good, but it went wrong: what did I/you do wrong' – when the problems are inherent in the material terms of our contract. Also, given the hypocritical space of the 'double-standard' which our male-dominated culture concedes to men and the romantic abandonment of other ties and consequent privatisation it concedes to women, monogamy has particular effects on women in terms of profound dependency and the containment and appropriation of their sexuality.

The Limits of Monogamy

Although of course it signifies much more, the main structuring principle of monogamy is its genital sexual definition. Around the central, consented appropriation of sexual practice by the Couple, all the terms are set. It's odd to think about it like that: but there it is. Sexuality itself is pronounced possible, celebrated, affirmed and 'free' within this space – but outside it, it is defined as threatening, resented, to-be-controlled, fear-inspiring, with a whole corollary of emotions under the rubric of 'jealousy'. So the space monogamy occupies politically is one in which central priority is given to the *sexual* connection as determining a hierarchy of social relations and powers of definition. Given the spectrum of romance, male control and violence the Women's Movement has alerted us to, it is clear that monogamy is related to key questions of women's survival and male control. Its conditions and consequences need particular attention.

> What feels natural and easy, is soft murder
> Of each other and of that mutant future
>
> *Marge Piercy*

Monogamy is a highly value-loaded term, affirming all sorts of emotional imaginings. In its aim to override tension and the threat of possibilities *outside* the limits of its definition, it harmonises sequences of *proofs* – proof that I am faithful, that I consent to its morality, that I am satisfied totally by you in some key, fundamental way, proof of security, stability, protection, loving dependencies, and most of all, of course, proof that I LOVE YOU in ways that only you will know, in ways so that your knowledge of me will be exclusive, uncontested, total. In reasserting those 'values', the monogamous construct is of course structuring terms of ULTIMATUM, it is establishing absolute criteria to which there must be acquiescence, or everything will be destroyed. A risky fragility, for if the sexual component is contravened, the whole edifice of proofs comes into question. Monogamy is a laying out of ramparts which want to pre-empt, at all costs (for its own survival is at stake) all risks of transgression. It lists the conditions for immersion, the conditions for betrayal. Here, in this territory, the assertion of self in autonomous practice is, by symbolic definition, to be abandoned, repressed and deprived of respect. Acquiescing to the monogamous sequence implies abandoning autonomy within sexuality. By the very terms of contract, it is already pervaded with the disturbing odours of anticipated violence.

> I do not want to live indefinitely
> in a world which you dominate
>
> *John Berger*

All images of strength in you . . .
. . . pull against me, till what feels right to you
wrongs me, and there is no rest from struggle.

We are equal if we make ourselves so, every day, every night
constantly renewing what the street destroys
We are equal only if you too open on your heavy hinges
And let your love come freely, freely where it will never be safe,
Where it can never possess.

Marge Piercy

Monogamy has however implicit in its historical materiality a basic equation of inequality. For in its integral ideological and institutional connection to marriage and to paternity, it is elaborated in terms of control on the man/woman model. And this locates it in terms of power/powerlessness, adequacy/inadequacy, achievement/nurturance. It never was a quiet alliance of equals. As a recognised institution, it endorsed imbalance in a claustrophobic circle, compensating loss with protection, if the terms of contract were complied with.

The allurement of terms of security (materially based in women's economic dependence and closely related to an individual sense of 'need') which monogamy offers, with its suggested elimination of tension of sexual decision and provision of dependable affirmation, conceal, more often than not, realities diametrically opposed to what was sought. The spontaneous 'attraction' pattern, the site of preliminary negotiations of sexuality, with the usual emotional idealism of our romantic heritage, inhibits many levels of negotiation around sexuality and its concomitant social structures. After the quest and yearning for 'true', 'committed' (i.e. proven-by-its-structure) relationship, the monogamous form embodies separation from others, isolation and the parallel effects of disablement and disempowering. By its very seclusion and its own internal sets of rights and non-rights, it lays ground for forms of abuse and devastation. As a student, Ann Holder, wrote in a text on sexuality, 'That's where the myth comes in; it felt safe and warm and it wasn't, it wasn't safe at all'. Or, as the poet Adrienne Rich invokes:

I cannot now lie down with a man
Who fears my power, or reaches for me as for death
Or with a lover who believes that we are not in danger.
('From an Old House in America')

For monogamy establishes terms of trust and respect in a frame of reference where the autonomy of the other is symbolically excluded or dramatically qualified. It defines a status of presence where the unit of the monogamous couple becomes the public, the known relationship versus the others which will be lesser known – the privatised, the more seen-to-be-subversive relationships. It establishes a public status where sexual connection indicates to others a context of closed discourse, representing a private consensus which goes way beyond the sexual contract – that is, the association that happens between the ideas of the two people involved once they are known to be in that kind of relationship. And it establishes formally a suspension of conflict, a 'final' decision, and the naming of self in terms of another whose ideologies one comes to connote (whether one likes it or not) in complex ways: that is, an assumed merging of knowledge and of 'reality' which the closed unit privileges. Now, this is, of course, unreal, and all that does not actually happen, but the monogamous format alludes to it continually. There is a building of identity and of codes of sexual availability involved as well: with this person *I do, I am* – with those *I do not, I am not*. We must ask what is rigidified in our perception of self and others and what is the potential for engaging with contradiction and the process of change, by the normative assumptions around monogamy? And, for women in particular, after more or less years of assenting to this and all the domestic, economic and psychological consequences that it brings with it, what grounds are established for the negation of so many levels of response and engagement? What is left for women in particular when the rules of monogamy are broken by them? What emotional and identity devastation is prepared when any enactment outside the monogamous island means evacuation, rejection, loss of sustenance – let alone the effects of years of patterning of relationships within the safety of monogamy, which means that the only thing to do is to replace it with *another monogamy* which still has similar terms set around it.

To concretise the issues at stake for a moment, I want to quote from a letter written to a friend by a woman a few years ago – in that it movingly and explicitly articulates the conjuncture of power and dependency written into the 'couple', the specific symbolic limiting of autonomy of the woman concerned, and the subjective consequences of the internal dynamics of monogamy on the female psyche. (The letter is authentic; names and geographical locations have been changed.)

> Sue, I have to tell you something that's impossible to tell anyone else, but I need to say it. In Paris, Denny and I slept together.

(By the way, this woman is married, to Jack; Denny's wife is Anne.)

> I feel so terrible about it now. I could and would tell Anne about it but I feel I can't if I can't tell Jack. That is totally out of the question. It happened in such an unexpected and pleasurable context. We felt very close for ages and liked each other but with no sex content. But spending that time together as strangers in a strange city, walking around and exploring with no tension and no arguments – just great fun – kind of led in a totally unthinking way to that kind of closeness. It really was unthinking – a kind of instinct for warmth that seems so divorced from home and everything else that I didn't want to work out rationally in relation to home in London and Jack. I have felt so desperate for that kind of physical kindness. Not leading to power or monogamy or quarrelling or to an ongoing situation of tension. But I do feel so awful now, Sue, I don't know quite what to do. I know that I could work it out with Anne

(which, in fact, she did)

> and that it would be OK, but it's with Jack that terrifies me. Just before I left, he looked into my washbag and he saw my diaphragm and because of that he refused to speak to me before I left. I worried about why for ages until I got back from my work in Paris. So when I came back and it was the same, I confronted him and he told me he believed I was planning to sleep with people while I was away. In fact, I wasn't at all and my diaphragm wasn't there because I'd deliberately put it there but because it's always there. But in fact then I had to lie to him because totally coincidentally I had slept with Denny. But God it's really such a mess, Sue, and I feel so bad I can't do anything. It would all totally explode if I tried to explain, in fact he wouldn't listen at all – he'd probably just go. I can't tell him it was meaningless at the level of love but it was fun and warmth and lovely and it gives me a strength in myself that makes me feel much happier and even more real in my relation to him. And if I can't say that, I can't have it degraded by his explanation and his ways of seeing. I'm trying to sort out where I am in all the mess that's here. I despair of ever being in a happy state again, just for odd weeks here and there.

What this text poignantly brings out, with the stalemate and fear it expresses, is a personal expression of the rules which 'spontaneously' evolve in a 'love' situation, but which over years become embedded destructively around the actual site of sexuality itself – which is where monogamy originates its key definition.

The question seems to me, then, to be how do we attempt to engage in finding viable ways of dislocating our own conservative practices and relating that process to other political articulations. In attempting to bring monogamy into question, the odds at work in us against that cannot be underestimated. We are all gendered subjects, and the gendering processes in our society imply certain positions of dependence and demand in the sexual and emotional connection. If we acknowledge the importance of the political implications of monogamy, not just the personal at an individual level but in the larger context of patriarchal power relations, we are going to have to learn the loss of certain kinds of relationships – which we value, but within which there is no space for certain kinds of questions to be confronted. A subjective imagining of territories of the self engaged with the socio-psychological territories of others – which are all at odds with the gendering processes, the nuclear family, and the social and economic positioning of the couple and the emotional hierarchies which our forms of male dominance institutionalise. And it is always easier and more paralysing to imagine the absence/negation of 'what is', of the normative expectation, than it is to imagine the absence of these as an affirmation of radically *other* fabrics of relationships and collaboration. Which brings us to a shifting territory where anxieties and reticence ensue; where there is a fear of loss of love; where intimacy is as constantly exposed to risk as to reassurance, and where there must be continual negotiation. And our growth within monogamous constructs (i.e. the family) which have utilised those fears as forms of control from our childhood, does not make it easy.

It seems to me that key aspects of the problems involved in the reproduction of monogamy are raised implicitly in an extremely important text, Nancy Chodorow's *The Reproduction of Mothering*. She examines the context of the psychic structures that are developed within men and women, and the way that gender is constructed in relationship to the way 'mothering' is organised (and enacted by women only) in the nuclear family and in the intimate and in the more public sexual divisions of labour in advanced capitalist societies (and in the dominant *white* culture). She looks at the formulation of psychoanalytic theory around gender in relationship to the fact (which she sees not as 'natural' but as social) that *women* mother. Her argument maintains that all aspects of psychic structure – character, emotional and erotic life – are socially constituted through a history of object choices which involve the material and ideological conditions of the family as a reproductive unit. She looks at the gendered organisation of parenting this implies and its effects in producing the psychological bases on which patriarchal forms can and do flourish. Key questions emerge concerning the nature of the mother-daughter relationship (an en-gendering tradition which involves specific dynamics of *lack of autonomy*) in a society where the father, the male figure, is absent yet powerful, and the boy enters masculinity by negating the mother, while the girl comes into femininity by never differentiating adequately from the mother. The mother's local power – dependent on the monogamous contract with the father – is enmeshed in the powerlessness this simultaneously implies for her in the larger society beyond the subjective and objective limits of that nuclear unit. Chodorow's enquiry raises along the way questions about the grounds for dependency (related to gender) which make monogamy the evident, if not the inevitable, *psychological* option for us. The politics of monogamy therefore relate back into politically re-examining the organisation of reproduction and parenting which form the institutional framework of our past and present lives (whether we parent or not). Individual sexual choice – lesbian alternatives or the individual renegotiation of the terms of heterosexuality – cannot *transcend* the complex infusions of patriarchal hegemony when the social realities of the way reproduction is institutionalised are ideologically prevalent in the conscious and unconscious of us all.

Yet the dislocation of the cohesive levels of sexual oppression must begin in all kinds of ways, with all kinds of risks at stake. In challenging monogamy there is the fear of losing the power of a defining knowledge of another person's intimacy; the fear of one's own sexual insecurities; and the competitive fantasies of the property scales. There is the fear of the *otherness* of someone else's sexual connections *elsewhere*, and the fear that if sexuality does not embody an extended, total giving, that our capacity for intimacy will be eroded altogether.

But, to conclude, if what is at stake is challenging the sets of power relations which raise political questions about all the relations of reproduction and of the patriarchal distribution of rights and authority, there are powerful incentives for us to engage in a disruptive exploration of anti-monogamous possibilities. And I would stress that this does not mean one major relationship versus minor secondary 'scenes', nor what somebody called 'multiple monogamies' with unchanged criteria within each, nor the indulgent escape into 'promiscuity for its own sake' which the sixties threw up in all kinds of forms. But it does mean recognising that all relationships have to be disinvested of the hierarchical ladder crowned by the royal couple. A desire to be consistent in relationships, combined with a political recognition of the destructive consequences which the normative forms available to us can give to that consistency, must make us conceive of them as dependent on non-exclusivity rather than exclusivity. So the question then is how do we attempt to engage in finding viable ways of dislocating our own conservative practices and relating that process to other forms of political struggles. There is, of course, no one correct line of action. I heard a man give an account recently of his sense of the different conditions around monogamy for men and women. He was saying,

> Men must learn to enact restraint on the licence which patriarchy has given them, that is to fuck women when they want, the *indiscriminate enactment of male sexual autonomy*, while women have to learn in their way what patriarchy refuses them – the right to have an autonomous sexuality and not be determined or controlled by sexuality itself. It is an imbalance of incompatible strategies and the weight of responsibility is heavy for all of us involved.

But there are other crucial dimensions too. There is the transmission of normative structures of power and property mediated by the experience of monogamy and its symbolic ramifications to children who are formed in and observe and reproduce the relationships that we construct. And it seems to me that it's so much the more urgent from that perspective. For if we are not trying to get some 'instant satisfaction' via simplistic changes of fragments of the power structure, or to change just ourselves, but are engaged in a longer, more complex and social process, it's so much more urgent for us to work on and affirm other forms of caring relationships, and to sustain each other in different ways within that, ways which do not produce conservative notions of monolith, but which enable an understanding of ongoing struggle, of dealing with contradictions, and of process, not repressing them – a model for all kinds of democratic struggle. My question is, if the emotional construct of monogamy does not change, how can the politics of reproduction be revolutionised? And how can sexual oppression and male dominance be ended and transformed if there is not an engaged struggle around the politics of reproduction?

References

Berger, John. *G.* Penguin, Harmondsworth. 1973

Chodorow, Nancy. *The Reproduction of Mothering: Psychoanalysis and the Sociology of Gender*. University of California Press, Berkeley. 1979.

Kollontai, Alexandra. *Selected Writings*. Allison and Busby, London. 1977.

Kollontai, Alexandra. *Love of Worker Bees*. Virago, London. 1977.

Piercy, Marge. *To Be of Use*. Doubleday, New York. 1973.

Piercy, Marge. *Living in the Open*. Knopf, New York, 1976.

Rich, Adrienne. *Poems: Selected and New 1950-1974*. Norton, New York. 1975.

Rich, Adrienne. *Of Woman Born: Motherhood As Experience and Institution*. Bantam, New York. 1977.

Rich, Adrienne. *The Dream of a Common Language*. Norton, New York. 1978.

Rich, Adrienne. *On Lies, Secrets and Silence: Selected Prose 1966-1978*. Norton, New York. 1979.

Stefan, Verena. *Shedding*. Women's Press, London, 1979.

HILARY GRAHAM

Coping: or How Mothers are Seen and Not Heard

This paper asks the question, 'What does it mean to be a mother?' 'What does the role entail?' 'What does it feel like?' [1] I attempt to answer these questions in two ways. The section below explores the question of motherhood in general terms, and suggests that the concept of coping can help us understand the way society sees mothers and how mothers see themselves. The subsequent section looks at the accounts that 200 women gave of being pregnant, giving birth and caring for children. It suggests some ways in which a concern with coping is woven into their experiences of reproduction.

Asking what it means to be a mother is important for several reasons: in particular, because of the theoretical centrality of reproduction within feminism and because of the changing social conditions of reproduction in the 1980s.

Expanding on these two issues in turn: it is important *first* because the question of reproduction holds a central place in the theory and practice of the Women's Movement. It is women's capacity to reproduce – to become pregnant and give birth – which is seen to lie at the heart of women's oppression. We therefore need to understand how this capacity is defined and controlled if we are to understand how women are 'kept in their place'.

The question of reproduction has been explored in different ways. It has been the subject of personal testimony, with women writing about their experiences of childbearing in the isolated world of the nuclear family. It has also been the subject of theoretical investigation, with debate centring on the relationship between the sexual and class divisions which scar capitalist societies. There is, however, a gap between the two types of analysis – between the everyday language through which women describe their experiences and the abstract language of feminist analysis. What is needed is a way of understanding the interconnections between the two: a way of linking the everyday and the analytical, a way of linking women's experiences to our analysis of the ideological and material structures which sustain them. As part of this task, we need to record the words and phrases through which women describe their lives. We need to identify everyday concepts which express the constraints and contradictions of being a mother. This paper suggests that one of these everyday 'linking' concepts is that of coping. It suggests that coping is a concept which enables us to see the structures which mould women's experiences not as abstract entities existing 'out there' in the social stratosphere but as everyday processes which infuse the way we think and act in our daily lives.

It is important to understand what motherhood means to women for a *second* reason: because of the current changes in the social conditions of reproduction. As most women are already acutely aware, we are presently living through a period of long-term economic decline, with a falling demand for labour and an increasing rate of inflation. Historically, economic recession has exacted a particularly heavy toll of women. Today, too, because of their position within the labour force and within the family, it is women who shoulder the burden of national decline. They act as buffers which deflect and absorb its effects both in the industrial and domestic domains. Through women's greater vulnerability within the labour market, female redundancy helps protect the jobs of male workers employed in less marginal sectors of the economy (Bruegel, 1979). Similarly, through their position within the home, housewives and mothers struggle to preserve the family's standard of living, compensating for any shortfall in the household income by going without themselves (Owen, 1974; Dobash & Dobash, 1979).

Again, as in previous periods, economic changes go hand in hand with ideological changes (Davis, 1978). In particular, the falling demand for labour and the decline in living standards are heralded by a resurgence of an ideology of female domesticity, in which woman's dependent and nurturative role as wife and mother is reasserted. Newspapers thus publicise campaigns to 're-establish the role of wife and mother as a worthwhile career' (*Guardian*, 1979) and bookstalls display a new range of books which proclaim that babies need mothers and mothers need babies (Leach, 1979). Behind the rhetoric of motherhood, we find the boundaries of the welfare state are being rapidly, and more stringently, redrawn. As the welfare state retracts, the role of the family (and specifically the role of the woman in the family) expands: it is the wife and mother who is expected to assume responsibility for the abandoned social priorities. It is she who is expected to cover for the missing school meals, to budget more carefully to compensate for the shrinking value of child benefits and to care for the sick, the elderly and the handicapped for whom the hospitals can no longer provide (Personal Social Services Council, 1980; Finch & Groves, 1979).

Listening to the way mothers talk about their lives is a means of understanding these changes in the economic and social organisation of the family. 'Listening to mother' may also help fill the theoretical vacuum within feminism, by illuminating the links between the conceptual tools of feminist analysis and the everyday experiences they seek to describe.

Defining Motherhood

This section looks at the language through which women voice their experiences of pregnancy, childbirth and motherhood. I focus on one word which runs through women's accounts of reproduction: coping. To cope, according to the dictionary, means to 'contend quietly' and to 'grapple successfully'. To cope is to handle the vicissitudes of your daily life with equanimity and efficiency. This idea of unobtrusive competence appears to express the essence of what it means and what it is to be a mother. Mothers are copers: they are individuals who can handle the pressures of their life calmly and effectively.

The concept of coping pervades the way we talk about mothers. The greatest compliment you can pay a mother is to shake your head in wonder and murmur 'I don't know how she copes': the most damning indictment you can pass is to suggest that 'she can't really cope'. A vocabulary of coping similarly provides the basis on which special exemptions and allowances are granted to women: a legal abortion for the patient who 'couldn't cope with a(nother) baby'; a prescription for a tranquilliser or mental hospital admission for the mother who is temporarily or permanently 'unable to cope'.

A medical advertisement for the tranquilliser, Stelazine, has a picture of a woman smiling as she pushes her trolley round the supermarket with her two children – shades of the Stepford Wives? The text of the advert reads

> Now she can cope. When she's suffering from anxiety and finds it difficult to cope, she comes to you needing effective relief that leaves her able to lead a normal life. Stelazine has been coping with anxiety for nearly 20 years.

The concept of coping is not new to the social sciences. It has been employed by social psychologists to explain how people respond to bereavement (Marris, 1958; Murray Parkes, 1972). It has been employed by sociologists to explain individual responses to illness (Gerhardt, 1979). In both contexts, coping is seen primarily as a process by which individuals survive short-term setbacks: a temporary expedient by which individuals can make out until their mind and body have returned to normal. By extending its usage from these transitional atypical conditions, I am not abandoning the social scientific model. Instead, I am suggesting that the qualities which social scientists have uncovered in their studies of bereavement and sickness are qualities which mothers are expected to display all the time. However, while we notice and admire the fortitude and tenacity of individuals whose lives are disrupted by illness and death, we have failed to notice that the same virtues are expected of women as they face the daily disruptions of family life.

Seen in the context of women's daily lives, coping has two dimensions. Firstly, coping involves responsibility: it involves taking on the obligations and duties which go with your role. For a mother to be complimented on her coping style, she needs to demonstrate an unrelenting concern for the physical and mental well-being of those in her care. Thus, the mother who fails to attend the ante-natal clinic during pregnancy, who fails to maintain her house to the accepted standard or who allows her children to wander the street can not be identified as a coper, since she is flagrantly shirking the responsibilities that her role entails. Secondly, coping involves culpability: it implies that the mother can be blamed for any faults and failings in herself and her family. Thus, to default on your ante-natal care, on your housework or on the supervision of your children is not only to break the rules of motherhood, it is also to risk being blamed for your irresponsible and inadequate behaviour (Crawford, 1977; Graham, 1979).

The definition of motherhood – as a state of perpetual coping – has important implications. First, it means that 'the maternal role', rather than being a fixed, biologically immutable condition, is open to constant redefinition. Since the essence of coping is the ability to adapt swiftly and efficiently to changing demands, the maternal role is one which is highly responsive to economic and social changes. It can relinquish and reabsorb a variety of obligations with little perceptible change in structure. While the experience of motherhood may change profoundly, its external appearance remains the same. This malleability of the mother's role is highlighted by the concept of 'child need'. If women are responsible for meeting the needs of their families, then their role alters and becomes more complex every time new needs are uncovered or old needs are reformulated. If children are identified as needing a stable, continuous and dependable relationship with their mother or mother-substitute (Pringle, 1974), then the mother is shirking her responsibilities if she fails to provide such a relationship. If unborn babies need to be protected from the hazards of smoking and alcohol, and if they need the facilities of a modern maternity hospital for their safe delivery, then their mothers can be blamed for irresponsibility in continuing to smoke and drink in pregnancy and insisting on a home confinement. Second, if coping is central to motherhood, it has important implications for the way in which our society assesses women's success at their number one role. Specifically, the more successful a mother is, the less apparent her presence becomes as she moves unobtrusively through the home, contending quietly with the demands of housework, husband and children. In other words, to cope successfully is to deny yourself a voice: the best mother is one who is seen but not heard. Coping thus involves low-profile living; it involves denying your role and denigrating yourself: 'I don't know how you cope with your husband and housework and your seventeen children', 'Oh, it's nothing really. I do very little.' If coping equals self-effacement, then women can only be made aware of themselves at times of failure. Mothers can only know what they should be doing when they are reprimanded for not doing it. Thus, a woman can only be confident that she has mastered the complexities of her role in retrospect, when she has stayed the course without comment and criticism. Yesterday, successful mothers were permitted to smoke in pregnancy, to reject breast feeding and to wean early: today such behaviour is seen to indicate an ignorance and irresponsibility incompatible with coping.

To summarise this section: it is suggested that coping is the everyday concept used to describe (and prescribe) what mothers do. The concept of coping thus represents the everyday face of ideology: it is the medium through which the ideology of motherhood is translated into individual experience. Further, it is suggested that through the concept of coping we can understand both the malleability and the invisibility of women within the family. On the one hand, the concept sensitises us to the way women's lives can be radically restructured in response to changing socio-economic conditions without their role being formally redefined; on the other, it sensitises us to the way in which women's roles are so constructed that their successful enactment commits the woman to a life of self-negation.

Women's Accounts of Reproduction

The comments presented in this section were collected during a survey of women's experiences of pregnancy, childbirth and motherhood carried out with Lorna McKee in 1976-7.[2] The women – 100 first-time mothers and 100 second-time mothers – were interviewed three times: during late pregnancy, in the first month after birth, and in the fifth month after birth. The experiences which the mothers reported have been summarised elsewhere (Graham & McKee, 1979): here, only a few aspects are described. Although only giving a glimpse into the world of motherhood, they indicate something of the pervasiveness of women's concern with coping. They point to the way in which a woman's experience of reproduction is essentially a lesson in dealing quietly and co-operatively with the conflicting needs of others.

1) Coping with pregnancy In many respects, pregnancy can be seen fundamentally to challenge taken-for-granted ways of coping with life. Being pregnant raises questions about your ability to remain in paid employment, to fulfill household duties and to participate in social activities. It even raises questions about your sanity: about your ability to think logically and make rational decisions. As the advice books warn expectant mothers,

> even the most highly competent and efficient woman may find that her judgment is impaired. She may be induced to make hasty decisions, her reasoning may not be as rational as it would normally be, and her conclusions may be inaccurate and incorrect. It would, of course, be wrong to suggest that pregnant women are incapable, but a word of warning about emotional instability should make them consider things more carefully (Bourne, 1975).

Pregnancy involves physical symptoms and a transformation in body shape which further threaten a woman's self-image and coping style. Women in the survey spoke of the struggle not to 'let yourself go', the struggle to maintain their femininity, and, for some, their economic independence, despite these changes. But the arena in which the struggle to cope was most acutely felt was within the womb. It was here that anxiety was focussed, and it was here that the issues of responsibility and culpability were highlighted. The most pervasive and enduring anxiety reported during pregnancy concerned the normality of their unborn baby. Altogether, 87 percent of the sample said that they worried that their baby might not be normal. Reading through the medical and psychological literature on pregnancy, we find women's anxieties often dismissed as irrational worries which reflect the psychic instability of pregnancy or the prevalence of old wives' tales. However, the anxieties of which women spoke had their basis not in the folklore of female culture, but in medical science: they worried because they were 'too old', because of smoking, because of drugs consumed, because of their exposure to German Measles, and because of their sexual activity:

> I'm more worried about this one (her second baby). I'm more worried this time. I'm just being silly with me having high blood, but you do get stillborn (babies) with high blood pressure.

> I hope it's alright. I hope it's quite normal and everything. But I mean, you know, they are on about your age and everything – you know 'you're sort of at a difficult age, in your thirties' you know? When you're 37, it becomes, you know, a little harder.

> I've thought about mongolism and things like that. When you get past 30, you're supposed to have all these genes that bring out this mongolism thing. Well you think, naturally, you're going to be the one. I try not to think about it.

> When I was on nerve tablets, well I possibly could have caught on when I was on those. You see my friend, she was on tablets when she had hers and they blame that on her (daughter) being retarded you know.

These comments suggest not only what women worried about, but why they worried. While medical theories help explain the substance of their worries, it is the notion of responsibility which explains the reasons for these worries. Typically, the abnormalities that troubled the respondents were those that they might cause themselves. In other words, it was not simply the possibility of abnormality which was disturbing, but the possibility of discovering a personal responsibility for the abnormality. One woman expecting her second baby described her anxieties during her first pregnancy in this way:

> I wasn't worried that he wouldn't be normal but I suppose I felt that if he was going to be, and there was nothing I could do about it, that would be that. But if it was going to be abnormal through my neglect, then that was inexcusable.

Coping with these anxieties involved not only privileging the needs of the baby, but reconciling these needs with those of other members of the family. The normality of your baby may be ensured by sexual abstinence, but only if this does not conflict with the sexual needs of your partner. Similarly, giving up smoking was a possible way of promoting the health of the unborn baby, but only if the costs for the rest of the family were not too high:[3]

> They say it can be born dead if you smoke, through coming on early. I've cut down and I'm down to ten a day. If I cut down any more, I take it out on him (her son) which isn't fair on him. So it's one bairn or the other.

> I'm always more scratchy when I'm carrying. I fly off the handle more and over little things. It's hard enough for Dave (her husband) and Louise (her daughter) as it is. I gave up smoking for a bit, and I was even more irritable and I don't think I can ask that of them again.

2) Coping with childbirth To understand women's attitudes to childbirth, it is important to distinguish between their expectations of labour and delivery in prospect and their experiences, as recounted in the weeks after birth. In prospect, women worried that they were not going to cope with two aspects of childbirth: first, that they would be unable to diagnose correctly the symptoms of labour, and second, that they would fail to handle adequately the symptoms of labour. To fail to cope with these two aspects involved the risk of public attention and personal embarrassment: it was to run the risk of 'showing yourself up' and 'making a fool of yourself'. Two women described their fears about going into labour as follows:

> I'm frightened to death I'll make a fool of myself. I'm frightened to death I'll have a false alarm, you know, that it isn't the real thing. I shall wait till the last minute I think.

> I'm frightened to go into hospital too soon. It's not starting that bothers me, but when to go in. I can see myself panicking and taking myself in straight away. I'd like someone with me who would take the decision.

Another woman described her fears about being in labour in a similar way:

> I'd rather be among people that I don't know and then if I make a fool of myself it doesn't matter. I do know a nurse at the hospital, I'm frightened I'll be there when she's there. I think it's a bit private – not private, but if you make a fool of yourself, I'd never forget it.

Women having their second baby expressed similar anxieties about their ability to cope, explaining how knowing about childbirth does not necessarily alleviate one's fears:

> I have a fear that I'm not going to be able to cope, because I had an easy labour last time. And there were women screaming and shouting and carrying on and I thought, how disgusting making a noise like that. I think it's the fact that perhaps I'm going to have a worse labour and show myself up. I think that's the frightening bit. That bit frightens me.

> I'm not frightened or anything like that. But I've been through it once before so I'm a bit more wary. People say you are more frightened the first time, but I think it's a case of what you don't know, you don't worry about; once you know what's going to happen, you know what to expect.

Having described their attitudes to childbirth in prospect, respondents were then asked about their experiences in the interview after the birth had taken place. From their accounts, it appears that their worries about recognising labour were well grounded. The symptoms by which labour was announced were vague and easily confused with 'everyday' symptoms like constipation, backache and indigestion. Nonetheless, most women managed to get to the hospital without 'making a fool of themselves' – usually by involving female friends and relatives in the decision-making process.

Women's second source of anxiety of labour – about their capacity to cope with childbirth – was also apparent in their retrospective accounts. Again, however, few found that they 'let themselves down'. This was not because all the mothers contended with the process of labour and delivery calmly and competently. Instead, it was because most women (57 percent of the sample) had pain-relieving drugs, and found they could not remember if they coped or not. Although pethidine was prescribed as an analgesic (pain-relieving) drug, it was experienced as an amnesic drug which induced loss of memory. As a result, pethidine provided a licence not to cope: it took away the woman's sense of responsibility for her performance and her sense of culpability for the outrages she committed while under its influence.

> I can't remember going into the delivery room. All I remember – I shouted, oh I remember that. I remember she kept telling me to push and I couldn't push any more, you know, I was exhausted. I wasn't very good, but I can't really remember much about it.

> I can't really remember 'cos they gave that – is it pethidine you get? I know I was floating. I didn't know where I was really. All I kept saying was 'what are you doing to me?' and Geoff said I was shouting. I think they give you that to knock you out really. You don't know what you're doing. I can't really remember. Geoff thought it was marvellous.

Both women admit to being unable to cope: an inability to contend quietly and obediently with the demands – physical and medical – being made upon their bodies. Both women recall in particlar the moments when the silence was broken by their shouts – 'I shouted, oh I remember that' 'All I kept saying was "What are you doing to me?" and Geoff said I was shouting.' Both women, however, felt distanced from their failure, exonerated from blame by the drugs they received: 'I wasn't very good, but I can't really remember' 'Geoff said I were shouting (but) you don't know what you're doing. I can't really remember.' Other women described their experiences in a similar way. Their accounts again focus on the breakdowns in coping, on the times when the mother ceased to suffer in silence. They bring out, too, the way in which the coping role is in some way surrendered to the husband and boy-friend, who takes on the task of monitoring the woman's behaviour and recording her misdemeanours:

> . . . and at half past twelve, they came in and gave me pethidine and from then I was out, and she was born at half past two. I can't remember a thing, out completely. Pete says I was playing hell, but I can't remember.

> I don't remember much about it. It was laid wrong and they gave me loads of injections to put me out. That's all I remember. He was there and he tells me all that happened. All that I was shouting – I was a bad bugger. He was giving me gas and air 'cos I didn't want to know, because I didn't remember much about it . . .

Not all respondents found themselves exempted from responsibility for their performances during labour and delivery. Many respondents (43 percent) received no analgesics, while others who had the drug found that pethidine provided little licence for deviant behaviour. Instead, they were able to remember – and assess – their behaviour. In these accounts, we glimpse the image of the ideal coper, the quiet, uncomplaining and co-operative patient who is seen and not heard:

> I was a bit of a coward you know. I don't think I actually screamed. I did sort of cry out a little bit and I didn't think I would. Not because I wouldn't feel pain but because I get embarrassed about anything like that. And that's why I kept the mask (gas and air) over my face, more than anything to stifle it sort of.

> I just had one injection, because I was quite good this time. I was determined I wasn't going to show myself up. I just sort of looked out of the window and breathed when they came and didn't make a murmur. Just lay on this bed looking out of the window, but I wasn't crying out or anything like that, I just kept on a spot in the sky outside the window, so I was pretty good.

> There was a girl in the other room and they played war with her and she screamed and screamed. And I kept saying to Martin 'Am I doing alright? Am I good?' because I thought 'Lord, I don't want anyone to come in and shout my name at me, you know.'

3) Coping with motherhood In the accounts described at the beginning of this section, it appeared that coping with the baby during pregnancy hinged around the question of normality, and the sense of responsibility and guilt women felt for any handicap which might develop. In women's accounts of motherhood, responsibility to the baby was again a recurrent theme. It came out in women's discussions of crying (by the fourth week after birth, 60 percent of the respondents found that the baby's crying upset them, 58 percent found that there were situations where they didn't know what to do when the baby cried, and 61 percent found that there were times when they felt angry with the baby). Two women spoke their feelings about the baby crying in this way:

> You get really upset because you think, 'What on earth is the matter?' Why is she crying? Haven't I done something right? She's utterly dependent on you and it's you she wants when she cries?

> The thing that really upsets me with this screaming business is you really don't know what it is and you can't do anything to console them. It upsets me. When she wasn't getting any better I felt terrible. I thought if anything happens to her it's my fault because I haven't done anything.

The feelings of responsibility which these comments reveal was not a uni-dimensional issue. Mothers felt a responsibility not only to their child but to their partners, their children, their housework and – sometimes – to themselves. These responsibilities often conflicted: to privilege the baby's needs involved sacrificing the needs of other members of the family. For example, breast-feeding might promote the wellbeing of the new member of the household but only by exacting its toll on the existing members. As women symbolically put it: they had to 'go on the bottle' because they 'did not have enough'.

> This time I was determined to succeed. I only did it for two months with Sophie and I thought this time I'm going to persevere. But I got so tired: you can't rest when you have two. I mean I let the housework go but I still had to do the washing and ironing. I just could not, I did not have enough.

> I fed her for about a month, but she messed me about that much and with Sarah being so young I just couldn't cope. So I thought I'd be better on the bottle. The baby's no different really, but I feel better in myself. I've got more patience.

Coping with motherhood, like coping with pregnancy, thus involved the ability to reconcile competing demands, balancing the needs of one family member against another. It was often achieved only at personal cost: through the mother sacrificing her time, her sleep, her health and her social life for her family. One month after childbirth, 88 percent of the sample reported feeling tired, 77 percent felt they had no time to themselves, and 24 percent had not been out at all without the baby. Meeting the demands of motherhood ate heavily into the mother's energy, pushing her 'past herself' into a state where she could no longer cope:

> I was really tired that night, and he was crying and I'd fed him but he still wasn't settling . . . I changed him again and fed him again and he still wouldn't go back. And I went to get another nappy 'cos

he'd wet again. And I just went and sat down with my head in the airing cupboard and I just started to cry 'Oh for God's sake, shut up!' That was just that night. It was just being tired. If I can get my sleep, I can cope with it.

I never thought I would get angry with children. I was past myself one night and I was really shouting at her. I felt sorry afterwards but I really did get cross with her. I'd been up that night, half past two I fed her; ten to seven, I was still there. I was past myself that night.

Aggression towards the baby, verbal and physical abuse, was the ultimate symbol of failure: the most dramatic sign that a mother can no longer cope calmly and quietly with the pressure of her role (Graham, 1980):

If after the 3.00 am feed, he had one of those gemmy times when he wouldn't settle, I'd get irritable with him and I felt dreadful about it. I said to Stan 'I'm a bad mother' you know, because I was picking him up and shouting at him. I felt awful about it.

Conclusion

This paper has asked the question, what does it mean to be a mother? It has suggested that part of the answer lies in the concept of coping: that mothers are women who cope. It has suggested that coping is the concept through which women describe their experiences of reproduction and further is a concept which illuminates the links between these experiences and the material and ideological forces which structure women's lives.

What implications does the concept of coping have for the way we organise and campaign? First, there are implications for the way women respond to feminist demands. There is the obvious implication that women's isolated position within the home minimises the possibility of mothers developing a political consciousness, in the same way that their role as the family coper leaves them with little time or energy for political action ('I'm too tied up coping with my life to try and change it'). In addition, and more subtly, the very definition of the mother's role militates against action, whether individual or collective. If women are socialised into an image of themselves as individuals who will grapple silently with the pressures of childbearing and childrearing, then certain possibilities are structured out of their role. Successful coping hinges around the quiet acceptance of your lot: to speak out, to criticise, to protest, to set up alternatives, lies outside the repertoire of the coper. To be vociferous in a campaign to change your situation is tantamount to a public admission of your failure as a woman-who-copes.

Second, therefore, the concept of coping has implications for the way we frame feminist demands. It appears vital that we tie our strategies (strategies all the more urgent because of the rapid erosion of gains made over the last decade) to an attack on the ideology of coping. At the same time as defending the 1967 Abortion Act and campaigning for abortion on demand, or defending child benefits and agitating for the abolition of the family wage, we must expose the way in which the abortion legislation and the provision of social security benefits rest on an image of mothers-as-copers. For example, when Corrie argues for a more restrictive abortion law, he assumes that somehow women will cope with the pregnancies that would previously have been terminated; he takes for granted that women will not violently protest against their enforced confinements but will quietly accept their newly defined responsibilities.[4] Similarly, built into the Government's decision to freeze child benefit is the assumption that women will cope with the reduction in income, smoothing over any shortfall by the appropriate self-sacrifices.

Putting 'coping' on to the political agenda thus appears to have implications for the way women frame, and the way women respond to, feminist demands. For to attack the image of women-as-copers would potentially liberate women who are presently locked into a state of perpetual self-denial, at the same time as exposing the cracks in the social system which are plugged only by women's tenacity and commitment to silent sacrifice.

Notes

1 I want to thank Mary Maynard and Jude Stoddart, for inspiring the ideas developed in this paper. However, since I coped with writing it, I take full responsibility for its contents.

2 The interviewing for the Survey was carried out by Margaret Beaumont, Hilary Graham, Flo Green and Lorna KcKee. The project was based at the Institute of Social and Economic Research, University of York. It was financed by the Health Education Council and directed by Professor Laurie Taylor.

3 These two comments are taken from an earlier study I carried out in 1974, based on a survey of 50 expectant mothers. (Graham, 1976).

4 John Corrie's private member's bill to amend the Abortion Act was introduced in Parliament in 1979.

References

Bland, L., Brundson, C., Hobson, D. & Winship, J. 'Women "inside and outside" the relations of production'. In Women's Studies Group (ed.) *Women Take Issue*. Hutchinson, London. 1978.

Bourne, G. *Pregnancy*. Pan, London. 1975.

Bruegel, I. 'Women as a reserve army of labour: a note on recent British experience'. *Feminist Review* 3. 1979.

Crawford, R. 'You are dangerous to your health: the ideology and politics of victim-blaming'. *International Journal of Health Services*, vol 7, no 4. 1977.

Davin, A. 'Imperialism and Motherhood'. *History Workshop* 5, Spring. 1978.

Dobash R.E. and Dobash, R. *Violence Against Wives*. Macmillan, New York. 1979.

Gerhardt, U. 'Coping and social action'. *Sociology of Health and Illness*, vol 1, no 2. 1979.

Finch, J. and Groves, D. 'Community Care and the family: a case for equal opportunities'. Paper presented at the Social Administration Conference, Cambridge. 1979.

Graham, H. 'Smoking in pregnancy: the attitudes of expectant mothers'. *Social Science and Medicine*, vol 10. 1979.

Graham, H. '"Prevention and health: every mother's business" : a comment on child health policies in the seventies'. In Harris, C.C. (ed.) *The Sociology of the Family: New Directions for Britain*. Sociological Review Monograph No 28, University of Keele. 1979.

Graham, H. 'Women's accounts of anger and aggression towards their babies'. In Frude, N. (ed.) *Psychological Approaches to Child Abuse*, Batsford, London. 1980.

Graham, H. and McKee, L. *The First Months of Motherhood*. Report on the Health Education Council project concerned with women's experiences of pregnancy, childbirth and the first six months after birth. University of York. 1979.

Guardian. Report on the Conservative Women's Conference on Caring for Children. November 20th. 1979.

Kuhn, A. and Wolpe, A. *Feminism and Materialism*. Routledge and Kegan Paul, London. 1978.

Land, H. 'Inequalities in large families'. In Chester R. and Peel, H. (eds.) *Equalities and Inequalities in Family Life*. Academic Press, London. 1977.

Leach, P. *Who Cares?* Penguin, Harmondsworth. 1979.

Marris, P. *Widows and their Families*. Routledge and Kegan Paul, London. 1958.

Murray Parkes, C. *Bereavement: Studies of Grief in Adult Life*. Tavistock, London. 1972.

Owen, L. 'The welfare of women in labouring families: England, 1860-1950'. In Hartman, M. and Banner, L. (eds.) *Clio's Consciousness Raised: New Perspectives on the History of Women*. Harper and Row, London. 1974.

Personal Social Services Council. *Reductions in Local Authority Expenditure on the Personal Social Services: Paper Three*. Personal Social Services Council, London. 1980.

Pringle, M. Kellmer. *The Needs of Children*. Hutchinson, London. 1974.

JO SUTTON AND SCARLET FRIEDMAN

Fatherhood: Bringing It All Back Home

The background for this paper was our gradual realisation that there is a growing movement towards improving the lot of fathers, and therefore, men. An increasing number of books about fatherhood have been appearing in parallel to the women's liberation movement. We have observed the growth of organisations like Families Need Fathers in England, whose Durham Branch was in close contact with a Member of Parliament, Leo Abse, over his Bill on illegitimacy, which fell just before the 1979 Labour Government. This was followed by the publication of the Law Commission Report on illegitimacy in June 1979. About this time we attended a talk given by a psychologist who claimed that men should have rights over children on the basis of a biological relation to pregnancy and birth: he supported this argument with evidence first of pregnancy symptoms in men, including morning sickness, swollen belly, depression and so on (which, had they occurred in women, would likely have been referred to as 'phantom pregnancies in hysterical women'), and second of increased manifestations of masculine behaviour expressing irritability, aggressiveness and sexual insecurity expressed as concern about 'prowess'. We began to notice that a significant change has been occurring throughout the seventies – a movement for the intensification of male power inside the home.

The old style of fatherhood – strict, harsh disciplinarian – is becoming increasingly intolerable to women. On the other hand, for the mother to become 'the principal agent of both discipline and support' is to render the male powerless, marriage less satisfying. This is the problem for modern *man* as set out by Leonard Benson (1968) and reiterated in various forms in most of the literature on fathers.

A number of reasons are proposed as to why this situation has come about. Industrialisation, with its separation of home and work, is said to have left the working-class man too tired to demonstrate his physical strength and power, and therefore authority in the home (Benson, 1968, p 96). (Let us assume for the sake of the argument that there are no battered wives amongst the working class.) Meanwhile, his middle-class brother, that is, 'even the most intelligent and intellectually oriented man', cannot keep up with all that is taught his children; 'his traditional role as the fountain of knowledge in the home' is thereby undermined (Lynn, 1974, p 8). Another brother, of the Against Sexism variety, explains that the permissive society has rendered the authoritarian rule maker no longer viable, such that 'the father today is regarded as a genuine authority by neither himself nor his children' (Fasteau, 1975, p 93). Finally, women are accused of robbing men of their fatherly privileges. The feminist movement is seen to have reduced the control men have over their wives (Lynn, 1974, p 71). Yet, behind the failure lies an ambition to succeed at the old game. For all these men the direction of change is to render the authority of men in the family more acceptable to women and children.

Since World War II we have witnessed a redefinition of family gender-linked tasks towards becoming increasingly 'symmetrical' (Young and Wilmott, 1973). Men and women are now expected to do things together, to be equally responsible for the fulfilment of the individual potential of each partner. We are also sold the possibility of an interpersonal exchange of rights and responsibilities.

The responsibility for parenthood too, has increasingly been presented as a mutual endeavour. Now the 'cement' in a marriage, and the fulfilment of the woman – having children – is seen to involve men as 'carers' who are present in the home and who share with the woman the happiness and the heartaches of childcare. The risk of not doing so is the loss of both wife and children:

> The absent husband has come to value status and power more highly than home and family, if time and energy devoted to them are anything to go by . . . And the man who concentrates on the rat-race to the virtual exclusion of his family may find, in the end, that he has no one to share the prizes with except the other rats. (Fenwick and Fenwick, 1979, p 182)

The democratisation of father's fireside seat is not, however, as unproblematic as this image of mutuality would imply. For the display of the so-called liberated woman within marriage engenders certain difficulties:

> The emancipation of women from the bed and kitchen stereotype and the decline of the authoritarian family, together with the growth of the democratic one ... (has brought) new tensions and queries. Few doubt that one of the main causes of present instability in marriage comes from the difficulty of adjustment to the rights of women, irresistibly and rightly gained in recent years. (Abse, 1979, para. 1863).

If we look more closely at what these tensions are, we find they are those of men. The problem for men is how to retain authority in the family in an atmosphere in which the traditional form of their authority is threatened. The problem is *not* how to change; it is how to *adjust* – and thereby, remain the same. Indeed, if women *were* equal, the family as we know it would not exist.

The rhetoric of mutual parenthood may seem to convey equality and exchange. However, just as the term 'domestic violence' obscures the fact that it is men who hit women (Dobash and Dobash, 1980), so the term 'parenthood' masks which parent retains control. Fatherhood and motherhood are not, in fact, merged: they are merely redefined.

Despite the modern picture of the ideal family with its caring, sharing parenthood, fatherhood and motherhood present two very different images. Fatherhood is an improved version of the stern disciplinarian, maintaining authority and control with a softer, cosier manner. Motherhood is an even cleaner, more efficient worker inside and outside the home and the maker of the parental bond with the child. A Motherhood mother copes lovingly and selflessly; a Fatherhood father enforces obedience. Of course, one qualifies for fatherhood or motherhood only by one's sex, having one or more live children and successful gender identification. The road is long and complex and, not surprisingly, not all men who make it to being fathers are of the ideal fatherhood standard – and the same for women and motherhood. True fatherhood and motherhood are not random occurrences; they are largely social achievements.

Fatherhood, the exercise of men's authority over women and children, is the position of men in the family. It is the means of instilling in the family members a recognition and acceptance of, and acquiescence to, male authority. As Peter and Elizabeth Fenwick suggest:

> The attitude a child develops towards men in general, and authority in particular (because most of the authority figures he will

> meet – teachers, policemen and later employers are likely to be men), will be founded on his attitude towards the 'male model' available. This is quite a responsibility for father (Fenwick and Fenwick, 1979, p 172).

The end is political self-perpetuation, that is, the continuation and reproduction of male supremacy.

One essential feature of this process is the maintenance of heterosexuality: this means, for boys, learning to dominate, and for girls, learning to submit to men. David Lynn explains that for sons:

> When a father combines nurturance with dominance and high participation in child care, he increases the likelihood of high masculinity in his son (Lynn, 1974, p 166).

while for daughters:

> Father-dominance in marriage often seems to have three unfortunate consequences for the development of daughters: it strains the father/daughter relationship; it seems to contribute to the psychological problems of daughters; and it promotes their adoption of the traditionally feminine role (Lynn, 1979, p 91).

Benson, too, maintains that father is important in 'developing his daughter's attractiveness to boys' (1968, p 210), and Fenwick and Fenwick propose:

> A woman's sexual response, her attitude towards men, whether or not she makes an eventual success of her marriage, all this can be laid at father's door (1979, p 178).

The assumptions indicated here are twofold: first, that boys need a figure of specifically male authority and dominance to imitate; if, for example, a boy was raised by his mother alone, he would be in danger of becoming confused in his future sexual relations to men and women generally – and in particular, in his future position as a male authority and father figure. Second, daughters are assumed to need to orient their lives and sexuality towards men. Father is seen to be a key figure – the first man in her life – who presents a male model and affects her relationship to all men. However, if a daughter's heterosexuality were as 'natural' as this assumption implies, then a man's presence would not be necessary to ensure it. It is more likely that this 'gentle' authoritarian figure – more directive than tyrannical, more subtle than blatant, more sophisticated than crude – is important in teaching daughters not simply 'natural' heterosexual urges, but to direct their primary loyalty to men, to adorn themselves with behaviour and clothing appealing to men, to service men well and, above all, to submit. The claim for the necessity of men in the raising of children is based, as Adrienne Rich (1980) points out, upon heterosexuality as a political institution.

Not only are fathers considered important in enforcing stereotypical masculinity and femininity, they are crucial as protectors. Primarily, this job consists of protecting male children from their mothers. Fathers encourage in young boys the recreation of their own image and discourage them from all things female:

> Boys are constantly reminded that they must avoid feminine behaviour and must show signs of being able to cut themselves loose from the world of women that surrounds them. They develop hostility towards girls and things feminine in very early childhood, and the hostility recurs throughout their lives as a fear of being identified with 'the enemy' (Benson, 1968, p 190).

A mother is seen to have little practical advice to offer her son in this matter. And further, she might attempt to introduce change into such a pattern of social relations. Fathers, therefore, are necessary components of patriarchal family life. For it is father who 'serves as an exacting coach, acting out masculine patterns of aggressiveness' (ibid., p 193). A coach is not somebody who sits on the sidelines, or is a mere visitor to the team's bench; rather he is, as Betty Lehan Harragan clearly describes, the boss, the unquestioned decision-maker (1977, p 108). The coach has his team's interests at heart, and encourages their loyalty and success at defeating any opposition.

In protecting boys from female influence and in coaching them in masculine aggressiveness, it can be seen that fatherhood is about teaching boys to ally with men, to join with and protect male control over women. These social relations are legitimated through the creation of competition with women, even in parenting. In 'proving his manhood' father must be seen to be better than women even at those tasks which are presumed to comprise 'a woman's role'. Benson, for example, proposed that the ideal father is one who is 'self-confident and directive' and 'better able than mother to cope' with difficulties that arise (1968, p 110). By this definition, for father to be ideal, mother must be inadequate.

It is not the case, though, that father is better at the routine, mundane tasks involved in caring for children. Rather, these are considered to be the appropriate sphere of a subordinate. Father's claim to be better is a claim of masculine objectivity and rationality qualifying him to decide who performs which tasks and then to ensure that the woman carries out her work to his satisfaction. As Margaret Polatnick points out:

> Fathers may default from the daily child-rearing routines, but, much like male principals supervising female teachers, they still tend to wield the ultimate decision making power (1975, p 224).

Whilst the mother, too, is seen to partake in the nurturance of stereotypical sexual behaviour – both in her treatment of the children and as a model of heterosexuality – it is father who is portrayed as the most important figure. The creation of another generation of masculine males and feminine females is primarily the responsibility of the father. Indeed it is he who has the most to gain from the club of males and the services of females. It is the father, and men in general, who would lose the most in any change of the power balance in favour of women. Men are therefore the people who maintain the status quo and are the most reactionary element in our society.

Although the individual man has power over his wife and children, all men are part of the social structure of male power over women. The child-care professions, claiming expertise in the knowledge of children's 'needs', are all male dominated and male oriented. Barbara Ehrenreich and Deirdre English (1979) show, for example, how the growth of the child-care expert was a process of male takeover and supervision of motherhood. The rank of father in relation to his family as a position of acting in for, yet remaining dependent upon, the guidance of the expert is described by Benson:

> Father is drawn into the toughest situations, the ones mother has been unable to handle . . . If he is called upon, the situation is imbued with a special atmosphere: his presence at this time is somewhat comparable to a doctor who is paying a sick call, although father's diagnosis is rarely the result of calm, professional reflection (1968, p 110).

In discussing so-called 'mother-child bonding', Christine Cooper (1978) indicates that where there is a 'failure' medical experts should be called upon. They, in turn, call upon the father to assist them to regulate the mother's care of the child. In their recent paper 'Is Dad an expert too?' Lorna McKee and Marion Kerr (1979) reported that in their own study, fathers tended to act as 'troubleshooters', taking decisions in the family as to when the experts should be called in, and intervening when they felt the mother was being mishandled or misguided by health visitors (women). In clinic sessions professionals never regarded fathers as irrelevant, and tended to offer explanations and refer to published material more often with fathers than with mothers. Fathers and professionals appear to regard fatherhood as an embodiment of rationality. It would seem that 'rationality' refers to the fact that the experts feel they can relate more easily to men: this is hardly surprising, since they are partners. For the partnership of child rearing is not between the mother and the father, but between the father and the male state, using and perpetuating their control over women.

The recent surge of legal interest in children is one example of increasing state involvement in this partnership. This development affects, as well as reflects recent changes in patriarchal relations. As Rhona Rapoport et al point out:

> By making it explicit what the boundaries of 'normal' behaviour are, and what the reasons are for enforcing those boundaries, the law defines qualitatively what is 'good' as well as what is 'bad' in relation to parenting (1977, p 76).

It is interesting that when the experts claim every child 'needs' a father, has a 'right' to have a father, the underlying concern is less with the actual effect upon children, than with the rights and privileges of men. For instance, the British Law Commission Report proposing to protect and improve the conditions affecting 'illegitimate' children reveals their primary concern with the rights of men:

> From a strictly legal point of view, the father of the illegitimate child is today at a greater disadvantage than the child himself (1979, para 2.11).

The content of the Report deals almost exclusively with the problem of how to introduce greater rights for men, giving them automatic rights of guardianship, custody and access to the child born of a woman with whom they have had sexual intercourse likely to have resulted in conception. The Rights of Women Illegitimacy Campaign Group exposes their expressed concern for the child to be a front for the extension of men's rights and the subordination of women:

> The real concern of the Law Commission's proposals is not with children's rights – as everyone is claiming – but with fathers' rights. The origin of women's oppression lies in male domination and control over women and children. As the illegitimacy rate has risen, women having children outside marriage, and outside the control of men, poses a severe threat to this patriarchal set up. It is no coincidence that the seemingly progressive move to abolish illegitimacy serves to extend fathers' rights, and hence male control, under the cover of supposedly benefitting the child (1979, p 2).

Significantly, although a woman with a child(ren) lives in a male dominated society, it is still advocated that each individual woman should be directly accessible to at least one man, a representative of the male state, on a daily basis. It is the experience of women in the 150 refuges for battered women in Britain that when a man has access to a child, he is able to use the child to further his own interests and to control that child's mother.

Institutionalising the rights of men to children, and through the children to mothers, is not so much the introduction of rights for men as the transfer of rights from women to men. Whilst men gain, women lose. The Law Commission recognises this fact and proposes to legalise it (again under the rubric of the child's best interests), for example:

> There will of course be many cases where mothers of children born out of wedlock are unwilling to allow the fathers to play, or continue to play, any part in the children's lives. In taking that attitude they will no doubt believe that they are acting in the child's best interests. But we think that the decision to exclude a father from all parental rights and duties is so important that it should not be the mother's alone; the final decision should lie with the courts, which are bound to regard the welfare of the child as paramount (1979, para 3.16).

Of the 18 people on the Law Commission working party who prepared this Report, two were women.

The assumptions which are to inform the courts are, first, the present 'disadvantaged' position of men in relation to a child born of a woman to whom they are not married (whether or not the pregnancy resulted from a one-off sexual encounter, including rape); and second, that fatherhood is an essential element in the development of every child who will grow up to fit within the existing social structure.

That this Report is to be influential in the drafting of new legislation in the near future is confirmed by the fact that the setting up of this Law Commission working party in 1976 followed the signing by the United Kingdom of the agreement set out by the Council of Europe in 1975. Article 3 of this document states:

> Paternal affiliation of every child born out of wedlock may be evidenced or established by voluntary recognition or by judicial decision.

The status of illegitimacy is at present conferred upon a child whose parents are not married. The Law Commission does not propose to enforce a state of legal marriage upon the biological parents. The child therefore remains a child of unmarried parents. To entitle an 'unwed father' to the same rights to children as one who is married enables a man to control women even further – to have a woman raise 'his' children, without having either to convince her to marry him or to provide any maintenance for her whilst she provides him with this service. And further, he could do this with several women (officially sanctioned polygamy?).

A woman who, at present, wants to prevent an individual man from having direct control over her but wants children, would be wise to remain unmarried. Under the proposed recommendations an unmarried woman would, in effect, be forced to give the biological father of her child rights over her. In this situation the man would be legally responsible for the maintenance of the child. If they were married he would also have to maintain her. Women will therefore be forced into marriage while raising children, whilst men will no longer need to marry to gain rights and privileges over women and children.

When feminists demanded that men become involved in childcare, it was a demand for men to be responsible – to take on their share of *responsibilities* for others. What has resulted is a minimal change in caring and a significant move by men to increase their *rights* and hence, control.

The recent reestablishment of fatherhood and the rights of men is a significant historical development in patriarchy. In revitalising the power of men over children the particular form of male control over women has altered, but not to the advantage of women – rather, distinctly to our disadvantage. We are not, of course, suggesting that the issue of fatherhood is the only area of increasing male control over women's lives. But we do feel that when we as feminists discuss, or even advocate, men in the domestic sphere, we need to take into account that in taking on an extra pair of male hands in a patriarchal society, male power is furthered. The issue is complex and has no doubt been reenacted many times: women are first divided from each other; the tasks are so many that they still need to be shared, but the burden appears to belong to the individual woman; and then a man(men) offers to solve 'our' problems. We would maintain that the offer is founded in self-interest and the consolidation of patriarchy.

References

Abse, Leo. Debate on Divorce Laws. *Hansard*, 22 March, para 1863. HMSO, London. 1979.

Benson, Leonard. *Fatherhood: A Sociological Perspective*. Random House, New York. 1968.

Cooper, Christine. 'Medical aspects of child abuse'. In Smith, S. (ed.) *The Maltreatment of Children*. MTP Press, Boston. 1978.

Council of Europe. *European Convention on the Legal Status of Children Born Out of Wedlock*. Strasbourg. 1975.

Dobash, Rebecca Emerson and Dobash, Russell. *Violence Against Wives*. Free Press, New York. 1980.

Ehrenreich, Barbara and English, Deirdre. *For Her Own Good: 150 years of the Experts' Advice to Women*. Pluto Press, London. 1979.

Fasteau, Marc F. *The Male Machine*. Delta, New York. 1975.

Fenwick, Peter and Fenwick, Elizabeth. *The Baby Book for Fathers*. Sphere Books, London. 1979.

Gieve, Katherine. 'Illegitimate proposal'. *New Statesman*, 13th July. 1979.

Harragan, Betty Lehan. *Games Mother Never Taught You*. Warner, New York. 1977.

Law Commission Working Paper No 74. *Family Law: Illegitimacy*. HMSO, London. 1979.

Lynn, David B. *The Father: His Role in Child Development*. Brooks/Cole, Monterey, California. 1974.

Lynn, David B. *Daughters and Parents: Past, Present and Future*. Brooks/Cole, Monterey, California. 1979.

McKee, Lorna and Kerr, Marion. 'Is Dad an expert too?' Paper presented at the University of Warwick, June. 1979.

Pleck, Joseph H. and Sawyer, Jack. (eds.) *Men and Masculinity*. Spectrum, Englewood Cliffs, New Jersey. 1974.

Polatnick, Margaret. 'Why men don't rear children: a power analysis.' In Petras, J.W. (ed.) *Sex: Male Gender: Masculine*. Alfred Knopf, New York. 1975.

Rapoport, Rhona, Rapoport, Robert, N. and Strelitz, Fiona with Kew, Stephen. *Fathers, Mothers and Others*. Routledge and Kegan Paul, London. 1977.

Rich, Adrienne. Compulsory heterosexuality and lesbian existence. *Signs: Journal of Women in Culture and Society*, vol 5, no 4. Summer. 1980.

Rights of Women Illegitimacy Campaign Group. *Illegitimacy: A Feminist View*. London. 1979.

Young, Michael and Willmott, Peter. *The Symmetrical Family*. Routledge and Kegan Paul, London. 1973.

Part Two
The Women's Liberation Movement and Men

Edited by Elizabeth Sarah

JAN BRADSHAW

Foreword: How it All Began . . .

We decided to have a conference that directly confronted problems about men and the WLM because we felt that on some levels the issues were being avoided, skirted around or approached from an increasingly oblique angle. On the other hand there was quite a bitter argument going on in the WLM about feminists relating to men, both as lovers and as mothers of sons. For some months prior to the conference internal WLM newsletters had been reeling under the swipes and blows from all sides. There was the issue of boy children, which eventually surfaced in the article 'Thinking About Boy Children' in *Spare Rib* (No 96, July 1980, pp 26-27), leading to discussion about whether women should 'put energy into men' of *any* age. And there was the debate surrounding the Leeds Revolutionary Feminists' article on 'political lesbiansim', which was published in a pamphlet *Love Your Enemy*? by Onlywomen Press (1981), together with a number of letters debating its arguments. There had also been disagreement about an article submitted for publication in *Spare Rib* by Ann Pettit, which some women felt was anti-lesbian. The article was rejected by *Spare Rib* but was later published in WIRES, a women-only internal newsletter.

About 250 women came, talked and listened to each other, occasionally yelled at each other, wept in the workshop on mothers and sons, and went home in various states of elation, bewilderment and despair. Amanda Sebestyen later wrote a report of the conference, 'Thinking About Men' in *Spare Rib* (No 94, May 1980, pp 23-24) which drew some letters from men to Amanda and myself – some good, some bad, some very very bad. At least three groups (to my knowledge) were formed from the conference – one on mothers of sons, one on making demands on men and one on sexuality, which is drawing together threads from lesbian, heterosexual and celibate women to be published in a book. The same summer, Onlywomen

Press initiated discussions between lesbian and heterosexual women to encourage further dialogue around the issue of sexuality. To those of us participating in all four groups it was a dizzying and exhausting experience. Of course we haven't by any means got it all sorted out, but we *did* begin to talk to each other.

ELIZABETH SARAH

Introduction

There is little doubt that feminists differ in both our analyses and our practices concerning 'men' and 'patriarchy'. However, on the whole, we are united in our commitment to an autonomous women's liberation movement as fundamental to the quest for social change in which women's interests are not subordinated to the interests of men.

The participation of males in our lives at any level is a threat to our autonomy and yet cannot be avoided at *some* level. What is the relative risk involved in engaging with men as 'lovers', as 'friends', as 'employers', as 'co-workers', as 'shop assistants', as 'bus conductors', as 'plumbers', as 'political comrades', as 'gay brothers', as 'friends of feminism' . . . ? Are some forms of interaction more dangerous (and more complex) than others? Why? On the face of it, a male 'friend of feminism' is less threatening than a male 'lover', but a male lover may accept his place *outside* the feminist struggle, and a male 'friend of feminism' may assume or insist on a place within it. On the face of it, a gay man is less oppressive than a heterosexual man, but for both, male experience and male bonding may be the dominant reality – the interests of women being completely subordinate (in the case of 'straight' men) or simply marginal (in the case of gay men).

Whatever choices we make regarding 'relationships' with men, the dominance of men, of male interests, and of male values, impinges on our lives as feminists. We may refuse to interact with men completely – sexually, socially and politically; we may demand that 'anti-sexist' men challenge male power and change their own assumptions and behaviour; we may reject heterosexual men as our oppressors and consider gay men our 'brothers'; we may dissociate ourselves from men sexually and work with them 'politically'; we may struggle with patriarchal conditioning to rear 'sons of the mothers' . . . We may choose any number of ways of confronting, surviving, dealing with the male world which structures our lives (and some will be more 'compromising' than others . . .), but it is impossible for us to make choices which are not shaped by the reality of male power.

The Women's Liberation Movement and Men does not claim to be uniform, comprehensive or definitive. Hopefully, the publication of these papers will encourage further exploration of the subject among feminists committed to the continued growth of an autonomous women's liberation movement.

ELIZABETH SARAH

Female Performers on a Male Stage: The First Women's Liberation Movement and the Authority of Men, 1890-1930[1]

Introduction

If I were writing this paper for a conference on women's history, it would be quite obvious why it was being written and what purposes it served. The task of establishing a tradition of articulated female experience in the world is an enormous one. If all our energy were directed towards making women *visible* in history, it would still take us years to uncover the evidence.

The creation of female history is a legitimate activity in itself. However, given that women today are involved in a movement for our liberation from male domination (once again), our central concern is to create the conditions for female autonomy so that we may be in a position to control our *future*. The question we are compelled to ask in this context is quite obvious in my opinion: can our knowledge of women's *past* experience help us to do this? It seems to me that our history is important to us not only as a *testament* to our activity in the past, but also as a *guide* to our activity in the present.

'In my opinion'; 'it seems to me': these are very cautious phrases. I am using them because I am not sure how many women share my ideas. Certainly, I am not laying some abstract claim to the notion of 'history repeating itself'; my conviction that women can learn from our history is based on a particular understanding of one of the few female historical events that has to a certain extent been visible to all of us: the 'Suffrage' movement.

From the outset, the relevance of the 'Suffrage' movement to modern feminism is immediately apparent. Feminists today are eager to recognise that then, as now, women took *action* to transform their lives. However, it is generally understood that First Wave Feminism was about different issues than those with which we are currently concerned, chiefly 'the vote', and it follows that the motivations and objectives of the early feminists must have been very different from ours. In other words, although we may be inspired by the knowledge of the determination of the early feminists, we do not consider that we are able to *use* their particular experience of struggle for our own purposes today.

In this paper, I intend to establish that the 'Suffrage' movement was a Women's Liberation Movement much like that of today, and to assert that in this case we are forced to address ourselves to how and why it *disappeared*. The modern WLM has not invented a feminist analysis of women's oppression in a male-dominated society. Rather, the major issues that we recognise today – the enslavement of marriage and the family, the tyranny of male sexuality, male violence against women, educational and employment inequality – have *reemerged* after fifty years of *silence*. It is not possible to be complacent about the gains of the WLM of the last ten years or so in the face of the fact that the first WLM, which attempted to challenge patriarchy, and which was in many ways so similar to current feminism, *failed*.

Examining the Evidence

There is no way we can experience events of the past 'as they happened'. Our only immediate connection is with the evidence which has survived the passage of time, for example, books, papers, artefacts and oral testimony (in the case of recent history), and since this is rarely accessible to all of us, we must rely on the word of the 'historian', the professional interpreter of the available historical evidence. What is more, of course, all the traditional historians have been (are) white, middle class, Christian and male: the 'history' presented to us in the classroom and in the textbooks reflects all these (particular) biases.

This is not a new revelation. For years, socialists, for example, have decried the pro-Imperialism bias in British history books. More recently, women, by uncovering the evidence and writing alternative female-centred accounts, have exposed the fact that men have literally written women out of history (Alexander, Davin and Hostettler, 1979; Branca, 1977; Davin 1972, 1980; Delamont and Duffin, 1978; Kamm, 1966; Liddington, 1977; Liddington and Norris, 1978; Raeburn, 1974; Ramelson, 1976; Rover, 1967, Rowbotham, 1974;[2] Vicinus, 1980).[3] But this is not the end of it. While patriarchal power may be the preserve of men, male *values* permeate the whole society. For women to write *women's* history, we must have established our own female-oriented framework of analysis, strictly speaking a *feminist* as opposed to *masculist* view of the world. Has this happened?

Reading some of the new women's history, I am aware of the preeminence of a *socialist* perspective (Alexander and Davin, 1976; Alexander, Davin and Hostettler, 1979; Davin, 1972; Liddington, 1977; Liddington and Norris, 1978; Ramelson, 1976; Rowbotham, 1974). Socialist feminist historians subscribe to the socialist (male) judgement of the first major feminist movement: it was essentially limited in its scope – concerned overwhelmingly with constitutional adjustments to accommodate women – because the majority of the early feminists failed to confront capitalism. Of all the more conspicuous feminists, for example, Sylvia Pankhurst (and her East London Federation of the Suffragettes) alone championed the cause of all women and appreciated the peculiar plight of working-class women. Moreover, she recognised the fundamental importance of *class* oppression and allied herself directly to the socialist movement (Rowbotham, 1974: pp 77-89; 114-7; 159-61).

A socialist analysis of First Wave Feminism fails to recognise that from a feminist point of view, it is *patriarchy*, not capitalism which is the root of the oppression of *all* women as a group. It is important to remember that the defeat of the first WLM was first and foremost a victory for *male power*: the male value system remained unchallenged and the male power structure remained intact.

My research is based on the assumption that the domination of women by men precedes and underlies all other forms of oppression and social hierarchy (for example, of race and class). I would call my analysis feminist by this definition, but to distinguish it from socialist feminist analyses (which also claim to be feminist), I shall label it *Radical Feminist*. In so far as a socialist feminist historical perspective selects 'women' as its subject, it is feminist. But this is a minimal definition and, what is more, socialist feminist history has made women visible *on male terms*. Socialist analysis denies the *communality* of female experience in the subordination of all women to men, by decreeing that since class oppression is fundamental, women must be *divided* by their class allegiances. Certainly, women occupy different class positions and command different resources (and middle-class women are relatively privileged in this respect). However, both capitalism and socialism are *male systems of power* (that is, created by men for their purposes); women do not have any stake in either system. Our only strength as a group is to be found in our bonds with one another: a radical critique of society in terms of class and radical action on the basis of conflicting class interests can only be antithetical to the interests of women *as a whole*.

My account of the first WLM is shaped by a Radical Feminist perspective. It is also limited by the evidence which I have chosen to examine. I have not attempted to seek out all the available evidence of the period – the letters, pamphlets, books and journals, to name only the *written* sources. I have looked at the journals alone (a fairly massive task in itself), and then again not all the journals. Since November 1979 I have been studying the 80-odd feminist periodicals (covering the period from about 1850 to 1930) which are available at the Fawcett Library in London.[4] Some of the periodicals are incomplete, the majority, however, are complete and go into several volumes. There are a few (about 20) journals which I have come across in references which are not available at the Fawcett,[5] and these, together with the missing issues of the other journals, are available at the Newspaper Division of the British Library.[6]

I would emphasise that my focus on the periodicals has enabled me to bring to light aspects of the first WLM which have been largely overlooked. These journals were published at close regular intervals (weekly or monthly) by the numerous women's groups which were engaged in struggle, and provide an immediate and ongoing account of activities and attitudes at the time.

However, written publications have their own limitations. Certainly, only women's groups which wanted to communicate to a public audience would have published journals.[7] There may have been groups of feminists around who, like the separatists of today, did not choose to participate in a public debate and were more concerned to establish autonomous communities apart from the mainstream of society. There is some evidence available which suggests that such communities did in fact exist, although they were few and far between.[8] But of course we can only have access to what has been *written* down and, if not circulated publicly at the time, at least preserved somewhere so that it may be discovered by feminists today. Ultimately, if I draw conclusions on the basis of the evidence that I have examined, I must be aware that much is missing and that grasping 'the whole truth' is not an option which is open to anyone.

Prelude to the Rise of the First Women's Liberation Movement: The Years 1850-90

Although I am aware of an almost continuous period of feminist agitation between about 1850 and 1930, the evidence of the periodicals[9] has led me to distinguish two distinct phases of the early feminist movement, 1850 to 1890 and 1890 to 1930, and to focus on the latter period in so far as it may be characterised as a *Women's Liberation Movement*, broadly similar to that in which we are involved today.

What was different about the first phase of the struggle? To answer this question, we must understand something about the nature of the power structure in nineteenth-century Britain.

In many ways the nineteenth century may be seen as a period in British history in which the *machinery* of the omnipotence of both patriarchy and capitalism was most violently and overtly displayed. From the point of view of women, this meant that not only were they completely subordinate to men in the conditions and circumstances of their lives, but their absolute powerlessness was enshrined in the legal code. For example, it is in the mighty text of the law at that time that the real meaning of 'marriage' is most explicitly stated. A woman, who from the moment of her birth was the charge and responsibility of her father, became, upon marriage, the property of her husband to be handled as he saw fit. Married women did not exist as independent persons in law and were not entitled to own their own property or to take responsibility for the welfare of their children (Strachey, 1979, pp 14-6; Ramelson, 1967, pp 47-53; Hollis, 1979, pp 8-14, 167-198; Bauer and Ritt, 1979, pp 166-205).

Both working-class and middle-class wives were defined as non-persons in terms of the legal code. However, they did not experience legal oppression in the same way since the circumstances of their daily lives were usually quite different. The majority of working-class wives, even after the establishment of the Factory Acts (The Factory and Workshop Act, 1877. See Rowbotham, 1974, p 61) which restricted women's manual employment, worked both outside and inside the home, and their wages were essential to the survival of their families. The working-class husband could not assume the role of 'breadwinner' and 'protector', and the working-class wife contributed to her own support and that of her children, thereby acquiring a measure of independence (Alexander, Davin and Hostetller, 1979, pp 175-9; Davin, 1972, pp 219-221; Pinchbeck, 1981; Ramelson, 1967, pp 25-31; Rowbotham, 1974, pp 55-9).

The life of the middle-class wife, on the other hand, was completely circumscribed. The majority of middle-class wives did not work, and since they were not allowed to have property or money of their own, they were totally dependent on their husbands for financial support (Branca, 1975, pp 1-59).

Of course, not all middle-class women were married. However, since the law assumed that women were either being governed by their fathers or by their husbands, it was extremely difficult for the 'single' middle-class woman to live independently and support herself. She was not entitled to any education beyond the acquisition of 'genteel accomplishments', and opportunities for employment were extremely limited. She could become a family governess, poorly paid and much abused, but little else (Peterson, 1973, 3-19; Ramelson, 1967, 35-6; Hollis, 1979, 90-9).

It was rare for the working-class woman to be in this position. Working women who were single were usually in paid employment and were financially, frequently quite well off by comparison with their married sisters (Davin, 1972, p 120). Of course, for those who were not in full-time paid employment, there was always the option (?) (in the winter months at least when there was very little else for *men* of the middle and upper classes to do in the way of leisure pursuits) of turning to a precarious 'independent' life as prostitutes 'on the streets' (Davin, 1972, pp 222-3; Hollis, 1979, 202-7; Sigsworth and Wyke, 1973, pp 77-99).

The determination on the part of middle-class women in the mid-nineteenth century to put an end to their legal bondage may be readily explained. It is not surprising that the issues of Married Women's Property and the Custody of Children were high priorities for those who were married, while the 'right' to education and employment became the central preoccupation for their single sisters (the rights of married women to education and employment were not generally considered at this time) (Bauer and Ritt, 1979, pp 108-165; Hollis, 1979, pp 100-156; Strachey, 1979, pp 64-186, 225-285. See also the periodicals of the time for details of the ongoing debates).

In fact the early legal struggles were dominated by middle-class women and this was also true of the fight for 'the vote' (Ramelson, 1967, pp 76-89; Hollis, 1979, pp 292-313; Bauer and Ritt, 1979, pp 206-235). Even the 'plight' of working-class women (that is, prostitution) was taken up by middle-class women on their behalf (Rowbotham, 1974, pp 51-4; Hollis, 1979, pp 208-219; Strachey, 1979, pp 187-224). However, working-class women did engage in their own forms of resistance: the agitation of women workers for better pay and conditions of employment became widespread during the 1870s and onwards, as restrictions on women's industrial work came into force (Alexander, Davin and Hostettler, 1979, pp 177, 180-1; Davin, 1972, pp 217-8; Hollis, 1979, pp 109-129; Rowbotham, 1974, pp 60-4).

With the fairly successful resolution of many of the legal battles in the late nineteenth century (for example, The Married Women's Property Act, 1882), feminist agitation took on a new meaning for all women. In spite of a large measure of legal equality, both working-class and middle-class women continued to be dominated by men in their daily lives. The issue was becoming one of *control*. How was women's control of their own lives to be achieved?

Understanding the 'Suffrage' Movement, 1980-1930[10]

From about 1890 onwards, 'the vote' began to emerge as the dominant *symbol* of women's liberation from male domination. While the central concern was women's subordination to men in law, the struggle for 'the vote' represented more than anything else the demand for legal equality. It was only when the bonds of the law became looser and women achieved a limited freedom, that the 'vote' began to take on a new significance:

> Our demand is primarily votes for women on the same terms as men, but ultimately absolute equality between the sexes – politically, socially and economically (*The Vote*, Vol 10, No 247, 17 July 1914).

In a sense, to label the feminist agitation after 1890 a 'Suffrage' campaign is grossly to misrepresent the struggle at that time. The word 'suffrage', both masks the fact that the movement was concerned with many other issues besides the vote – marriage, sexuality, male violence, education and employment, for example – and imposes a far too literal meaning on the fight for 'the vote'. On the whole, the vote was not seen as an end in itself. The majority of feminists regarded the achievement of 'the vote' as a beginning only: as the acceptance of the *principle* of the freedom of every woman, not as the *actuality* of that freedom.

Many of the feminist periodicals that were published between the years 1890 and 1930, have the word 'suffrage', 'franchise', or 'vote' in the title. The average list of contents, on the other hand, reveals that this did not mean that feminists believed that women were oppressed *because* they didn't have the vote. The early feminists were very well aware that it was patriarchal power that was responsible for women's subordination to men in every area of their lives, and the issues discussed in the periodicals reflect this understanding: women are oppressed because they are not entitled to a comprehensive education, and if taught anything at all beyond reading and writing, acquire 'accomplishments' only, to be used for the entertainment and enhancement of others and not real skills with which to enrich their own lives; women are oppressed because the institution of marriage restricts their sphere of independent activity and forces them to serve men; women are oppressed because they are victims of rampant male sexuality which renders them mere vessels of male sexual pleasure, either 'on the streets' or in the marriage bed; women are oppressed because employment opportunities are severely limited and even when women are doing the same work as men, they do not receive equal pay. These are the sorts of insights that I have found repeated again and again inside the pages of the feminist periodicals. Reading through, I am left in no doubt that the 'Suffrage' movement was a Women's Liberation Movement.

Of course, the excitement of this 'discovery' is somewhat dampened by the recognition that, in spite of its extraordinary breadth and the depth of feminist analysis of the position of women, the first WLM *failed*. If we try to examine why it failed, we may well learn something which we can use in our current struggle. What should/can we do and not do to ensure that the process of women's liberation continues?

The Quest for Equality

While acknowledging the enormous similarities between the first WLM and the WLM today, it is important not to adopt a 'cycle' interpretation of history. The circumstances in which the early feminists found themselves were not identical with ours and it follows that in some respects their understandings, priorities and practices differed from ours as well.

However, the differences between the two movements do not suggest that we should evaluate the second as more 'advanced' than the first, and consequently more likely to prove successful (a 'progress' interpretation of history). There is nothing inevitable about the success of the current movement. We are struggling in a context which is broadly similar to that of the first WLM, and we could fail just as *easily*. We must be aware of patriarchy, not only as representing the nature of the society we wish to transform today, but also as the organisational form of male domination which has existed for thousands of years and which may continue to exist well into the future. It is the context of a patriarchal society and the determination of women to confront male supremacy which unites us with our sisters of ninety years ago.

What are the main differences between the two movements and

how do/should we interpret them? At the outset, a fairly superficial reading of the periodicals reveals that some of our assumptions concerning the nature of freedom for women and how it may be achieved differ from those of the early feminists. What were their assumptions? Why did they make them? What were the consequences for their action, of their beliefs about 'equality' and about how male domination could be undermined?

Of course, neither the first WLM nor the modern WLM may be characterised as homogeneous. There were differences in the ways feminists perceived the 'problem' then, as there are differences today. However, my principal concern here is with identifying the *major ideological* impulse of the first movement and attempting to explain it.

During the time of the first WLM, there were a large number of women who believed that significant changes in the position of women could be brought about within the context of the existing (capitalist) society. Those who rejected capitalism as inherently oppressive believed, in turn, that the liberation of women could be achieved within the context of a socialist society. Today, the potential of a capitalist society for sustaining sexual equality has probably been fully exploited (The Equal Pay and Sex Discrimination Acts, 1970 and 1975 respectively) and men remain in control of women's lives. At the same time, the evidence of the socialist experiments (Croll, 1978; Scott, 1976) has demonstrated that any society which is conceived and created by men will serve male interests. The main impetus of the current WLM is towards *autonomy* from male control rather than *equality* with men in *their* world.

There are feminists today who believe that equality with men may be obtained, if not within capitalism, then certainly in a socialist society (socialist feminists), and there were feminists in the past who recognised that equality with men was impossible in a man-made world and that women had to create a new society on the basis of their own values. However, there is a fundamental difference in the central assumptions underlying the two movements. The question is what were the repercussions of the 'quest for equality', for the development of the first WLM ?

The Quest for Equality: Equal Rights with Men under Capitalism

The dominant impulse of the first WLM was for women to become full and equal citizens with men, thereby abolishing the *double standard* in every area of social life – sexuality, marriage, education, employment and politics. In the sexual sphere alone, women pressed for men to adopt the female standard, or rather, the standard established for females by males, that is, moral purity. In all else, they strove for women to be *included* in the male standard of manhood/personhood, that is, economic independence, political citizenship and so on.

The issue of sexuality highlights the main point of contrast between the two movements. The majority of the early feminists did not claim sexuality for themselves, they accepted that 'sexuality' was synonymous with the way men had defined it and so, on the whole, they rejected it. Only a small minority of women attempted to redefine sexuality on their own terms.

Although the majority of feminists were critical of certain aspects of the man-made world in which they lived, for example, male violence (especially as perpetrated against women – battering and rape – and war) and male sexuality (the 'tyranny' of which was evidenced in prostitution and widespread Venereal Disease – Pankhurst, 1913), they did not fundamentally question the male value system. The society which men had created was *redeemable* so long as women were included as equal members in it.

The majority of feminists not only accepted the structure of society as men had organised it, but also the 'differences' between the two sexes as men had defined them. However, they used the notion of 'separate spheres' of interest for men and women to arrive at very different conclusions. From the point of view of men, it was the 'natural' difference between men and women which justified male domination and the exclusion of women from the decision-making process (Conway, 1973; Duffin, 1978). The feminists used a very similar conception of 'natural' difference to argue for the equality of the sexes. It was because the sexes were different that equality was essential for a healthy, well balanced society. If the man-made world was rife with injustice and suffering, this was because of the absence of women's influence in public affairs. The attitudes and priorities of the two sexes were different (men: aggressive and thing-oriented; women: nurturing and person-oriented) and both were needed in order for society to be complete:

> The woman's demand for the vote . . . is also the demand that the mother-half of humanity should be given its proper place: that the preserver and producer of life, the maker of men, should be as highly honoured as the destroyer of life, the maker of things. (*The Common Cause*, Vol 1, No 1, 9 April, 1909: 3).

The Quest for Equality: Equal Rights with Men under Socialism

It was the determination of a considerable number of the early feminists to achieve equality with men within the existing social system which has prompted socialist feminist historians to dismiss the mainstream of the movement as middle-class, exclusive, elitist and accommodationist (Liddington, 1977, pp 192-201; Rowbotham, 1974, pp 77-89). The 'suffragettes' may have been militant but they were not revolutionary: they were *liberal* reformers intent on modifying, rather than overthrowing, the society in which they lived.

While it is certainly the case that the majority of feminists did strive for acceptance in the existing society on equal terms with men, it does not follow that this indicates that they were essentially conservative and concerned solely with moderate social change. It was not that they chose to limit their goals within the confines of a capitalist society, rather they believed that the possibilities of the established social order were *limitless*.

For the minority of women who rejected the existing social structure as inherently oppressive, the 'problem' was capitalism, not patriarchy, and the main issue at stake was class *allegiance*. Moreover, their motivation in becoming socialists derived less from the recognition that equality for women was impossible in a capitalist society, than from the belief that *class* oppression was more fundamental than the domination of women by men. In other words, they accepted a male framework for confronting the system.

The socialist feminists saw the liberal feminists as being identified with capitalist interests (that is, being middle-class and helping to perpetuate class oppression), while they sought their allegiance with the working class and socialism. This conflict came to a head in the debate around 'the vote'. The socialist feminists, criticising the liberal feminists for failing to attack the *class* nature of the franchise, in their demand for the vote 'as it is or may be granted to men' (that is, accepting existing property qualifications), eventually followed their male comrades in raising the demand for *Universal* Suffrage. In practice, this meant giving equal priority to *Manhood* Suffrage and denying the existence of any significant conflict of interest between female and male workers (see *The Woman's Dreadnought*, 1914-1917 and *The Worker's Dreadnought* 1917-1924, both edited by Sylvia Pankhurst, for discussion of the socialist feminist position regarding 'the vote'):

> Held back by their traditional demand for the vote for women on the present terms, and their rigid refusal to ally themselves with the

> forces of democracy, the older suffrage societies cannot take part in a general movement for franchise reform. (*The Woman's Dreadnought*, Vol 2, No 52, 18 March 1916, p 443).

In the same way that the liberal feminists assumed that equality with men was possible under capitalism, the socialist feminists assumed that equality with men would be a central feature of socialist society. The explicit demands of both factions were extremely radical, but essentially naive in so far as an understanding of the nature of patriarchy was concerned: it did not occur to either faction that a society in which men determined the priorities and the goals (both capitalism and socialism) *must* be a society in which women's interests and purposes are subordinated.

Of course, some of the criticisms made of the liberal feminists by the socialist feminists were justified; in an immediate sense, working-class women were in a different situation (in economic terms) from middle-class women, and as a result had separate grievances. However, in confronting capitalism rather than patriarchy, the socialist feminists failed to recognise the extent to which all women shared a *common* oppression; an understanding that the liberal feminists, on the other hand, took for granted:

> Sex monopoly has worse aspects than class monopoly. But let them be of good cheer. Arrayed against sex monopoly on the one side, and sex disabilities on the other is a great world-wide combination, daily gathering force and momentum consisting of women of all classes, workers and non-workers . . . (*Women's Franchise*, Vol 1, No 14, 3 October 1907, p 145).

The Quest for Equality and the Departure of the Free Woman

While the majority of feminist periodicals published between the years 1890 and 1930 issued from a framework in which the present structure of society was accepted as a given, and a much smaller number rejected capitalism in favour of socialism (most notably, Sylvia Pankhurst's paper *The Woman's Dreadnought*, first published on 8 March 1914, which changed its name to *The Worker's Dreadnought* on 28 July 1917), on careful inspection it is possible to discern isolated gestures towards a woman-centred view of the world inside the pages of most of them. Indeed, the irony of the situation is that most of the liberal feminist journals were published completely by women only (including the printing), and the groups which they represented and the campaigns which they ran were also generally organised by women alone. Moreover, many feminists made a conscious decision to work on their own and several groups refused to be allied to any existing political party, since none could be seen to promote women's interests. However, in spite of the relative autonomy of their movement, most feminists saw 'independence' as a short-term *means* to an end, not as an *end* in itself. The 'end' was equality with men. All that was required was for women to prove their determination and their worthiness, and men would accept them as equal *partners* in every sphere of social life.

As I worked my way through the periodicals at the Fawcett Library, I came across one paper which in the first six months of its publication (23 November 1911 to 30 May 1912) revealed a type of feminist understanding which I have not found in a concentrated form in any other single journal. This paper was *The Freewoman: a Weekly Feminist Review*, edited by Dora Marsden and Mary Gawthorpe. Unlike all the other periodicals at the time, *The Freewoman* totally rejected pragmatism and any interest in accruing gains from men. Feminism was seen primarily as an ideological weapon in the fight against male-dominated society.

I would like to quote two short pieces from the first issues of *The Freewoman* which convey an analysis strikingly similar to that of *radical feminism* as we know it today:

> . . . though some men must be servants, all women are servants and all the masters are men. That is the difference and distinction. The servile condition is common to all women . . . freedom will consist in appraising their own worth, in setting up their own standards and living up to them and putting behind them forever the role of complacent self-sacrifice. (Vol 1, No 1, 23 November 1911, p 1-2).

> The sex war is going to be the biggest thing civilisation has seen . . . its effects will be gigantic. And let no (one) be deceived by the circumstances that men are fighting on women's side and women on men's, here and there, in meetings and societies and in articles . . . The great mass of the armies on the two sides are similar. Men are on one side. Women on the other. Watch for the clash – or watch for the guerilla warfare, as the case may be. Open battle or long-range quiet shooting – whichever it be, will produce results from which civilisation will never recover. (Vol 1, No 4, 14 December 1911, p 65).

Unfortunately, *The Freewoman* was isolated, not only in being the only periodical of its kind, but also in having no roots in concrete autonomous feminist activity (it was not the organ of a particular group, as were most of the other papers) and consequently its pronouncements became increasingly idealistic, individualistic and finally, extremely elitist. On 30 May 1912, the subtitle of *The Freewoman* became *A Humanist Review*; on 15 June 1913 it was re-named *The New Freewoman: An Individualist Review*; on 1 January 1914 it became *The Egoist: An Individualist Review*. The paper ceased publication in September 1916. The name changes were parallelled by an increasing involvement of men as writers and editors, and the increasing expression of abstract male, at first humanist, later egoist, philosopy.

Our Brothers in Struggle: The Common Cause[11]

> Ours is a common cause. The right relationship between the sexes can never be the affair of women alone . . . more and more as the days go on men and women will work together as equals, till at last there is no artificial barrier between them, and each sex makes its contribution freely and fully to the common human task. (*The Woman's Leader*, Vol 12, No 1, 6 February 1920, p 7).

Although the early feminists faced almost total opposition from the male power structure in the first two decades of the twentieth century (the struggle is well documented in the literature, the most interesting accounts being as follows: Pankhurst, E., 1979; Pankhurst, S., 1977; Strachey, 1979; Rover, 1967), there is no doubt that the apparently liberal attitude of the minority of male suffragists[12] influenced them in the belief that they would be accepted by men (if not in the capitalist present, then certainly in the socialist future), and militated against the possibility of women challenging the structure of society in their own terms. The liberal feminists did not stop to question the motives of their male supporters (who came increasingly from the ranks of the traditional opposition as the crisis escalated), although it became obvious, with the prospect of war looming on the horizon, that women would be granted the vote, would be allowed to work, would be furnished with technical knowledge, if it served the *interests* of men and helped to *stabilise* male-dominated society.

The advent of the First World War had a dramatic effect on the first WLM: it *collapsed*. Feminism evaporated, not so much because, in the pragmatic flurry of the war, the demands of the feminists were acceded to in return for much needed 'services', but rather because, having failed to develop an autonomous framework for their activity and their purposes, it was impossible for women to dissociate themselves from the only context they knew – the male world. Because of the *emphasis* that the liberal feminists put on taking an equal part in society as it was, as opposed to questioning the nature of society as men had created it, it was almost inevitable that when the war came the majority of these women would abandon feminism to support the war effort and identify themselves with their country*men*.

Within a few months of war being declared, the majority of the periodicals changed their stance from righteous condemnation of male war to complete support for 'our nation's noble struggle against "the Huns" (Germans)'.

Most liberal feminists saw the war (and the employment and training opportunities arising from it) as a not-to-be-missed opportunity for women to prove their worthiness for equality. The most dramatic shift in policy and subsequent strategy can be discerned in the pages of *The Suffragette* (edited by Christabel Pankhurst). On the eve of war:

> Women of the world, witnesses and victims of this man-made civilisation, are being roused to the knowledge that in their emancipation and participation in the government of the world lies humanity's one hope of release from the barbarism of war. (Vol 3, No 95, 7 August 1914, p 295).

In the next issue but one, eight months later:

> Naturally and logically in the present national crisis, our appeal is to the patriotism of women. In the militant woman, the love of country is necessarily strong . . . Our country . . . is our temple, and he who seeks in force to destroy it is our enemy. (Vol 4, No 97, 16 April 1915, p 3).

On 15 October 1915, *The Suffragette* was re-named *The Britannia* – 'For King – For Country'.

Among the thousands of women who sacrificed their feminism to patriotism, there were those who refused to identify themselves with the 'cause' of the war and left the feminist organisations in which they had worked rather than support the war effort. The non-militant National Union of Women's Suffrage Societies, led by Millicent Garrett Fawcett, was completely split by the issue: half the executive members and large numbers of other officers resigned in protest against its chauvinist policy (See *The Common Cause*, July 1914 to

April 1915 for details of the debate; also Strachey, 1979, p 351). These women wanted to educate for peace and together with women in other countries became involved in the Women's International League for that purpose.

However, in spite of this independent female initiative, the majority of women who opposed the war (for the most part socialist feminists) tended to join forces with male objectors (for example, working together with men in the Anti-Conscription League) and in doing so confronted the war on male terms. They became pacifists first, feminists second: the 'problem' was war, it was not male power. Like their patriotic sisters, the women who became supporters of the pacifist movement (which was led by socialist men) also abandoned feminism for a 'higher' cause.

Women's Liberation in Two Movements?

The first WLM failed because the impulse toward female *autonomy* from male control over women's lives was submerged by the impulse towards *equality* with men in *their* world, be it a capitalist present or a projected socialist future. Women chose men as their *reference group* and feminism was abandoned. What is more, they chose men as their reference group because, although they recognised the impact of male domination in every area of their lives, they were reluctant to see men as the 'enemy', especially when there were so many liberal men around, willing to assist them in their struggle.

Clearly, there is a marked contrast between the first WLM and the present WLM, in so far as radical feminism (as I have defined it in this paper) has now become the keynote, in contrast to its existence as a sporadic and isolated impulse eighty-odd years ago.[13] Today's radical feminists do not believe that it is possible for women to participate in a male-controlled society on equal terms with men – both because it is not desirable (rejection of male values), and because we know that men will not voluntarily relinquish their power.

While most feminists who are involved in the current movement are determined to define ourselves and recreate the world on our own terms, there are women who call themselves feminists who reject the present structure of society primarily on the basis that it is capitalistic (socialist feminists: see Eisenstein, 1979, for an exposition of the socialist feminist 'case'). Within the context of the 'struggle for socialism', the feminist movement is but one feature of a wider progressive movement in which the conflict of interest between the two main social classes is the central moving force in social change.

There have been numerous attempts to 'fit' an analysis of women's oppression inside a marxist framework, or rather to modify the latter so that it may be seen to provide an explanation for women's subordination (for example, the *Domestic Labour* debate, see Beechey, 1979 and Taylor, 1978; and the *Patriarchal power as 'the oppressor in our heads'* debate, see Adams, 1979; Adams and Minson, 1978; Coward, Lipshitz and Cowie, 1978). However it is the recent socialist feminist discussion of feminist organisation and strategy which has been most explicit concerning the primacy of *The Socialist Revolution* (Rowbotham, Segal and Wainwright, 1980; Wilson, 1980; Margolis, 1980). Needless to say, there is no need for a male conspiracy to co-opt the current WLM so long as women themselves believe that feminism is less important than, or contingent upon, the achievement of 'loftier' goals.

Whatever women do we must have a reference point which exists *outside* the male framework – our *own* understanding of our experience in a patriarchal world – otherwise we will be absorbed into male-directed struggles based on male-defined priorities, and the second WLM, like the first WLM before it, will become a *past event*. The issue is not that women should not participate or try to gain a place in the existing structure of society, nor that we should not identify with some aspects of the socialist alternative. Women can do these things so long as we do them from an *independent* perspective in which women's interests come *first*. The fact remains that *wherever* we look in the world today, Patriarchy *still* rules – O.K?

Notes

1 Paper presented at the Women's Research and Resources Centre one day conference: *The Women's Liberation Movement and Men*, London, March 1980. Re-worked in places following workshop discussion. Acknowledgements to the latter can be found in footnotes 7 and 8. Some of the references have also been updated.

2 *Hidden From History* was re-printed by Pluto Press in 1980. I have used the 1974 edition throughout the paper.

3 I am not including here books written by the early feminists themselves, for example Ray Strachey's *The Cause: A Short History of the Women's Movement in Britain*, Virago, London, 1979. First published in 1928 by Bell and Sons, London. See bibliography for details of the others.

4 *The Fawcett Library* is the national historical collection of women's writings and is currently housed at the City of London Polytechnic, Old Castle Street, London, E.1.

5 See the bibliography listing the periodicals that were published by women involved in feminist issues between the years 1850 and 1930. For reasons of space, I am supplying the *names* of the periodicals and the *dates* of publication (of the issues that are available) *only*. I am currently preparing a manuscript for a book entitled: *A Cautionary Tale for Modern Feminism: Women's Liberation the first time round, 1890 – 1930*, which will include a full annotated list of the periodicals.

6 The Newspaper division of the British Library, Colindale Avenue, London, NW9. Access only by special reader's ticket (you must be over twenty-one) obtained by application to the Reading Room of the British Museum, Great Russell Street, London, WC1.

7 My thanks to the workshop discussion for raising this point.

8 My thanks to Liz Stanley for the following references: The Edward Carpenter Collection, Sheffield City Library Archives; the Suffragist Collection, Manchester City Library Archives; various collections of letters and papers in the John Rylands University Library, Manchester.

9 The major periodicals published during the early period (1850-1890) were as follows: *The English Woman's Journal*, 1856-64; *The Alexandra Magazine*, 1864-65; *The English Woman's Review*, 1866-1909; *The Victoria Magazine*, 1863-80; *The Women's Suffrage Journal*, 1870-90.

10 The following argument which comprises the remainder of the paper is informed by my reading of the feminist periodicals (1890-1930) which are available at the Fawcett Library and the British Library. The discussion is an overview based on my own interpretation of the material and I shall be supplying very few individual references.

11 *The Common Cause* (1909-20) was the official organ of the women's movement for reform, the non-militant National Union of Women's Suffrage Societies, led by Millicent Garrett Fawcett, who saw women and men in partnership striving towards a better society for all.

12 There were several male pro-suffrage publications and societies. The publications tended to link women's suffrage with moral regeneration in society as a whole and their main concern was to abolish vice: for example, *The Sentinel*, established in 1879, was 'a monthly journal devoted to the exposition and advancement of public morality and the suppression of vice'. Another periodical was the *Eye Opener*, soon re-named *The Awakener*, 1912-14, a monthly publication of the Men's Society for Women's Rights.

13 Since writing this paper and discussing it at the conference, I have begun to re-evaluate the feminist understandings developed

in the militant suffrage movement – particularly those of Christabel Pankhurst (see my article 'Reclaiming Christabel Pankhurst', in Spender, Dale, (ed.), *Feminist Theorists* – forthcoming from The Women's Press, London in 1982). Although by no means identical with radical feminism as we know it today, a re-examination of the ideas of the militant suffragettes, reveals an analysis of the man-made world and the subjection of women through male sexual control which is closely akin to current radical and revolutionary feminist thinking (see especially: *The Great Scourge and How to End It* by Christabel Pankhurst. The Women's Press, London, 1913). For a recent discussion of women's campaigns against male sexuality in the nineteenth and early twentieth century, see Sheila Jeffreys' article in *Women's Studies International Forum*, special issue on Reassessments of First Wave Feminism, forthcoming, 5(5) 1982.

Bibliography of the Feminist Periodicals (1850-1930).

The following is a list of the periodicals which, with the exception of two, the *Victoria Magazine* and the *Alexandra Magazine*, are available at the Fawcett Library and the British Library in London. Periodicals which are available only at the BL are marked:*. The dates shown are those of the issues which remain (in years only). The periodicals which are incomplete are marked: +.

The Alexandra Magazine, 1864-1865: Bodleian Library, Oxford University.

Association Notes, 1909-1920.

The Britannia, 1915-1917.

The Catholic Citizen, 1918-1930.

The Catholic Suffragist, 1915-1918.

The Church League for Women's Suffrage, 1912-1917.

The Church Militant, 1910-1927.

The Coming Day, 1914: +.

The Common Cause, 1909-1920.

The Conservative and Unionist Franchise Review, 1910-1915.

The Cons. and Unionist Women's Franchise Association Monthly News, 1915-1918.

The Conservative Women's Reform Association Monthly News, 1919-1914(?): +.

The Dawn, 1888-1896.

The Egoist, 1914-1916.

The English Woman, 1909-1921.

The English Woman's Journal, 1856-1864.

The English Woman's Review, 1866-1909.

Everywoman, 1911-1914: *.

The Free Church Suffrage Times, 1914: +.

The Freewoman, 1911-1913.

The Independent Suffragette, 1916(?) 1918(?): +.

International Woman Suffrage News, 1917-1930.

International Women's News, 1930-1954.

Jus Suffrugii, 1906-1916.

Labour Woman, 1913-1971: *.

The League Leaflet, 1911-1913.

The Liberal Women's News, 1926-1936.

The Liberal Women's Review, 1914: +.

The Link, 1888: *.

The Link (The organ of the women's socialist movement), 1911-1913: *.

The National Council of Women News, 1918-1930.

The New Freewoman, 1913.

The Only Way, 1909: +.

Opportunity, 1921-1940.

The Pioneer, 1887-1898.

Quarterly Leaflet of the Women's National Liberal Association, 1907: +.

Shafts, 1892-1898.

The Shield, 1970-1970.

The Storm Bell, 1898-1900.

The Suffragette, 1912-1914.

The Suffragette News Sheet, 1916: *.

The Suffragist, 1909: *.

The Victoria Magazine, 1863-1880 (Vol. 1-3: *; vols. 1-9, 11, 13-32, Bodleian, Oxford Univ.

The Victoria Times, 1873: *.

The Vote, 1909-1933.

Votes for Women, 1907-1918 (1913-1918: *).

The Woman Citizen, 1908-1913: *.

The Woman Clerk, 1919-1921: *.

The Woman Engineer, 1919-1942.

The Woman of the World, 1908: *.

The Woman Teacher, 1919-1961.

The Woman Worker, 1908-1910. 1916-1921.

The Woman's Charter, 1909: *.

The Woman's Dreadnought, 1914-1917.

The Woman's Gazette and Weekly News, 1876-1879.

The Woman's Herald, 1891-1893.

The Woman's Leader, 1920-1931.

Woman's Opinion, 1874: *.

The Woman's Signal, 1894-1899 (Jan-June 1898: *).

The Woman's Signal Budget, 1894-1895: *.

The Woman's Times, 1920-1922: *.

The Woman's Union Journal, 1876-1890.

Womenfolk, 1910.

Women and Progress, 1906-1907.

Women and Work, 1874-1876: *.

The Women's Charter Review, 1913: +.

Women's Employment, 1900 onwards: *.

Women's Franchise, 1907-1909.

The Women's Gazette and Weekly News, 1888-1891: *.

The Women's Industrial News, 1898-1919.

Women's Penny Paper, 1888-1890.

Women's International League Monthly Newsheet, 1926: +.

The Women's Local Government News, 1921-1925.

The Women's Protestant Union Monthly Paper, 1893: *.

Women's Suffrage, 1907: *.

The Women's Suffrage Journal, 1870-1890.

Women's Suffrage Record, 1913: +.

The Women's Trade Union Review, 1891-1906, 1911-1913, 1917-1919: +.

The Women's Tribune, 1906.

Work and Leisure, 1880s.

The Worker's Dreadnought, 1917-1924.

The Young Woman, 1894-1900.

DIANA LEONARD

Male Feminists and Divided Women

This paper derives from two overlapping sources:
One was the publication of an article in the *Morning Star* by 'Professor Vic Allen, of Leeds University' entitled 'Male feminism is a reality' (Tuesday, 20 November 1979) in which he claimed:

> It is the common purpose of the feminist movement to eliminate sexual discrimination and as I identify myself with this I am a feminist just as much as women who support it are.

I have known Vic Allen for some years and had numerous skirmishes with him on this subject, for such is his concern with feminism that he can seldom resist giving women the benefit of his opinion. But his ignorance has always been so obvious, and his political involvement and astuteness in other areas such, that I never imagined he would be rash enough to put his ideas down in cold print. His arrogance did not however disturb the editor of the women's page of the *Morning Star*, nor the paper's regular readers, for there was little follow-up protest.[1]

The second source was my work (with Linnie Price) on translating an article by Christine Delphy called 'Our Friends and Ourselves: the hidden foundations of various pseudo-feminist accounts' (*Questions féministes*, 1 Nov. 1977), which, amongst other things, is a critique of a short book by a French leftist sociology professor (Vic's homologue) Claude Alzon, and the tactics he uses to weaken the WLM whilst presenting himself as women's best friend (Alzon, 1973). So much of what Christine Delphy had to say was relevant to Vic Allen's stance, and to that of various other of our 'friends', that I decided to borrow liberally from her (especially as it will be a while before her article is widely available in England),[2] and to try to take Vic Allen's article seriously and answer it – not because its author is a particularly important opponent of the women's movement, but because he is close to us and typical of what can undermine us. (All quotations are from his article unless otherwise indicated.)

First, as Christine points out, such self-styled male feminists, these good friends of ours, not only talk about women, they actually *use up* the spaces we have opened up to do it in. Vic Allen is quite typical in his paternalism: having given the matter his acute political attention for a few hours, he can see where we are going wrong, and as an expert and a friend it is his duty to let us know where we are deviating. What matter that thousands of women have worked on the problem for years, feminism is too serious a matter to be left to women. He will happily use the Women's Page to put us straight – now that this part of the paper is no longer concerned only with culture and cookery but also with politics:

> (T)he separatists in the women's movement are on a track like that trodden by Marilyn French's women in *The Women's Room*. It is one which leads back to oppression, with nothing solved.
>
> It starts off rightly in a blaze about abortion, rape and battered wives [sic] but ends with biological determinism, with a preoccupation with the womb, the vagina, menstruation and the penis. Along this path women end in isolation, frustration and neurosis [so watch it, ladies], for there are no individualistic solutions to problems created by social forces.
>
> I realise that there are many aspects concerning the position of women, for example the relationship between domestic and wage labour and the different class positions of women which are unclear. But it is not a solution to side-step the issues as is done by the radical and revolutionary feminists. I also realise that structural changes in society are no more than a necessary condition for substantive changes in the position of women.
>
> We have to counter an ideology which is so powerful and pervasive that it disarms women at the same time as it arms men. *In all of this working-class men are as much victims as women, and are much exploited* [my stress].
>
> In the end it will only be through revolutionary forces which encompass men and women that freedom for both will be achieved for it is as clear as daylight to me that one cannot be freed without the other.

This sort of argument is pernicious – not for seeking to 'give' us support generally, not for saying that

> For [men as well as women] feminism is a political position which has to be fought out and, therefore, lived out. Sexism is something to identify in oneself as well as in others, to abhor, to root out and do so in those areas of life where one has effective decision-making power and responsibilities;[3]

but because, in exchange for their support, our friends want actually to be allowed inside, to infiltrate, the WLM – the one real bastion which exists against their privilege.

Initially it is a little difficult to see why they are so concerned to be in the lead here, as well as everywhere else. They make it seem as if we are where we are now, after a hundred and fifty years of feminism and twelve years of the WLM, through some process of inevitable progress, rather than because of any changes pushed for by women, and achieved by the movement. They may nowadays assert that

> there is no evidence, either of an analytical or an empirical kind, to prove that the intellectual and physical differences between men and women in matters that relate to the distribution of power are any greater than the range of differences between males alone;

but who was it who fought against the plethora of studies which purported to show precisely that there *were* such differences? (And who continue to have to fight, since the issue is *not dead*.) Women or men?

However, concerned to get into the WLM our friends certainly are, and they even try to justify their demand by pulling the age-old trick of suggesting they are particularly suitable members because *they are above the fray*, they are the cool, calm voice of reason, and *disinterested*, even self-sacrificing:

> I accept no basis for discriminating between men and women. This is not a theoretical position for me. It would be easy enough to adopt a stance which had few practical implications.

But of course they are sure as hell *not* disinterested, nor are they above the fray. They are busying away with the women's movement and feminist analyses with one aim in view – *exonerating men*. To do this they want to have a say in feminist concerns in order to direct the movement away from focussing on men, on men's behaviour to women, and on male advantage.

When Christine Delphy was looking at Claude Alzon, she showed how he tried to divert attention from men by suggesting that the dividing line was not between men and women, but between 'feminists' (men and women) and non- or anti-feminists (of both sexes). He then concluded that

(a) 'feminist men' could play an equal role in the WLM with feminist women; and that
(b) feminist women should treat anti-feminist women as the enemy.

However, as she stressed, there is no symmetry between feminist men and anti-feminist women – one is the oppressor and the other the oppressed, whatever their politics – and so it would not follow at all that if we wanted to keep anti-feminist women out we would agree to let 'feminist men' in.

And in any case, we do not want to keep anti-feminist women out of the movement. Anti-feminism in women is simply false-consciousness and self-hatred, whereas it is a defence of objective interests and self-love in men. All of us *in* the movement have some anti-feminism in us. Becoming a feminist is a long and painful process, so there is no line separating 'us' from 'them' – merely a continuum of views and a *shared experience* of oppression. What Christine Delphy stresses is that although Alzon's real reason for advancing this argument is probably a concern not to be left out himself, a concern to push into the WLM under cover of his 'feminism', *he is prepared to accept dividing women from one another if this is the price that has to be paid.*

Vic Allen pursues a different, but parallel, line which is very common in England: he spends much of his time warning the *Morning Star's* (women) readers against other women – against (parodied) radical and revolutionary feminists and separatists:

> I put other men who oppose sexual discrimination in the same category as myself, not simply as supporters of the feminist movement but as part of it equally with women. Unfortunately it is not as simple as this. The position of men is both unclear and ambiguous.
>
> The problems stem from the fact that the oppression of women is always *mediated* through men. Men are *seen as* the oppressors, providing daily mental and physical evidence. *It is easy*, therefore, *to blame men* and active groups of women who describe themselves as radical or revolutionary feminists do just this (my stresses).

> These women locate the source of female oppression in patriarchy and, therefore, in the marriage contract. They make no distinction in the treatment of women between different types of societies throughout history or in the contemporary world. Men, because they are physically men and despite what they might be as social beings, are 'the main enemy'. [The contradiction between his first and last sentence *cannot* go unremarked.]
>
> It follows that the solutions for women must lie in separating themselves from men for one cannot live, talk, fraternise with the enemy. This means a complete denial of my own perception and identity as a feminist. Indeed, for the separatists, the term male feminist is a contradiction in terms.

As Christine Delphy says, it is always a joy to hear men who describe themselves as marxists asserting that which side you are on is not a question of whether you exert or suffer oppression, but what values you hold. And it is classic to turn the accusation of sexism and biologism back on the victims, as if hostility to the oppressor is the same as hostility to the oppressed, and as if it were radical and revolutionary feminists who had invented the crazy idea that having or not having a penis/phallus should be the source of significant differences in the way in which society treats 'individuals'!

Because our friends believe that the whole gender problem is 'just' a question of false values and consciousness, they are prepared to be tolerant of women meeting together autonomously for the moment:

> I can see short-term tactical reasons for women organising themselves autonomously. It may be difficult, even impossible, for them to raise their consciousness in the presence of apparent oppressors.
>
> There are many examples of women failing to communicate with each other when men are present. Much the same argument has been used in connection with the development of black consciousness. The autonomous organisation of women, however, is not for me an issue of principle.

But they are not prepared to accept the *real* reasons why blacks and women need non-mixed movements (and why workers need to kick our their petty bourgeois leaders if we are ever to have a socialist movement). They are prepared to accept separatism as a short-term tactic and consciousness-raising as a means to boost morale; they accept 'autonomy' for a time so we can bind up our wounds, talk to and see other women as people, and gather some self-confidence: a kind of half-time while we recover our strength. What they choose not to comprehend is that our oppression is so deep we are *not able to see what it is while in the company of men*.

The old civil rights groups (and the short-lived mixed anti-sexist groups) tried to pretend that whites (and men) shed their superior resources (access to powerful positions in outside bodies, more money, and dominants' psychology) when they went to meetings or on demonstrations – or, as many now like to pretend in respect of men and women, when entering into a sexual and/or love relationship. But of course they did and do not. Men always have at least better access to occupations, higher pay, the right sexually to objectify women, to take initiatives, and not to do domestic work – even if certain liberal men choose not to exercise some of their rights, or not to exercise them fully, within a given heterosexual relationship. They do not have to lift a finger to have them: they come with the social position of being a man – just as I do not seek, but I still get, all the advantages of being white in a racist culture, and of living in a country which exploits the third world. No one can stop having male advantages, even if he fights against them, any more than I can stop myself gettng whites' advantages by joining the Anti-Nazi League and supporting my (one) black colleague.

The power that dominant groups (whites, men, the bourgeoisie) have to determine and define the dominated groups' subjective experience is one of the most insidious and potent aspects of their control. We need non-mixed groups therefore not 'just' to change our values and raise our self-confidence and perception of other women, but primarily – and here it *is* a question of *principle* – so as to establish together as women exactly what it is we are fighting: to work out the extent and nature of our oppression. Hassling on the street, then domestic violence, then rape, and now sexual harassment at work were not 'obvious' forms of oppression, even if they seem so now. We had slowly and laboriously to recognise them, and then to establish them as forms of male power and hence as new areas for political struggle. Certainly, once we have worked things out, we can put them to men and some will be willing to support our fight. But it is not a question of men and women linking arms to advance across a battlefield to victory, since a major part of the struggle is precisely concerned with locating the very areas where the fight is to take place. Men cannot help in this since they do not have the experience on which to draw, nor the will to knowledge. And experience suggests men will not, initially anyway, be excited by our discoveries, since they do not speak to men's experience: they do not get the same release of guilt and sense of self-discovery which we have experienced in the movement. In the short-term, even liberal men will object to what we say and require forceful and sustained arguments to convince them it is worth the bother, that they cannot legitimately maintain their advantage or continue their particular behaviour, and indeed that they must fight it in themselves *and* in other men. (Recall Pat Mainardi's account of the resistance to her arguments about housework. And Goddess knows we haven't made much *practical* progress on the sexual division of housework – one of the very first areas feminism explored – in the last ten years.)

Our friends are not only prepared to divide women while trying to assert their own rights to be feminists, to be part of the women's movement; they also, and paradoxically, manage to divide women while arguing that there is really no need for a *women's* movement at all anyway, since women as such have nothing in common: gender is not the point at issue. The magic concept which they use here is 'class'.

> If the cause of women's oppression is located in male and female relationships, then it implies that being a woman in physical terms transcends all class and ethnic differences. This is reflected in the activities of the radical and revolutionary feminists, for they pay little or no attention to working-class women and black women.
>
> They exist as caucuses of white, largely middle-class intellectual women, defining oppression as an internalised, subjective matter, and taking it out of the context of the objective conditions in which women live.
>
> This perception of women contradicts all the everyday experiences of most women. Being black is not a peripheral matter for a woman. If it is, then racism must itself be peripheral. Being a double-loaded working-class mother on supplementary benefit is not the same as being a double-loaded female university lecturer or the wife of an oil magnate.
>
> The assumption that all women constitute a homogeneous group is as much nonsense as the assumption that all men do and it leads to equally nonsensical, self-defeating activities.

Ignoring both our friend's ignorance of the activities of any feminists outside his own white middle-class intellectual location, and the fact that to the extent that his criticisms do apply equally to socialist feminists – these being but further instances of a blithe disregard for what any *actual* feminists may be, do or say – let us note merely that he goes for political efficacy – he goes straight for our guilt complexes. As Christine Delphy says, when the left waves the red flag, conditioned cows charge.

The above quotation, please note, goes from the movement's assertion that women are oppressed as women (socially defined category), to saying, quite gratuitously, that we therefore do not recognise that there are *any* differences between women. It then shows its true colours by contrasting the working-class mother, the female university lecturer and the wife of an oil magnate, for it fails to note that the very adjective used of two of them – 'double-loaded' – gives the lie to their having nothing in common. Further, the fact that it can be implied that the 'bourgeois wife' is not oppressed, and that she is the enemy of the proletarian's wife since both will rally behind their men – without the contradictions which exist between the first and last assertions being recognised – shows the depth of the author's prejudice.

If we look again at the three women contrasted, we see that they are not described in equal or value-free ways, and that certain very important things are left vague. For instance,

1 The working-class woman is 'a double-loaded mother', the rich woman is 'a wife'. Could it be that what is being avoided in the former case is any suggestion that some of the 'double-load' might be due to her (working-class) husband? While it is also suggested that the bourgeois wife has no domestic or childcare responsibilities at all.
2 Only in the third case, with the oil magnet, do we know what the husband (if present) does for a living. Perhaps a female university lecturer is married to a male university professor? If so, why is *she* 'double-loaded'? Or perhaps she is married to the oil magnate, who supports her with the sweat of his dividends, provided she uses her university salary to pay for the domestic work she should have done for free?
3 The working-class mother is even more of a problem since
either a she is a single woman with children, claiming Supplementary Benefit (so why is she 'double-loaded'? *Poor* she will be, but the terms 'double shift' etc. usually imply doing housework *and* paid work);
or b she is a single woman, with children, who has paid employment (and also claims SB? and why not give her occupation?);
or c she is the wife/cohabitee, with children, of a man who is

> working-class and on SB (so why call her 'a mother' rather than 'a wife'? and why omit to mention that it is not she but the man who is eligible to claim SB?).

I suggest the underlying reason for these difficulties is that at a gut-level our friends experience university women and the wives of rich men as distasteful anomalies; as transgressors of the ideal rule which says that *all women* should submit to *all men*. Left intellectuals are rarely conscious of their attachment to this norm – they assure us repeatedly that they themselves are not at all sexist – and even more rarely do they put such consciousness into words. This attachment is, however, revealed in negative, by the indignation and double-thinking which any transgression of the norm produces in them. For them the only OK woman is working-class and/or black.

As Christine Delphy shows, two ideological processes are at play:

1 Pure and simple sexism. Hatred for the oppressor, the capitalist oil magnate, is displaced on to his possession, his wife:
   a because she is easier to attack, and
   b because to attack her is also to attack part of the rich man's power and privilege: his right to monopolise the 'best' women. (cf. Susan Brownmiller's interesting parallel analysis on the role played by the – fantasised or real – rape of white women by black men. See *Against Our Will*, 1977).

2 A more complex sexism. For a woman to have an easy life is seen as even less legitimate than for her husband to have one. The authority the rich man's wife exercises and the money she spends and the goods and services she consumes (though less than and different from the authority, money and consumption of her husband) is resented even more than his, because it is seen as less legitimate: because she gets it not from the classic (accepted) source – economic control – but from being a possession.

Women having bourgeois standards of living as wives, or interesting, well paid managerial jobs of their own, goes against their rightful status, which as women should be lower than that of men – all men. Their class protection as wives, or their being on the lower rungs of the professions, therefore prevents them from being where they should be – according to Stokely Carmichael's term, 'prone'. The fury which men – all men, and many women – show when sex status is mitigated by class status shows that *they believe gender should outweigh class*. The wives of bourgeois men and women with professional (university lecturer) jobs are seen, and resented, as usurpers.

This hostility is therefore based on the opposite of what is actually being *said*. What is said is that the wife of the oil magnate, the double-burdened woman lecturer, and the double-loaded working-class mother are different because their class *outweighs* their *gender*. But, *on the contrary*, the first two women are particularly odious to left men precisely because they *are not*, and *should not be*, bourgeois or middle-class like men, and yet somehow or other, they have managed to get bourgeois or middle-class privileges: as wives or by somehow worming their way on to the lower rungs of a profession. The former are no better than whores, and the latter are uppity women.

This sort of attack therefore shows

a that the wives of bourgeois men are seen (correctly) as not of the same class as their husbands;
b that female lecturers and the wives of bourgeois men are seen as women rather than bourgeois or lecturers; and
c that gender should and/or does outweigh class.

A related line of attack is the suggestion that while all women are 'oppressed', working-class women are also 'exploited'. This is just a polite way of saying that what women suffer as women (even if it is accepted that 'women in British society are subordinate to men in all areas of social activity which relate to the distribution of power') is secondary to – is less then – what is suffered by 'the working class' (of both sexes). This is just a refined insult. What is also being said, however, is that while the working-class woman-wife (and the black woman) *works*, the oil magnate's wife, like indeed all white middle-class women, does *nothing*. They are the idle rich personified. In fact, of course, even the wives of really wealthy men work: they do what is required of them as the wives of those particular individual men. We may not *like* what they do, and we may take a very puritan attitude to the grossly extravagant standard of living they are given in return for hostessing cocktail parties, being the president of the women's branch of the Rotary Club, or chauffeuring children to dancing classes and private school. But this does not mean that what they do is not work, nor that they are not dependent on their husbands – any more than the fact that some receptionists are merely required to sit at a desk looking good (and getting bored) all day, stops these women from being wage-workers along with nurses and car-workers. The ideology which is being developed by not mentioning any 'burden' as resti on the wife of the oil magnate is the one which suggests that such women are total parasites. The oil magnate at least has an *occupation*: he earns his bread more than she earns hers.

Our friends have thus accepted some of the feminist analysis of housework. They have accepted that some women carry a heavy load – *some, but not all.* They try to divide women from women by refusing to see that *all* women are dependents in marriage, even if some get a very good return for (what Alzon equates to) their de-luxe prostitution, because they have rich and generous husbands, whereas others get a very poor one. They therefore wilfully refuse to concede or to comprehend – or more likely they do not bother to read – what radical and revolutionary feminists and (yes, also) socialist feminists have said about housework and marriage.

They make this division between women because they want to direct attention

a away from the 'seeming' oppressors of women – men; and
b on to the class which oppresses most men as well as women.

They are quite happy, in the process, to paint a quite false picture of the WLM – as made up of women who are indifferent to, indeed so bound up in the minutiae of their own subjective experience as to be quite unaware of, the very existence of race, class or the trade union movement. There is *not one* mention of any feminist initiatives in any of these fields in the *Morning Star* article.

But what I want to end by considering is the fact that this attack does actually touch on a raw nerve within the movement, and thus expose a problem for feminists, because we also at some level share the dominant ideological view which they are playing on: the view that women usurp class power, and that we should really under no circumstances possess it. Our guilty consciences are both the product and the sign of our oppression.

Women think that we share the class of our fathers and husbands, when in fact very few daughters end up earning as much, or in as statusful occupations, as their fathers (or brothers); and very, very few indeed end up owning or controlling capital or in senior management or politics (i.e. becoming upper or middle-class or bourgeois *in their own right*). Some may make it to be university lecturers – though far fewer will get through to join Alzon and Allen in the professoriat – and those of us in such positions are indeed privileged women, who generally recognise our advantages very well. (A lot better than most of our liberal/socialist male colleagues, let me add, for the simple reason that, as women, we are a lot luckier to have got them.) But how many women are oil magnates – as against the numbers who end up on Supplementary Benefit? Women may *sometimes* have privileges and class protection, but this is almost invariably due to our husband's (or father's) position: we get it as dependents on men.

It is only by identifying with men (and this process of identification is pre-emptive proof that *we are not the same* as men) that most women can think we (or other women) are of the same class as the men to whom we belong; hence that we are as privileged, as oppressive, as exploitative, and in the same way, of the working class as our fathers, brothers and husbands. But, by a further turn of the screw, it is because we are *not* men, because we are in the middle class as objects and not as subjects, because most of us are in it only through our relationships with men, that 'middle-class' women who are socialists feel so bad. We combine false consciousness about our class position with a really guilty conscience, because what we get is derived and not ours in our own right. We feel that the oppression to which we (think we) make the proletariat submit is even less legitimate than that which our men produce. That is, we feel guilty for having class privileges while not being of the class. And we feel guilty because, as women, we accept the dominant ideology which says that nothing should ever put a woman in a position to dominate *any* man.

In some aligned left groups, women's guilt is systematically expressed in an attempt to reconcile the class struggle and the women's struggle. But this reconciliation is not effected by suggesting how the oppression of women *as such* articulates with the oppression of the workers *as such* – for this would grant the oppression of women an autonomy and an attention which is unacceptable. Instead the articulation is effected by simply focussing on working-class women, since they are oppressed by *both* patriarchy and capitalism (and the relationship between domestic and wage labour can thus be left 'unclear'). The fact that Vic Allen, for example, does not distinguish between women in working-class jobs and the wives of working-class men – that he is so unclear how or why the working-class mother is both 'double-loaded' and on SB – says worlds about the unclarity of his analysis of the position of women.

Women in the movement (as, indeed, all women) are much more aware than our friends that the status of women depends on their husband's class (and goodwill) and that the lot of a rich man's wife is materially much better than that of the wife of a man on SB. We have been taught from early in our lives the importance of making a 'good' marriage. What is of concern, though, is why certain movement women go along with the leftist line: why, while calling *themselves* middle-class or bourgeois (even if sometimes falsely), and feeling (correctly) that they are *themselves* oppressed and recognising indeed that it is women like them who comprise the bulk of the WLM, do they *still* go along with the line which suggests that middle-class/bourgeois women are not oppressed? Why, when all their experience suggests that men as men enjoy real advantages from the oppression of women, do they work so hard to support the claim that men merely *mediate* capitalist oppression?

In part it may be because, knowing themselves to be middle-class, yet politically despising the middle class, they give themselves an objective, theoretically-founded basis for the self-hatred which all women have internalised in this sexist society. Christine Delphy however has another suggestion which I find even more pertinent. Women accept this line because, as she says:

> Not content with feeling themselves *particularly unworthy of oppressing others*, women feel themselves *unworthy of being oppressed*. The idea that women form a class is never refuted with theoretical or logical arguments, but always in an emotional fashion. What this emotion reveals is a deep refusal to consider themselves on the same footing as other oppressed groups, in particular as the typical oppressed group, the proletariat . . . (T)he 'working class' . . . are always represented by a group of *men*, and men in particularly 'virile' attitudes: wearing helmets, armed and shaking their fists . . .
>
> To think of yourself (as exploited) i.e. as a class is primarily to think of yourself as a *man*, and . . . a man of the most glorious category . . . this, in its double claim, is psychologically impossible and unthinkable for the majority of (revolutionary) women. It would be a double sacrilege, a double profanity: it would defame the dignity of men and the dignity of the proletariat . . . Here again, women's feeling of unworthiness leads them to fear that they are usurping power, and it is this feeling which invalidates the account which tries to rationalise their feelings. This account rests on the opposite premises; it explains their refusal to see themselves as equally oppressed on the basis of the pre-eminence of class over gender; but their refusal itself rests on the pre-eminence of gender.

She also suggests that this same feeling of unworthiness in women is shown in women's acceptance of one or other of the various masculine theories on the reason for women's oppression in the family. In Vic Allen's version

> The position of women cannot sensibly or usefully be separated from the organisation and function of the family on the one hand and labour markets on the other. The function of the family in British capitalism has always been concerned with the social reproduction of labour power, with the transformation of sons into miners and daughters into typists.
>
> The organisation of the family serves this purpose and, at the same time, maintains women as a reserve army of labour. The family and labour markets are thus inter-related.

That is, women's oppression in the family is due to capital's need for labour power, and for a special sub-section of the labour force: a reserve army.

What is striking about such theories is that *even the oppression which women suffer is not aimed at them*. The family is simply there to reproduce the proletariat. As Christine Delphy says, the

> material and very concrete oppression of women is nothing but a means or a consequence – in any case nothing but a by-product – of an oppression which is aimed at the workers.
>
> (W)omen . . . are . . . removed from the objective – from what is posited as the ultimate end – of the process which oppresses them . . . Not only are they exploited, but they are only exploited to the extent that their exploitation serves *another exploitation*: one which does not concern *women as such*.
>
> In other words, it is clear that women are preconceived as *unworthy of even being exploited*. Their oppression can only be explained, given theoretical status, if it is put forward as mediating another oppression. This clearly means that they are *no more thought worthy of being exploited for themselves than of living for themselves*. Their exploitation, like their existence, must be justified by something other than itself: by its usefulness for the lives or for the exploitation of men . . . The deeper meaning of (such 'theories') is that if men were not oppressed, women would not be oppressed; which means that the question is put in the following terms: Why oppress women if not so as to oppress men?

In accepting such theories, we merely affirm the general ideology that women are worthless in themselves, but may be turned to use for and by men.

I trust readers do not feel this paper has been just a continuous pummelling of one short article, because, as I said at the start, this particular article raises wider issues and exemplifies a line of thinking which can be found inside the movement as well as outside it. The article shows a concern to get men accepted as feminists; but it also exemplifies the lines which are used by such men, and also by others who are not arguing they should be seen as feminists, *and by women within the WLM*, to push women apart and to prevent us discovering the nature and extent of our specific oppression. If there is one thing better for male dominance than women remaining silent about their experience, it is men talking about it – subtly selecting from and twisting feminist ideas to their own ends – or women mouthing the same sentiments. And where better for this to come from than our friends – or even from within the WLM – and in those very mass media which, thanks to our efforts, have now recognised 'women' as a topic of wide appeal and concern.

The lines men use to divide us are varied. To propose a division between feminist and anti-feminist women, or to exacerbate the difference between 'tendencies' in the movement, is pretty unsubtle, even though, sad to say, it generally works. But the line on class divisions between women is more complex and therefore more insidious.

I know no one in the WLM who does not recognise and is not concerned about racism, and the differences between the life experiences of women from working-class and middle-class backgrounds, in working-class and middle-class jobs, and married to working-class and middle-class men (not to speak of bourgeois backgrounds, ownership of property, and marriages). We do not, in other words, regard women as a 'homogeneous group' abstracted from the forces which shape and mould their social relationships. But we *do* know that gender cuts across race and class, and that *all* men (i.e. men of all classes and races) treat, or feel they ought to be able to treat, all women as inferiors in this society. What is not so generally recognised is that this same assumption underpins those very analyses which try to deny it: which purport to show that class over-rides or out-weighs gender. To quote Christine Delphy one final time:

> This is very clear from the fact that popular, like academic,

> sociology attributes to women the class *of their husbands*: that for women we use a criterion of 'class membership' different from that used for men (hence for husbands). We use a criterion which is moreover not only totally estranged from marxist definitions of class, but also from every other definition of social categories. For women, and only for women, marriage (or daughterhood) on the one hand replaces a position in the processes of production as the criterion of class membership; and, on the other, even when women have their own place in the capitalist mode of production (i.e. when they work for wages outside as well as unpaid within the family) it outweighs their paid work nevertheless. 'Bourgeois women' are thus so called, and identified with their bourgeois spouses, not because the same criteria are used to class them as their husbands, but, on the contrary, because a criterion is used *which distinguishes them*: that of marriage. In other words, before claiming and in order to be able to claim that they are identical with their husbands, they must first be considered and treated as radically different. Thus, in putting bourgeois men and their wives in the same bag they show, *by this very operation*, that they are not in the same bag. The one can be assimilated to the other only by treating them differently – by classing one set by their place in the production process, and the other by their (familial) status. What distinguishes bourgeois men from 'bourgeois' women in the classing process is precisely what unites 'bourgeois' women to 'proletarian' women, who are also classified by the class of their husbands (or fathers). We therefore cannot speak of class *differences* between women – which it seems is the source of eventual political *divisions* – except by first of all treating them in the same way: by determining their 'class' by their relationship to a man. These differences of classification are thus based on what all women have in common – the fact of being 'someone's (actual or potential) wife/woman/daughter'.

Hostility towards a capitalist's wife rests, in the final analysis, on the correct perception that she does not '*really*' belong to the bourgeois class, i.e. she does not belong to the class as classically defined by male marxists and sociologists. Which is to say, she belongs to it in a different way from 'her man'. She 'belongs' to the bourgeoisie as *a* 'belonging': as a dependent of a bourgeois man.

The fact that our friends are so hostile to such women and to women who have got interesting and well paid jobs – the fact that they bother to write silly attacks on radical and revolutionary feminists as 'white, largely middle-class intellectual women' – reveals that for them gender should outweigh race and class. This happens, however, to be the case not only in the 'political' (read emotional) line they adopt; it also happens to be the case in reality. But their gut reaction and empirical reality are in absolute contradiction to what they *appear* to be arguing. *They are saying, vehemently, that race and class outweigh gender*: that black women and working-class women (be they women in working-class jobs, or the wives of working-class men) have nothing in common with women lecturers, or the wife of the director of British Petroleum. *But, on the contrary, as women well recognise, and as our friend's hysteria shows, women have a great deal in common: gender outweighs class.*

If our friends argue that class outweighs gender – if they try to persuade us that there is no division between the sexes across the class barrier – it is because they want to justify a reactionary position: they are seeking support for the view that men, all men, themselves included, are innocent of responsibility for the oppression and exploitation suffered by women. *They fix on class to deny gender and excuse themselves.*

But their actions speak louder than their words, for when any woman escapes some element of male domination – through getting the protection of a really powerful husband and playing the dependence-cum-identification game to the hilt, or by being lucky enough to get a well paid job and hence some independence from men – and consequently has a standard of living, social status, and occasionally even a personal class position higher than their own, or when a woman does not respond to them (and all other men) deferentially, they find it *insupportable*. They know that gender *should* (as it generally *does*) cut across and outweigh class,[4] and they are enraged when this rule (their rule) is broken.

Notes

1 See reply by Vicki Sedden, 27 November, and letter from B Craigh, 11 December 1979.

2 Articles from *Questions féministes* are being translated and published in America in *Feminist Issues*, which started in Summer 1980.

3 Though unfortunately there is little evidence that our friends do actually practice what they preach when it would actually *hurt* them or other men.

4 When I say that gender cuts across class, I do not mean that gender is not differently constituted in different classes, but rather that *structurally* patriarchal power is common throughout society.

JAN BRADSHAW

Now What Are They Up To? Men in the 'Men's Movement'!

This paper is neither an indictment of the men's movement as a whole nor an apology for it. The question 'Now what are they up to?' comes from other feminists' reactions to me when I say the man I live with is in a men's group. Usually the immediate reactions are (understandably) extreme suspicion, hostility, curiosity and bewilderment – although two or three women I know have tried actively to coerce their men into the movement. I'm not proposing to allay anyone's suspicions about the men's movement as I think these are, and will continue to be, vital. What I *am* hoping to do is to dispel as much as possible of the bewilderment.

Men's groups began to form around 1971-2 in this country, largely as a response to the Women's Liberation Movement. Most of the heterosexual men in the groups had been influenced by feminist friends and lovers. Other men came in from the gay movements or left groups, dissatisfied with both the style and content of these groups, and feeling that the importance of sexism and of feminist arguments and analyses were being ignored or underestimated. Some men have taken a fairly strong radical feminist line – I'm thinking in particular of some of the American 'Men Against Sexism' groups and their British counterparts. Some men continue to be in left groups as well, and attempt to deal with what they see as a 'split between their lives as political activists . . . and their "personal" lives and problems as expressed in men's groups'. (*Achilles Heel* Collective, 1978, p 6).

In the early days there were three basic reasons for men forming groups. First, they wanted to take action against the institutionalised ways in which men oppress women; second, they wanted to explore ways in which men too were distorted by rigid sex stereotyping, so that they could attempt to break down hierarchy and competitiveness amongst themselves and learn to express themselves emotionally;

third, they wanted to overcome the ways in which they, as individual men, were oppressing individual women every day. These areas were given differing emphases in each group, and some men remained almost unaware of their own personal responsibility for sexism and the importance of making changes central to their own lives – while other groups were particularly concerned with this issue. (Personal Communication, Cohen, 1980).

In organisation and structure, the men's movement is broadly similar to the WLM, but very much smaller. There are local small groups which are seen as the most important elements by most men, and as the *only* elements by those who discount the wider movement. And there is a loose network held together by regional and national conferences and meetings around specific topics. There is also a men's centre in London (also in Brighton now, and perhaps in other parts of the country) which acts as a kind of clearing house for information and groups and also holds meetings. The London Men's Centre can be contacted by women in the WLM wanting men to run crêches for meetings and conferences. There are also fairly regular publications: *Achilles Heel*, which looks on the surface like an equivalent to *Spare Rib*, open and pluralistic, but which in fact is dominated by a particular group; and the *Anti-Sexist Men's Newsletter* which aims to represent a more specifically anti-sexist tendency, but which I find is often full of Men's Liberationist ideas. Because of the inherent contradictions of men trying to organise against their own power, the larger network is even less structured than the WLM. For example, something I'll be going into in more detail later on is the question of the 'commitments'. There is no question of the commitments being accepted by the Men's Movement as a whole, say at a conference like the seven demands of the WLM, because all men are not united on the question of whether or not to have commitments at all, let alone on their content. And the whole existence of a Men's Movement is constantly under attack from men who say they thought 'women would make the feminist revolution' and the job of the men was to 'get out of the way' rather than 'professing to make revolution on behalf of someone else' (Smith, 1980: p 35). It is also attacked by men who see dangers in more male bonding taking place.

I want to take some parts of the Men's Movement separately now and look at them in more detail.

The Small Group

The purpose of the small group is consciousness-raising. Some feminists have been very curious about this, asking me what the men talk about and *how* they talk to each other, suspecting that the men would be competing with each other and spend the whole evening ego-tripping and putting women down, and so on. It is true that there are dangers of 'more anti-sexist than thou ego games' (Goldsbury, 1979a, p 13). An American man has written a paper identifying what he sees as the four main dangers of men's consciousness-raising (Schein, 1977, p 129-135), and later on I am going to look in detail at some of the problems encountered by one British man against sexism.

In the group that I know most about, they began discussing their expectations of the group and went on to discuss homosexuality; defences between men; body image; close relationships outside the group (to women and to other men); pornography; misogyny, including their own; sexual fantasies; their own life histories; power and ownership; alternatives to penetration including celibacy; monogamy and non-monogamy; and contraception and vasectomy. They have also discussed feminist literature, particularly on sexuality and matriarchy.[1]

I think the reasons men feel the need to raise their consciousness are fairly obvious. Again, feminist friends have said to me that they can't understand why men need to get together in this way, it's different for women because we've been isolated from each other and we need to make bonds and build things together – but men, they say, have always worked together anyway. While this is true, men have never really looked into themselves or related to each other deeply in the way the groups attempt to do. The main reason that I was hopeful when the man I relate to joined a men's group was the prospect of being relieved of the choice of either shouldering all his emotional needs myself, or having him go off and lay it on some other woman – supposedly by way of giving me freedom. To quote from *Achilles Heel*, 'In our men's groups we have begun to fracture those barriers of privacy, of competitiveness and control that were part of our upbringing. We have learned to admit our need for one another as men; we have begun to re-examine our gayness; we have gained a confidence in our inner lives and in ourselves. In doing so, we have begun to transform our relationships with the women we are close to'. (*Achilles Heel* Collective, 1978, p 5).

But I think already we can see the potential dangers in this kind of thinking. While it may be true that 'men are too easily drawn into activism and too easily scared of introspection' (M.A.S. National Conference, 2nd Newsletter, 1978), the stage is set here for the men's liberationists to move in. In a discussion of the Men's Liberation vs. Men Against Sexism tendencies, one man wrote:

> If we can get from each other the nurturing formerly got from women only, this could be very liberating . . . But we also gain from the economic and material oppression of women. So if we no longer need women emotionally, because of the support we get from each other, and if women are invisible to us, we might keep our eyes closed to the oppression of women and so be more oppressive than ever . . . we must face this as individuals and not put the blame on men or society. We must learn that 'we have met the enemy, and he is us'. (Cohen, 1978, p 2-3).

Therapy and Guilt-Tripping

Other related issues in small groups (and something that is also argued about in the wider network) include the role of therapy and the value (negative or positive) of guilt. Therapy is an issue that, alongside men's liberation vs. anti-sexist men, seems to split groups up. Some men have learnt skills in Red Therapy groups, the 'human potential' or 'growth' movements etc. and want to use these skills on each other in the context of the men's movement. The rationale behind therapy goes along these lines: men have relationship blocks and need to work through and face up to patterns of past hurts which get in the way of changing themselves in the present. They need to rediscover their feelings, face their anger and violence in order to accept them and be able to dissolve them etc. etc. This sounds valid enough, but in practice it can lead to a whole group getting bogged down while one or two men wallow self-indulgently in their feelings, never getting any further forward – which was the reason for therapy in the first place. And I suspect that where therapy *is* successful, it might be *too* successful. In co-counselling men are discouraged from feeling any responsibility for their own sexist behaviour – they should think positively, sexism is not their fault. Personally, I can't see the point of the Men's Movement being a therapeutic refuge for emotionally battered men unless some real anti-sexist action is forthcoming.

The guilt-tripping issue is something I have found difficult to relate to, thinking that men *ought* to feel guilty, what could be wrong with that? But what is usually meant is that dwelling on guilt can be yet another way of avoiding change. That men can become paralysed by guilt and do nothing. 'In its extreme form it becomes another form of being dependent on women, allowing them to do all the work in making the changes that we need' (*Achilles Heel* Collective, 1978, p 7). Some men, though, seem to accuse others of guilt-tripping whenever they try to face up to their own sexism and misogyny. For example a socialist man wrote to the *Anti-Sexist Men's Newsletter* accusing the commitments of being guilt-ridden and penitential. I was delighted to see this reply in the next issue:

> Well, is Paul Kelly going to tell women they're going to have to put up with rape and no childcare from men until the revolution because it's just too much of a guilt-trip for men to turn round, draw the line for themselves and take responsibility? (Scott, 1980, p 25).

And Keith Motherson has written very movingly, I think, about a situation where guilt-tripping was used as an excuse for avoiding issues in his men's group. This quote comes from a piece he wrote called 'Devolving Our Power' and was part of a discussion of the commitments:

> One week we were all to think about what sexism meant to us personally. When the meeting came I talked about shouting at L. that morning, about how I vent my rage and frustration and negativity on M. and L., not on other men, including ruling men. I was still *doing* sexism. The four others also talked of 'my experience of sexism' – only for each of them this seemed to mean 'my experience of sexist treatment at the hands of others' (mostly women). That seemed to me to be very significant . . . we didn't really try to understand the sexism of our society by challenging it practically, by theorising around our individual insights. We 'kept politics out of it', we maintained unspoken norms against change, against action, against moving, against really letting go of our privilege as men . . . We didn't respect women's intelligence enough to study feminist writing together . . . I felt that the other men were quick to point to 'paranoia' in the women's liberation movement – refusing to have solidarity with women's painful experience and anger and justifiable and very often healthy suspicion of what we in the 'men's movement' were up to. Hence we didn't need to think deeply about their criticisms, whether their criticisms were true and what we could do on our part to allay any unnecessary suspicions some women might have. We almost seemed to take it that 'women were just naturally like that, hostile and suspicious'. Several times, as I was describing events in my relationships with women, I felt disconcerted by sudden laughter in unexpected places. I felt that people were getting off on things which they were taking as *against* women, when I didn't intend them that way, more descriptively, or in anguish, sorrow, perplexity at the knots *between* us. I felt almost

egged on to assert my 'manhood' – why didn't I put my foot down or belt her back? I began to watch what I would say.

Every so often I'd try to talk about my dissatisfaction with the group, with unfocussed anecdotes, about feeling we were too much of a men's club, how I wanted us to change. Sometimes this led to a crisis meeting but nothing ever seemed to come of them: three weeks later we'd fall into the same habits which I felt I colluded in too much, but didn't know whether I was being pushy, or heavy, guilt-tripping etc . . . When I voiced my criticisms nothing was resolved, patchings up were effected but no underlying unity of perspective on our conflicts was achieved. I felt like an institutionalised dissident . . . Also over a corresponding period of time, I had two or three conversations with feminists in which I found that who I was in with and what we were doing or not doing collectively affected the level of communication admissible between us. 'Stop going on about small details . . . Go off and get something solid together with men, take the pressure off us, hassle men to change'. They *weren't* against a strong and large men against sexism movement developing, they wanted it urgently. But they were perturbed at how we weren't growing personally or politically, at how we didn't move against sexism, how we mostly got stuck in men-ism, a night out with the boys, swapping notes about the state of play in the sex war. I want to have solidarity with these women's perspective – if necessary at the risk of creating difficulties in our relationships as and between men. I think that moving beyond guilt-impasses to action is in our best interests too. (Motherson, 1979, p 3-5).

Gay Men

I have said very little about gay men in the movement so far – but something that comes over time and time again in the literature is the reference to the women's and gay movements as if they were equally important. I think heterosexual men have been made to feel guilty of oppressing gay men as well as all women. And because gay men are actually present in the Men's Movement the emphasis seems to get distorted. So much so that a few years ago the movement reached an impasse and almost faded away when gays demanded that straight men could stop oppressing women and gay men only if they came out as gay themselves (Cohen, 1980). Either you're the oppressor or the oppressed, went the argument, and becoming gay was the only way out. Straight men felt they disagreed but found this argument difficult to resolve – hence the impasse.

More recently, a man wrote to the *Anti-Sexist Men's Newsletter* about the revolutionary impulse of gay feelings and claiming that 'Feeling gay is the revolutionary imperative, the essential way for people to personally commit themselves to fighting against sexism. Feeling straight is the lynchpin on which sexist society hangs, is the basis of patriarchal domination' (Pickering, 1980, p 7). And he went on to say that 'as a male I can seek to abolish my sexual and emotional demands on women, and consequently allow them the space to develop their own autonomous collective reality, free of male distortion. And I must seek to fulfil my emotional and sexual needs amongst men' (Pickering, 1980, p 7).

I get the feeling that he's missing the point somewhat!! And coming out for these reasons can be copping out of taking responsibilities, a way of rejecting women altogether. I know men who have gone through all kinds of contortions trying to sort that one out – coming out can be copping out, but relating to women sexually can't help but oppress them, becoming celibate might also be a cop out, to penetrate or not to penetrate, and so on . . .

The Commitments

I'd like to go into the commitments drawn up by the M.A.S. tendency in more detail now. The commitments have now reached their third draft and have been severely criticised for representing a rigid party line, although they're intended rather to be directions, to focus on what needs to be done for the men themselves, and to give an idea of intentions and commitment to the WLM. It's important to look at the commitments as they now stand:

1 *Commitment to a M.A.S. group* – to acknowledge the importance of men against sexism politics and anti-sexist activities: being in a M.A.S. group where possible and having a whole-hearted commitment to the group (or M.A.S. events) expressed in punctuality, reliability, consideration, sensitivity: to face up to and learn from the resolution of conflicts in the group and seeking to ensure an atmosphere of mutual equality and 'soft' solidarity.

2 *Consciousness Raising* being central and continuous, done rigorously and involving intimacy and risk based on personal experience, and leading to a shared understanding of patriarchal conditioning. Consciousness-raising and constructive anti-sexist actions being interdependent.

3 *Importance of Therapy* – Exploring ourselves and our lives, working conscientiously and thoroughly on relationship blocks with

other people. Dissolving patterns of past hurts (and put-downs) that are oppressive in our present lives and relinquishing power plays of all sorts. Re-discovering and owning our feelings and self-worth and exploring body-work, physical taboos and our relationships with our own families. Encountering the patriarch in ourselves, facing our anger, rage and violence in order to accept them and thus dissolve them through open but not oppressive expression. Struggling to re-connect increasingly with our love, warmth, nurturing, caring for others and a true sense of human equality.

4 *Relating to Women* (in everyday life) – outgrowing the deeply ingrained assumptions we have been conditioned into, that we always know best and that women are blameworthy. Not taking advantage for our own selfish ends of privileges and power not accorded to women in patriarchal society. We accept all women's rights to explore, define and act out their autonomous sexuality. Not seeking 'sexual liberation' at women's expense or in ignorance of or indifference to how life and its situations *are* and have been for women in society at large. Sharing responsibility for contraception (where welcome) rather than assuming it is women's sole burden. Dissolving our fears of menstruation and learning from women about women's bodies and bodily rhythms. Not taking our anger at what has been done to us and others out on women we live with or around. Sharing in housework and domestic life generally, including in the nurturance of emotional life and group relationships. Not stopping women having space and time to themselves.

5 *The Women's Movement* – To support the Women's Liberation Movement. To participate in WLM campaigns where possible when invited, and to be open to requests for support from the WLM. Learning to confront and question in creative and non-polarising ways sexist put-downs of women, feminism and the WLM.

6 *Gay Liberation* – Support for Gay Movement campaigns and community social life. Confronting sexist put-downs about gay people, gayness and gay liberation. Confronting our own and other men's deep-rooted homophobia and heterosexist attitudes. Exploring our sexuality unashamedly and with joy, acceptance, and eroticism with brothers.

7 *Relating to Children* – Taking responsibility for and involving ourselves in child care and the breaking down of the traditional father /mother/child roles, e.g. involving ourselves in crêches/playgroups/ babysitting etc. Discovering the positive benefits to us from being with and learning from children. They can teach us so much. Relating openly and honestly, without laying our ageist oppressions on them.

Recognising children's rights and supporting their struggles for them, including their right for autonomy and freely chosen sexual expression. Finding and cherishing the natural and playful child within ourselves.

8 *Renouncing Oppressor Violence* – towards women and other oppressed people (be it physical, emotional or verbal): exploring the psychic roots of rage, destructiveness and guilt so as to dissolve our violence and liberate our gentleness; learning to negotiate our differences where possible in a non-violent spirit (listening, not interrupting, not caricaturing, not intimidating with self-indulgent displays of anger).

9 *Reading Studying and Learning* from feminist and gay culture in all its forms, tuning into the positive benefits for oneself in appreciating novels, art, photography, theory, pamphlets, video, films, plays and music. In turn, contributing to the future gay/feminist culture.

10 *Action on our own behalf* – Contesting and transforming the stereotypes and restricted life options offered us in a patriarchal society. We will devise campaigns – cleared where necessary with the women's and gay movements – to oppose degrading images of women and men in the media; to reclaim knowledge and responsibility about our bodies and health; to re-integrate our work lives and work identities in a feminist community context. In the short-term this last will mean campaigns around unemployment, job sharing, flexible part time work, paternity leave.

11 *Reaching out to other men* in non-patronising/paternalistic ways, going beyond our own limited circles by talking with men informally about MAS and also communicating with men in particular spheres whose experience complements our own (e.g. via black or old people's organisations). Making use of the media, and producing our own pamphlets, leaflets, exhibitions, films etc. to reach a wider audience. Showing positive honest images of ourselves in the process of change, with lows as well as highs. Creating open forums where men can join in for the first time.

12 *Linking up* – locally, regionally, nationally and through interest groups. Participating in dialogues with more general 'men's' groups. Finding forms of organisation to facilitate what needs to be done without being attached to traditional models or preconceptions of structureless-ness. Links where welcome with women's and gay movements; readiness to accept their leads in wider political culture. (Huddersfield Commitments Group, 1980, pp 19-20).

I think most of the criticism of the commitments comes from the men's liberationist tendency and from men trying hard not to repeat the errors of rigid, hierarchical left groups, and hence falling over backwards not to be committed to anything at all. In America there is now a complete split between men's liberation, which is really a part of the backlash propping up damaged male egos in the wake of feminism, and the anti-sexist men. The differences can be seen fairly clearly in the two main books to come out of the two movements: *Men and Masculinity* edited by Pleck and Sawyer (1974) and *Readings For Men Against Sexism* edited by Jon Snodgrass (1977). The latter is explicitly anti-sexist and pro-feminist, and there are good articles from women and men in it, criticising the men's liberation tendency and putting forward very positive ideas as well. Carol Ehrlich's article, for example, goes into the self-indulgent emphasis on men and masculinity in Pleck and Sawyer, and points to how the 'politically aware reader has to struggle with contradictory reactions of sympathy for the personal pain expressed by these men, and anger at their apolitical self-indulgence' (Ehrlich, 1977, p 143). Men's liberationists talk of women *and men* being oppressed by sexism, trivialising and patronising the WLM and not recognising the importance of institutional sexism. Carol Ehrlich puts the counter argument like this:

> A man may refuse to oppress the women he knows; he may share housework and childcare; he may reject every unsavoury element of machismo. Yet, if he makes more money than his female co-worker or is hired in preference to an equally qualified woman, or is promoted because he has a family to support, or qualifies for a job because of an irrelevant height requirement or is listened to in a discussion because he is a man, or sees that men are featured in the mass media, or can pick up a textbook in his high school or college class and know that all human achievement is ascribed to him, or can routinely walk past strangers without being whistled at or propositioned or fearing rape, or doesn't have to cope with the horrors of trying to stretch welfare payments so he and his children can survive another day, or need never worry about the ill effects of contraceptives to his body – he is still part of a privileged group. (Ehrlich 1977, pp 144-145).

She goes on to say that 'men must work simultaneously to change their individual relationships with women (and with other men) and to change our political economic system that thrives on the power of a few privileged men over the masses of Americans, both men and women' (Ehrlich, 1977, p 145).

Kirsten Grimstad and Susan Rennie (also excerpted in Snodgrass) say that we must 'insist that the only kind of men's movement which we can take seriously is one which explicitly recognises that the oppression of women is the lynchpin of sexual politics' (Grimstad and Rennie, 1977, p 153) and that 'however desirable the reduction of machismo may be for the enrichment of the individual male personality, it has nothing to do with women's freedom if it is divorced from the struggle to dismantle institutionalised patriarchal privilege' (Grimstad and Rennie 1977, pp 152-3).

'Men's Politics'

This brings me on to the 'men's politics' tendency that superficially might seem to be doing just that. In one of the *Anti-Sexist Men's Newsletters* there is a letter from a member of the *Achilles Heel* Collective about some of the letters *Achilles Heel* receives:

> Men are writing to us saying 'Why don't you write about the inequalities suffered by men, for example in relation to pensions, divorce, etc'. These are men who are not necessarily part of the extreme backlash – though that exists too – but who are at least ambiguous about the Women's Movement and would see a men's movement as 'parallel' to it, if not competitive with it or counterposed to it. (Morrison, 1979).

And he goes on to re-affirm commitment to the WLM and gay movement etc. But despite this lip-service paid to the women's movement, what in fact *appears* in *Achilles Heel* (and frequently in the *Anti-Sexist Men's Newsletter* too) is often men's liberationist rubbish about how hard it is to shoulder the burdens of power and lots of wallowing in poetry, and what I see as a peculiar kind of inward looking mimicry of the WLM. For example, the very concepts of 'men's politics', 'men's movement'. *Achilles Heel* is published by the 'Men's Free Press', and it's gone further than this in the States – there are Men's Studies collections in US college libraries! And doesn't this from the Men's Free Press ring an odd sort of bell?

> We have started to feel the need for a new culture – a socialist men's culture – of songs, poems, books, plays, pictures and analysis that lend support to our struggle to re-define ourselves, and a need to re-examine our histories, personal and social . . .

Co-Option

The Men's Free Press also publish a set of notes and poems by Paul Morrison which must be the ultimate in co-option and outright takeover of control. The title is *Pregnant Fatherhood* (Morrison, 1977). I can't resist picking up quotes from this, like his constant references to 'the birth of *my* baby' (p 2), 'in *my* ante-natal class' (p 5), '*my* baby and her mother' (p 26) – one of the few references to the woman who was actually giving birth while he sat there scribbling notes (emphasis mine). After the birth, he's so excited he says 'I want to tell everybody, everybody, Everybody I've had my baby' (p 12), 'I gave her life I say to myself, and try to grasp the meaning' (p 14). And my favourite quote of all is this one:

> If only people realised
> How hard it is, for a man,
> To have a baby. (p 19)

As well as that (if it isn't enough) there are horrendous references to the nurses and midwives being 'All women together, keeping me out'. And about the doctor who did a forceps delivery:

> Hard woman doctor, hard face,
> You've got to be tough, in this job.
> God what does she feel. About her own body.
> How can she ever enjoy to fuck.
> This lady butcher. (p 21)

And this man is supposed to be on our side?

Something which I think gives their game away comes from the *Achilles Heel* Editorial Collective – supposedly about how 'feminism has been the most important source of self-discovery and political change for us, slowly transforming our understandings of ourselves as political men and our convictions about socialism and political organising.' They go on to say this:

> Men can put feminism up on a pedestal just as they do women in general. Feminism is idealised, which serves to distance it and put it on one side rather than having to bring it into our lives through the changes it stimulates . . . we want to raise carefully – the possibilities of active engagement, rather than passive support, in women's struggles with which we identify, for example questions of daycare provision, contraception and abortion, housing, health, and equal pay. (Achilles Heel Collective, 1978, p 7)

I'd like to contrast that kind of approach with some of what the three men who wrote the *Effeminist Manifesto* (also Snodgrass' book) say:

> Only that revolution that strikes at the root of all oppression can end any and all its forms. That is why we are gynarchists; that is we are among those who believe that women will seize power from the patriarchy and, thereby, totally change life on this planet as we know it. . . . Exactly how women will go about seizing power is no business of ours, being men. But as effeminate men oppressed by masculinist standards, we ourselves have a stake in the destruction of the patriarchy, and thus we *must* struggle with the dilemma of being partisans – as effeminists – of a revolution opposed to us – as men. To conceal our partisanship and remain inactive for fear of offending would be despicable; to act independently of women's leadership or to tamper with questions which women will decide would be no less despicable. Therefore we have a duty to take sides, to struggle to change ourselves, but also, necessarily to act. (Dansky, Knoebel and Pitchford, 1977, pp 116-7)

The Movement

Given these differences, it's difficult to understand how and why these different tendencies (there are men in Britain who would endorse the view of the American effeminists) keep together in a movement. I think partly men are putting up with marked differences because it is a tiny, tiny movement so far – 300 is a good turnout for a *national* conference. And partly there's a lot of overly liberal tolerance going on. Some of the more radical men have the idea that the men's liberationists have to start somewhere and that they will be slowly radicalised after enough brotherly crying on shoulders, therapy and poetry readings. And also there's a lot of double-think and contradiction going on within the same man. So that the same MAS man who has said some (I think) quite good things about the commitments, can almost in the next breath come out with terrifyingly ignorant stuff about brotherly love and get-togethers. After a long wallowing description of how sixteen singing, chanting men moved a telegraph pole (I've always wanted to know why!), he says:

> One brother said how like an ancient men-bond it felt to have done that together. Great. (Goldsbury, 1979b, p 26)

And as I've already said, the supposedly strongly anti-sexist *Newsletter* has had appalling things in it about supporting men fighting women over child custody, and an article by a man claiming that 'women have all the power in society to dominate childcare', and so on.

It seems some men would prefer to keep a men's movement together at all costs rather than actually *do* anything positive, and I think this comes out very clearly in the debate about the commitments. One man actually said:

> By avoiding drawing up a list of commitments we might also avoid a division between the politicos and the non-politicos . . . such a division would be immensely sad. (Letter, 1979, *Anti-Sexist Men's Newsletter*, 4)

And you can see in the re-drafts of the commitments, how they are falling over backwards to accommodate the criticisms of the more reactionary tendencies. I think it would be salutary for them to remind themselves here of what Keith Motherson has said about wanting to have solidarity with women's perspective at the risk of creating difficulties in our relationships as and between men. From what men have said to me, I think that very radical men are put off by the other tendencies and either don't participate or become frustrated and drop out of groups. Talking about a similar situation in the USA in 1975, Bob Lamm wrote:

> It is tempting to state the men's movement has no formal or unified commitment to anything. Some see the men's movement as a diverse, open movement without a political line. If this were really the case, we could at least praise the men's movement for its spontaneous, decentralised, anarchistic spirit. But it is not true, it is a deception. (Lamm 1977, p 155)

He says the men's movement is really concerned with creating awareness among men about men's issues, with no concern about women's issues or feminism or male supremacy. This, he says, reveals the 'essential male bonding of the men's movement' (Lamm 1977, p 155).

It seems to me, as an outsider, that Men Against Sexism are going to have problems if they don't dis-associate themselves from other groups in the movement. It is utterly ludicrous that the commitments people, for example, have been criticised as a take-over bid for the men's movement; and accused of being too heavy and too soon, of steering *away* from the centrally important therapy/bodywork and spirituality towards (horror of horrors) politics and action, and of guilt-tripping and ingratiating themselves with the WLM. Reading the *Anti-Sexist Men's Newsletter* you can see the commitment groups being intimidated into trying to accommodate everyone, including – and I quote – 'Men who don't at present support the WLM and feel threatened by it' (Motherson, 1979, p 5). Recently, a woman wrote to the newsletter to say she felt the 'usefulness of the men's movement depended on its capacity to clarify and define what it is doing, what role men see themselves having, what links they have/would like with the Women's Movement and continual discussion and criticism' (Clements, 1980, p 9). Let us hope they take that plea to their newly melted hearts.

Between those women who feel we can't make any bargains with our enemy, those men who won't take any responsibility for change and think this is respecting the autonomy of the WLM, and those who would love to take over the reins, surely we can make demands on men who declare themselves our partisans. The line between co-option and sitting back passively, letting us, as usual, do all the shit-work, is a very thin one – and while some may see it as further oppression for us to make demands on men, I think we should be thinking about what we *do* want men to do – and as they have taken the initiative and drawn up the commitments, I think it's worth our while to examine and criticise them.

Both Grimstad and Rennie in their article, and the men who wrote the *Effeminist Manifesto* (both in Snodgrass, 1977), have drawn up checklists of what men can do, including taking part in the drudgery, housework, childcare, typing etc. for feminist publications, listening to what women say, and supporting us without getting in our way, expecting rewards, diverting our energies or trying to take control. I think we might also ask them to put their money and power where their mouths are and put money into feminist projects, and use their power to discriminate positively in favour of women.

Author's Afterword

I have left the paper unedited as I think it should read as it was at the conference. However there are some points I would like to add. In the discussion following the paper, some women expressed grave doubts about the advisability of letting men be involved in childcare. Given the way many fathers and other men abuse their power, this is understandable. On the other hand this leaves women, yet again, doing the work. Any discussions around men who 'want to help' in any way seem to run up against a brick wall of this nature.

After the conference a group of us started to formulate 'Demands on Men'. This arose partly from my paper and partly from Amanda Sebestyen's paper. We drew up a list of areas in which demands were to be made, including money, power, sexual relationships, domestic arrangements, fatherhood, public actions and emotional needs of women. We also began to draw up a checklist for men on the point of taking any action, called 'Stop and Think!'. As well as this we formulated 14 actual demands. Many of these ran into similar problems to the childcare issue: for example, if we pushed for women's financial independence and autonomy, what about women who desperately need maintenance? At this point we were beginning to be invited to publish our demands by some men in the 'men's movement' who were very keen to have feedback and to see what we wanted done. This gave rise to all kinds of ambivalent feelings, including doubts about channelling ourselves through these few men rather than (in some way) addressing *all* men in society.

This is my own personal view of how the group went.

From reading the British men's publications and judging from letters Amanda and I received after her report on the conference in *Spare Rib* (No. 94 May 1980 – 'Thinking About Men'), it seems there are very few men of the Effeminist Manifesto genre around – and they have their contradictions too.

The London Men's Centre lost its premises some time ago and the only formal grouping left calls itself 'Crêches Against Sexism'. Many feminists continue to express anger and anxiety about men running crêches at conferences.

Finally I no longer have a relationship with a man in the men's movement, or indeed with any man, which perhaps accounts in part for my decreasing interest in the topic.

Notes

1 Paul Carlo Hornacek in his article on anti-sexist CR groups in Snodgrass (ed), 1977, recommends several other topics as essential for CR, including childhood training for sex roles; marriage; work and housework; fathers and sons; rape; the nuclear family as a bastion of sexism; maleness and masculinity; intimacy with women and with men; and so on. (Hornacek, 1977, p 129).

LIZ STANLEY

'Male Needs': The Problems and Problems of Working with Gay Men[1]

Then – and Now

Once upon a time I experienced my relationships with gay men as a paradigm of what 'liberated relationships' between women and men might be like. Now I find it difficult even to think of gay men without a groan, without thinking that in some respects they are more sexist, and certainly more phallocentric, than many heterosexual men. This paper is an attempt to explain, to other feminists and myself, why I (and perhaps other lesbian feminists) now feel like this. I will try to do this by looking at a series of experiences I went through while involved in the gay movement.

The relevance of this paper to a more general discussion of the relationship of men to the women's liberation movement may appear problematic. The gay movement is not the women's movement; has no *necessary* relationship with feminism. Nevertheless I think that my experience in the gay movement raises problems and issues which are of importance to feminism. Many gay men, like many straight men, want their 'consciousness raised'. But, I shall argue, they want this to occur in such a way that it leaves quite untouched their everyday attitudes, behaviours and feelings. 'The personal is political' remains at the level of rhetoric in their lives, a slogan to be mouthed but not something which leads them to change those lives. In this too gay men and straight men react similarly: they want change without themselves being changed.

Recently I described myself to someone as a separatist. Now I feel that this is in many ways a ridiculous description, because there is little opportunity for even the most determined of women to be separatist in our everyday lives. But later on in this paper I shall argue that 'being separatist' is one of the main characteristics of the lifestyles of gay men. It's easy for most men – and particularly so for gay men – to have almost no interaction with women, but it's almost impossible for women to have no interaction with men. Nevertheless there is a sense in which to describe myself as a separatist is both useful and accurate. I am a separatist in the sense that I have decided that I will no longer work towards the 'feminist revolution' with gay men (I made a similar decision about straight men in 1970). I feel this because of my experiences within the so-called 'mixed' gay movement in this country from 1971 until 1977.

Part and parcel of this understanding of myself as a separatist is the feeling that distinctions and divisions between different 'kinds' of men on the basis of sexual orientation is largely irrelevant. I also believe that there is just one kind of man in another sense: all men share in a basic phallocentric attitude to themselves, to women and to the world. Some men may share in this to a lesser extent, others to a greater, but this is an essential aspect of being 'male' in our society at this point in time. I don't think that this derives from anything innate about being male, anything biologically determined, but it will do for those of us living now rather than in some future utopia.

I also believe that the oppression of lesbians (I include in this both bisexual and homosexual women) occurs around a reaction to us as a particular kind of woman. I don't believe that lesbians are oppressed because we are homosexual, but because we are particularly threatening (and I mean to both men and many women). More than any other women, I shall suggest, lesbians threaten something essential to the definition and construction of masculinity and male power within sexist society.

But I haven't always felt like this. I discovered feminism, the gay movement, and the possibility of living my life openly as a lesbian and a feminist, at the same time. This was in approximately the middle of 1971, when the Gay Liberation Front (GLF) began in this country and open demonstrations of the existence of gay people – and angry gay people at that – became more common. At that time, although I thought of myself as a feminist and wanted to live out the ideals and analyses of feminism as I understood these, I also wanted to do this without working within the organised women's liberation movement. What I wanted to do was to work within the organised gay movement on gay issues as these concerned gay women.

At that time I quite specifically wanted to work with gay men as well as with gay women. I felt that gay women and gay men were similarly oppressed – the roots of our oppression were the same, although how this oppression was exhibited might differ. I also wanted to work with gay women of *all* kinds, not just those who defined themselves as feminists. All gay women were oppressed, I reasoned, and therefore we can all of us work together with gay men in order to fight that oppression. Whether we did so as feminists or not was not all that important. But more than simply feeling that we shared an oppression and should therefore work together over our common interests, I also saw homosexual and bisexual men, with some heterosexual men, as a different *kind* of man from the ordinary sexist-man-in-the-street.

In my mind I suppose I used some kind of a spectrum in order to differentiate among men. At one end of this was the totally machismo sexist man, at the other end a feminist man, and somewhere in the middle were non-sexist men. Generally I believed that most gay men were non-sexist, and a number were feminist. In more everyday terms, I experienced relationships with the gay men I knew as liberating: they did not treat me in the way that all heterosexual men I had ever met had done. This seemed a reasonably good reason for wanting to work with gay men – they could be worked with because not only were our political interests the same, but they were not like other men. They didn't treat women as sexual objects.

I should like to stress this point, because without understanding my feelings about these men then, what follows makes less sense. How these men treated women, related to me, was a revelation. It was the promise of comtradeship, of a relationship between true equals. And sexism appeared to be banished both from their words and from their behaviour. But at that time 'sexism' was a word used to describe how chauvinist men treated women, not to conceptualise relationships between men and men, and women and women, as well.

Part of this was the feeling that the non-sexist and feminist gay men I knew in the gay movement would both welcome and support the involvement of feminists within it. This was important because I wanted women to form an autonomous part of the gay movement – within it, but within it as women and organised as such within women's groups. I came to feel that this was necessary because I believed that the oppression of lesbians came in two 'parts'. The first of these I've already mentioned – because we are homosexual and therefore 'failed' members of our sex. But I also understood that lesbians were oppressed as women, in exactly the same way that all other women were oppressed. Part of the oppression of lesbians was simply that of other women, the other part was simply that of other homosexuals. It wasn't different in kind or degree from either of these, it simply included both.

How I got to 'Now'

So then, from being a non-separatist, believing that there were different kinds of men and that many men could be non-sexist or even feminist, and understanding the oppression of lesbians in the way I've just described, I have changed to the position I outlined at the beginning of this paper. I am a separatist, who rejects the idea that there are different kinds of men, and I see the oppression of lesbians as different in kind from that of gay men and different in degree from that of other women. How I got to where I am now is the substance of this paper. I shall describe some of the experiences and involvements which influenced and so helped change me from one to the other.

Describing these will necessitate providing a personal account of some aspects of the history of the gay movement in this country. I make no claims for the exact chronological accuracy of this; nor would I ever suggest that this is an 'objective' account of what happened. 'Objectivity' is for men; it is their weapon against those of us so foolish as to disagree with what they say. But it does perfectly accurately describe what I think happened and how I feel about it retrospectively. So it describes 'then' from the vantage point of 'now', which is all we can ever do.

That this is necessary, I feel, comes from two observations. The first of these is that surprisingly few such accounts exist. Those of us who were involved in the gay movement in the early 1970s appear to be stunned by our experiences, incapable of writing about them. Or perhaps some of us have simply kept quiet from a mistaken sense of loyalty – this is certainly so for me. And so I think it's time that those involved began to write about this – and in a direct and personal way. But I have no doubt that most of what will appear (and is beginning to appear) will be carefully prepared 'objective' histories. And this is really my second observation – what has appeared to date is often inaccurate about very basic things, like whether an event happened or not, and always sexist. Reflecting male accounts of what happened, looking at the world through male eyes, such accounts paint careful pictures of some men as different from others, some groups within the gay movement able to work with feminists, with lesbians.

One such account of the recent gay movement in this country writes about the experiences of lesbians within it (Weeks, 1977a). Discussing events and feelings concerning the lesbians within the Campaign for Homosexual Equality (CHE) this account presents something quite unrecognisable to those of us who were involved in it. Relying heavily on information from the *Guardian* and *Gay News*, the writer failed to get information and views from those of us who were personally involved. The result is that men in CHE (and the organisation itself) are painted as more sexist than they actually were; and other gay groups less sexist and more sympathetic than they appeared to the women around at the time (Weeks, 1977b, pp 7-9). My purpose is not to provide a critique of this and other similar accounts, although this undoubtably needs to be done. It is rather to make the point that it is now no longer possible to take for granted that anyone knows about these things as they were experienced by the *women* who were involved in them, other than these women themselves.

I have mentioned both CHE and GLF; and I think that a brief thumbnail sketch of each and of my relationship to them would be useful at this point. GLF came into existence in this country in 1971 as a revolutionary organisation (but organisation only in a very loose sense), borrowing a large part of its analysis of the oppression of gay people from the women's liberation movement in the USA, and also adopting a 'lifestyle' approach to political action. As part of its revolutionary ethos it emphasised the need for gay people to 'come-out' and live openly as homosexuals in each and every aspect of our lives. But also its analysis insisted that gay people should not set up sexual relationships which aped those of heterosexual sexist capitalist society. More specifically, couple relationships based on monogamy and sexual jealousy, with not only a division of labour but also a division of attributes and sexual 'roles', were seen as intrinsically oppressive. Another important feature of its analysis was an emphasis on participation and communality. This emphasis covered both living arrangements and also organisations and the participation of people within these. It emphasised that liberation depended on the full participation of everyone, not the leadership of an elite.

CHE was set up as quite a different kind of organisation, and predates GLF by about a decade. Initially its primary concern was with changing the law concerning male homosexual sexual relationships so that these were no longer illegal. With the passing of the 1967 Sexual Offences Act its activities became less concerned with law reform and more concerned with other apsects of social interaction. It too, although in a slightly different way, became involved in lifestyle politics. Stressing the need to provide social groups, CHE also saw these as inevitably political because it realised not only that gay people needed to meet each other, but that it was also necessary for them to live openly as homosexual – to come out, in other words. And it saw that the strength to do this was to be found in group support.

My early involvement in the gay movement was in GLF, mainly in

Leeds. Although not disagreeing with the basic analysis and sentiments then to be found in GLF, I nevertheless decided that my own longterm involvement would be in CHE. My lover of that time was more involved in CHE than she was in GLF, but there were other reasons. The most important was that GLF, like most other revolutionary organisations, attracted predominantly young, white, middle class, well-off people. It didn't attract ordinary everyday people. I felt, and feel, that the first concern of gay organisations should be to reach out to those gay people who are lonely, old, not stereotypically 'attractive', to people who are frightened, ashamed, worried and isolated. Such people weren't attracted to GLF.

Now, this doesn't mean that I'm arguing that the gay movement should be quiet, safe, conventional and eminently respectable in order not to scare people off. I don't feel that this is the most useful or efficient way of doing what needs to be done. What I am arguing is that campaigns, policies and activities should be those which enjoyably and efficiently do what they are supposed to do, not those which best inflate the egos of those participating in them. Much of GLF seemed to me to be about ego-inflation on a rather grand scale. And herein lies the second major reason why I decided to become involved in CHE. This was that there was a large measure of hypocrisy present in GLF. A large number of revolutionaries who preached the need to come out, to reject capitalism, and live the free, liberated life, were people whose own relatives and workmates (if they worked) didn't know they were gay, or who lived off the profits of capitalism via private income, and whose ideas about 'the revolution' seemed to me to be little short of ridiculous.

The feeling in GLF at the time I was involved was that the revolution would happen soon, maybe next year, maybe even next month. All we had to do was shout a little, dance a little, show we were there, express our solidarity and love for each other. Our existence, as openly and liberatedly gay, would dissolve heterosexism and smash capitalism. I felt euphorically about the existence of the gay movement at that time. For me, as for many other people, it provided both the rationale and the support necessary for things we wanted to do, like living openly and proudly as gay. But I still couldn't accept the kinds of ideas about 'the revolution' that many people in GLF seemed to hold.

So then I felt that CHE was more down-to-earth, more bread-and-butter, and so more likely to reach the vast majority of gay women and men than GLF was. GLF and its activities were necessary to CHE because it demonstrated that a gay movement existed, but CHE could do things with and for people that GLF couldn't. Although CHE was a quintessentially liberal organisation (I have no knowledge of what it's like now) I still felt that the *implication* of liberal policies, in CHE and elsewhere, was revolutionary. A situation in which sexual orientation is an unremarkable irrelevancy, in which sexism doesn't exist, in which the family as we know it doesn't exist, must be a situation in which change of revolutionary proportions has occurred. And each of these things became part of CHE's policies.

It has been said many times that the women's movement isn't something which can be 'joined' in any formal sense. It doesn't have paid officials, a hierarchy based on an internal division of power, and other symptoms of bureaucratic organisation. However, CHE had all of these things and was a very good example of a bureaucratic organisation. But I felt that, considering the task it was concerned with and that most gay people (then and now) do not live openly as such, having such a formal structure was probably the most efficient and reasonable way of doing what it was trying to do. What it was trying to do was to provide a social milieu in which gay people could meet each other and so escape from living totally isolated lives in which they passed as heterosexual; and at the same time to campaign around a range of issues that were of concern to gay people. In other words, it wanted to do different but linked things. What I shall now do is briefly to describe this 'bureaucratic organisation' in order to locate myself within it.

As I have said, CHE employed paid officials who acted as its fulltime bureaucracy. They were responsible for day-to-day organisational matters, including much overtly political work. They were responsible to an elected executive committee (known as the EC) of some ten or twelve people. The EC was elected by the entire membership, through a system of proportional representation, for three years. During this time they were responsible, in a formal sense, to no one. Each local group within CHE sent delegates/representatives to a quarterly meeting between the EC and groups known as 'National Councils', while remaining quite autonomous within the overall structure.

Soon after joining CHE I stood for election to its EC and, once a member of it, became involved in a number of campaigning activities. Then later on in 1972 I became 'Women's Organiser' and remained this for the length of my involvement in CHE, which was from 1972 until 1976 on the EC and until 1977 as a member.

As Women's Organiser I was responsible for attempting to involve many more women in CHE; and as part of this I was concerned to make it less sexist and more feminist. Originally I worked alone, liasing with local group officials and members. Then we set up something which became known as the 'Women's Campaign Committee' (WCC), a group of about ten women from all over the country, most of whom had come out and all of whom considered themselves to be feminists. These women, through me, had responsibility for specific parts of the women's campaign: for local groups, for writing to women living in isolated areas, for producing leaflets, and so on.

At the time of my initial involvement in CHE only about a tenth of its members were women, although women formed a higher proportion of its politically active members. In a direct sense the women's campaign was concerned with increasing this so that at least half of the people involved were women. Indirectly it was quite obvious that the achievement of this would involve a whole series of changes nationally and locally. CHE was based upon and worked around male interests of various kinds – the law reform issue was but one of these. Another manifestation of male interests was the organisation of its local groups. The form this took was extremely formal, hierarchical, and was based upon an organisational power structure in the same way that CHE was nationally. But most local groups were not 'political' in a conventional sense – they were mainly concerned with meeting new members and introducing them into group social activities.

Such a concern with formal organisation is sexism in a sense. But much of what went on in CHE (and elsewhere in the gay movement) was sexist in another and much more obvious sense. Gay men treated each other in what seemed an almost invariably sexist way. By this I mean treating each other as sexual objects, objectifying the young and stereotypically attractive, and making use of involvements with new members in order to exploit them sexually.

As part of the women's campaign's attempt to make CHE less sexist and so encourage more women to become involved in it, we became concerned with its structure.[2] We encouraged the local groups to operate in less bureaucratic and hierarchical ways, to discourage sexual exploitation of new members and the young, and prevent the isolation of the 'less attractive' and old. We also encouraged consciousness-raising activities within the local groups. These were of a very basic kind, like suggesting that meetings should be used to talk to each other, not just to listen to speakers talk about astrology and climbing the Alps.

Effecting some changes in CHE at a national level was comparatively easy. Its paid officials of that time (but not later) were among the least sexist of men I have met. Similarly most of the male EC members were easy to work with, politically aware and openly gay. But later more men were elected to the EC, or were employed in the national office, who were incredibly sexist to women and vilely sexist and exploitative to other men. My and the WCC's relationship with the EC and the national office 'deteriorated'. But this was in the future.

At the beginning of my 'career' as Women's Organiser a major problem seemed to be the relationship between me and the local groups. My early involvement on the EC was disastrous, and my activities attracted a series of insulting and, it might be said, obscene letters from some male members of CHE. These were not so much about me as about how some men felt about women generally and, more particularly, women mucking around with 'their' organisation. I became CHE's 'castrating woman', the embodiment of vile womanhood for so many men it now seems incredible. Frequently when I went to visit local groups I was warned about myself by men who told me they knew Liz Stanley well (so well they didn't recognise me). She was horrid, they said, and a nice girl like me didn't want to have anything to do with a man-hater like her. The whole of the women's campaign became interpreted in this way. We, the WCC and I, wanted to do things about women in CHE; we obviously hated men; we should therefore leave *their* organisation. Why this happened is interesting. But at the time it was extremely painful and upsetting for me and the other women involved in the WCC who had similar experiences.

I have described the organisation of most of the local groups. These were, in the main, 'run' – and I use this word quite deliberately – by men who were interested in having power over an organisation and the people within it. Groups of thirty or forty people were run like ICI or Unilever, and produced about as much paper. As a large element in what the women's campaign tried to do was to dismantle this power-structure, it isn't surprising we upset and angered a great many men. But what we proposed also seemed to upset many of the (few) women involved in CHE's groups. Of course, some women were as involved in the existing hierarchies as the men and used them in similar ways. But more than this, the mere proposal that CHE ought to be 'feminist' in some sense seemed to threaten both men and women at a more basic level, and produced a range of responses.

Some of these responses were odd in the light of what you might expect from men who've lived essentially separatist lives. At the beginning of this paper I pointed out that using this term of women is in some respect inappropriate. But it can be appropriately applied to men; and I would say that perhaps the majority of gay men in this country who are in contact with other gay men, through gay groups and the commercial 'gay scene', live separatist lives. Women are not only absent from their lives in terms of friendship, but absent in other ways because few postmen, electricity men, television repair men, and so on are *women*. They have no need to have women involved in their lives *at all* unless they want to, and most decidedly do not.

Indeed, not so long ago a gay man who had been very active in opposing the women's campaign and accusing us of separatism (a boo word, of course) told me that I was the first woman to enter his house in the two years he had lived there. Counting up how many men had entered my home in the same period of time I found it impossible to do, there were too many. Nevertheless, for other people we were the separatists and he was not – we wanted separate women's groups in CHE, he wanted groups to remain 'mixed'. That this meant that they remained relentlessly male was, of course, irrelevant.

But some, perhaps most, of these responses were odd in a way that you wouldn't expect. Persistently I and other women in the WCC received complaints that the women in local groups smelled. This was a feature of all women who, literally, stank. Women's cunts were suppurating wounds, full of crawling worms. They should not be permitted in the same rooms with men. Lesbians didn't want to have sex with men; this meant they hated men, all men, including gay men, and wanted to castrate them. Attempting to get women involved in CHE was an attack on the gay movement, which belonged to men. All women should be barred from it.

Verbal attacks were made on us at any and every political and social event we went to, locally and nationally. Over and over we were accused: you want more women in CHE, you want separate women's groups, you must hate men to want to do this, you *do* hate men. Local groups refused to 'allow' separate women's activities of any kind, refused to include 'and women' in advertisements because this would put off gay men. CHE's early policies, supporting the women's liberation movement, the National Abortion Campaign, and stating that separate women's groups should exist, were constantly attacked.

I have talked about these responses in a very general way. But I should also say that a great many more personal reactions occurred over a very long period of time – some three or four years. From 1972 to 1976 I was, as the 'name' associated with the women's campaign, constantly attacked, vilified, insulted and, quite literally, hated by hundreds, possibly even thousands, of gay men in this country – and not just those in CHE either. A possibility is, of course, that I am a singularly vile and disgusting person; and I accept that this is a possibility. But I reject this as an explanation of the reactions of these gay men towards me. Most had never met me, talked to me or even seen me. All they knew is what other men told them, and the existence of the women's campaign: 'Liz Stanley wants separate groups, she must hate men'. As I've said, I've been told this of myself by men who claimed to know 'Liz Stanley' well, and wanted to protect me from 'her'. But also all of the other members of the WCC would have to be as awful and as castrating as I, because all the women who became associated with the women's campaign were similarly reacted to. The more they were associated with such policies, the stronger the reaction.

And so I suggest the most reasonable explanation of these reactions is to interpret them as they were explained by the men who made them. What they felt and why they felt it was expressed within their reactions. I see no reason to reject this as a valid explanation. They were reacting towards women who were identified as *women*, not just as 'gay'; but also towards women who were politically concerned with *organising women*, women who were not concerned with, or involved with, the interests and activities of gay men. We were women who were not 'for men' and so we must be 'against' them. In other words, they said we were interested in other women more than we were interested in them; and it was for this that we were condemned.[3]

Everyday Life and Men

What I would now like to do is to pull together some of the themes and arguments which have been largely implicit in what I have said so far. I shall do this by tying them into a discussion of four sets of experiences which occurred in Manchester and which, taken together, brought into the open some of the conflicts and problems faced by feminists who wish to work with gay men. Because of the nature of male reactions to lesbians, I shall discuss experiences concerned with straight men as well. Then I shall go on to examine some gay men's response to the opening up of the problems in the form of their analysis of 'male needs'. The first set of experiences concerns reactions to the setting up of a lesbian group; the second set concerns experiences with straight men; the third concerns the exclusion of lesbians from a number of gay clubs; and the fourth concerns gay men's involvements in befriending activities.

1. *A separate lesbian group* Living in Manchester, a number of lesbians, including me, decided that we would set up a separate lesbian group, rather than attempt to get women into 'mixed' groups. Our experience of the then existing 'mixed' groups in Manchester was that two or three women were involved in each and sometimes a few more

would come to particular meetings or social events. But as soon as we set up the Manchester Gay Women's Group (MGWG) we found that it attracted large numbers of women who came regularly, were interested, involved and active within it. We had a subscription list for those women who wanted newsletters sent to them and at one time we had over a hundred paid-up members. In most people's terms the MGWG was extremely successful.

It attracted into it large numbers of women, many of whom were married, many working class, quite a few black women, and some older women, where previously people had said it was impossible to do this. But also many of the lesbians joining the group became involved in its organisation, and through a series of consciousness-raising and other similar activities decided to come out. I'm not saying that the MGWG had no problems, that there was nothing wrong with it. Neither of these things would be true. But it was good at doing things that the gay movement ought to have welcomed: it attracted women and it encouraged political awareness and activism.

But as soon as the group was set up we were approached by people involved in the CHE 'Town' group in Manchester, a 'mixed' group. We were told that we should have asked their permission to set up our group, that the MGWG had no right to exist. They emphasised that I, because I was an EC member of CHE, should not have done something which was against the interests of CHE. As a group we of course rejected the idea that we had to ask the permission of anyone to do anything. Also I personally felt and said that the existence of the MGWG was definitely in the best interests of CHE, not least because it soon became an autonomous group within it, just like the Town group. The furore caused by the existence of the MGWG went on for as long as I was involved in CHE. We were never forgiven for having set up a women's group in Manchester; even less were we forgiven for its successes.

The reactions we experienced from the CHE Town group were replicated elsewhere in Manchester. Soon after the MGWG was set up a number of other groups came into existence or were resuscitated. These were all 'mixed' groups composed of men with the occasional woman who attended; and we experienced similar reactions from the men involved in these. Being women and more concerned with each other than we were with them, we were experienced as the apotheosis of the threatening. Wherever the MGWG went where there were gay men from other groups in Manchester, there were problems. We were met by anger, opposition, sexism. As long as we remained quiet, did nothing specifically for women, didn't object to their sexism to each other, things were fine. But as soon as we became 'difficult', wanted to do any of these things, we were reacted to as aggressive, castrating, man-hating.

2. *Sex and the straight man* This second set of experiences concerns the activities of straight men in and around the gay movement.[4] Throughout my involvement in the gay movement, and still now, many straight men have attempted to make use of lesbians in order to find sexual partners and/or sexual titillation for themselves. The ways in which they attempt to do this are many and varied, but the main ones are two. First, they either ring a contact number for gay groups staffed by a lesbian and pretend to be a woman, or they get a woman friend to ring, to arrange a meeting with one/some lesbians. Or, second, they use the phone service in order to make obscene phone calls.

The purpose of the first approach is to try to get the lesbians who may meet them to have sex with them. Their female friend is 'bait' to get the lesbians to enter such sexual encounters. The purpose of the second is to ejaculate or at least get turned-on. Obviously the experience of receiving obscene phone calls isn't confined to lesbians, but contact telephone numbers staffed by lesbians receive an inordinate number of a specific kind of such calls. I have written elsewhere about the obscene phone calls I received when my telephone was the contact number for the MGWG (Stanley, 1976a; Stanley, 1976b; Stanley & Wise, 1979; Stanley and Wise, forthcoming 1982) and don't wish to repeat this here. What I will say is this.

The content of such phone calls on the one hand suggests something extremely interesting about the reactions of a large number of straight men to the existence of lesbians and lesbianism. But on the other hand the experience of receiving such calls over a very long period of time is one which, for me, had great importance. It changed the way I felt about men, and my involvement in 'mixed' organisations of all kinds. It changed the way I felt about meeting men in everyday situations. And it also changed my understanding of the basis of the oppression of both women in general and lesbians in particular. I shall come back to this later; but here I'd like to say something about why the obscene phone calls had this effect.

The content of the obscene phone calls, and the reactions of gay and straight men to talks and papers given about them, were remarkably similar. The obscene phone callers, gay men in the gay movement, and straight men in academic circles and in left groups all found the calls sexually arousing. What they found arousing was the phallic imagery, the violence, and the insistence on 'doing' sex to other people. It was nothing, or only peripherally, to do with anything about women in the calls – instead it was the cock, the almighty penis, that they all reacted to.

What, in particular, they found arousing was the power the penis gave them, its centrality in the lives of all people, its ability to be used so as to impose their will on other people. In a poem by Don Marquis, Warty Bliggins the toad 'considers himself to be/the centre of the said /universe/the earth exists to grow toadstools for him/to sit under' (Marquis, 1958, p 47). Similarly, phallocentrism seems to me to be at the centre of the universe as conceptualised by men.[5] The penis exists so as to give men power, and they articulate this belief in their relationships with women and with each other. I see little reason for not accepting this belief as a consequential fact in their lives and so, whether we will or not, in ours too.

3. *The 'gay scene' and lesbians* Both CHE and GLF recognised the need to set up various alternatives to the commercial 'gay scene' of pubs, clubs, bars, saunas and so on. Both recognised the exploitative nature of these: their relentless commercialism, outrageous prices, lethal alcohol, subservience to the police, their racism and their sexism. Both insisted on the necessity to provide alternatives which weren't economically exploitative and dependent on the continued existence of gay oppression and self-oppression. In Manchester there were, and are, clubs, pubs and other 'gay' commercial establishments which do not allow women to enter them or to be members of them. Both the gay movement and people working within it had indeed been aware of such sexism within commercial facilities for a long time. There was also a recognition that within them gay men treated each other in sexist ways and that their prime use was and is as means to quick and easy sex. To use them for 'easy sex' is not a bad thing in itself, but the manner in which this occurs in such places is the very opposite of reasonable. So not only does the gay scene blatantly discriminate against women, it is also not particularly pleasant in other ways.

Some lesbians in Manchester had close relationships with gay men who we construed as non-sexist or even as feminist because of the words that they spoke; and earlier I emphasised the importance of this to me personally. We were amazed to find that many of these men were living 'double lives' in a sense. We would all leave the discos, meetings, cinemas, meals, that we went to together. But the women left to go home or to each other's homes, while the men went to gay clubs that wouldn't allow women in, or only token women signed in by male members.

Most of these men identified themselves as gay liberationists. They preached the gay revolution, were involved in exhorting others to come out, to be non-sexist; and they are still doing so. At the same time as they did this during the day, at night, sometimes covertly, sometimes overtly, they were involved in regular attendance in the very places their spoken daytime words were concerned with abolishing.

I want to stress that in what I now say I'm not talking about the majority of gay men who go to such places, just those who claimed to be friends with us, to be gay liberationists, and to object to and fight sexism. It hurt that they should continue to mouth the sentiments of lifestyle politics while living unchanged and largely unrepentant lives. It wasn't that we weren't allowed in these clubs that hurt, that we protested about. Being barred from them is a compliment more than anything else. It was that *friends* should feel that it was outrageous and unreasonable of us to protest at their hypocrisy. But more than this, it was their total inability to grasp exactly what it was that we objected to.

When our gay male friends' involvement in such clubs became a talking point, what we said was interpreted in a curious way, and this is still the substance of their feelings on this matter. Basically they suggested this: 'Don't just complain about this discrimination, do something about it so that you can go into these places. We will even help you to do this'. This is in effect the same response as the one they made to our objections to 'cottaging', to having sex with strangers in public lavatories. Come the revolution, sisters, they suggested, you too will be liberated enough to do this.

What they seemed and seem incapable of understanding is that we don't want any involvement in such places. What we wanted was for them to put their principles, their political analyses, into operation in everyday life. We wanted them to take a stand against sexism to women and to men, and not go to the sexist clubs themselves. This they construed only as sour grapes – if we couldn't then they shouldn't either – rather than as a wish that they should not be hypocrites. Their presence in such places wasn't to spread the gay liberationist message, encourage political action, protest about sexism and racism in them. Their presence was for the same reasons as the other men present, and was basically sexually exploitative. They were there to see who they might get off with, and they were willing to forgo the possibility that some particularly tasty titbit (I use their objectifying ways of speaking here) might turn up that they might have sex with.

4. *Gay men, sex and befriending* The fourth set of experiences I outline is closely related to what I have just said about gay men and the

gay scene. It concerns the involvement of gay men (largely the same gay men I have referred to above) within befriending activities organised through local gay groups.[6] Befriending activities are particularly vulnerable to people who wish to use them for sexual purposes. This has little to do with the attractiveness or niceness of the befriender, much more to do with the nature of gay oppression and the consequences for the befriended of meeting another gay person after years of isolation. Nevertheless the problem remains. The problem is, of course, that befriending involves a power relationship which shouldn't be exploited, sexually or any other way, by befrienders but often is.

In the FRIEND befriending group in Manchester in the early and mid-1970s this problem was recognised, and a very definite policy about it existed. People weren't accepted as befrienders unless they agreed that in no circumstances should a member of FRIEND have sex with someone they were befriending. But gradually, over a long period of time, we found that many of the men involved had done precisely that, regularly and for as long as they did befriending. Their mouths constantly stated that for sexual political reasons no one should have sex with people they were befriending, but their bodies did differently.

We knew that most other men involved in befriending did this, and that they subscribed to an ideology which legitimated it: this was the belief that having sex dissolves the power relationship between befriender and befriended. But we didn't know that the men then involved in FRIEND subscribed to this ideology and its practice because these were the men, we believed, who rejected sexism and sexual exploitation. It was somewhat shattering to find out what they had been doing, partly because of what it said about the men concerned, but also for what it might have done to the people contacting FRIEND. Most women contacting it went to gay group meetings. Few of the men who were befriended ever did so. At the time a host of reasons were given to account for this. Now it seems likely that many of them were put off by their initial experiences of 'gay liberation'. Even later still, this impression was corroborated when we found a series of complaints had been made about this very thing – that male befrienders had been involved in the sexual exploitation of people contacting groups for help.

Of course, sexual exploitation is by no means something invented by gay men. But what was so surprising and so difficult to cope with was the fact that these activities were conducted in secret by men who were close friends and who spoke constantly of their condemnation of sexism. And we only found out about these things piece by piece over a long period of time, when we were also finding out about their involvement in the gay scene.

'Male Needs'

During the period when we were finding out about our gay male friends' sexual activities in the gay scene and in befriending, we obviously talked to them about this. I have already said that they saw the issue about the clubs as 'our problem'. But this suggests that a bland and unified response existed. It didn't of course, and many of them were upset and apologetic about what they too experienced as a 'contradiction' in their lives. For a long time, singly and together, they floundered around, accusing us, each other, themselves, then us again. And then they produced an explanation of their activities which, absolving them of responsibility, convinced them if not us.

This explanation appears in two written statements produced by a gay man living in Manchester; and, as I go on to discuss both of these, perhaps too much emphasis is directed at this one person. Without wishing to deny him responsibility for what he has written, I should like to point out that what he has written must also be seen as a communal rationale for a communal problem. That is, the concept of 'male needs' has an importance beyond its conceptual use in these two articles. It expresses an important piece of ideology used by many gay men as a rationale for their activities, more particularly for any which might be described as sexist or anti-women.

The first of these two articles dealing with the idea of 'male needs' discusses the fragmenting of gay men's 'political' selves from their 'sexual' selves. This is discussed in relation to, among other things, gay men's participation in the commercial gay scene. What now follows is a fairly long quotation from this article, which expresses more clearly than any paraphrase could what is meant by the idea of 'male needs':

> However much I have solidarity with the oppression of lesbians, however much I enjoy the friendship of women, I remain a man and as such need the company of other gay men . . . This really hit home when it became obvious that lesbians were being discriminated against in admission to the two gay clubs in Manchester . . . When it came to the crunch, none of us, including myself, was prepared to take action which would result in our being expelled from the clubs, or to boycott them as an individual protest. We valued

> our gay social lives more than the principle of outright opposition to misogynist male managements. The one disco per week which comprises the sole remnants of an alternative gay scene simply did not provide us with sufficient opportunities to mix with other gay men. We could not cut ourselves off from the only places where it is possible to meet and relax with one another. (Shiers, 1978, p 11)

This quotation states or implies a number of interesting and important things. One, the company of other gay men is needed by gay men, and can only be found in gay clubs. Two, 'gay social lives' are to be found in gay clubs. Three, the alternative gay scene is not sufficient for gay men. Four, it is possible to both meet and to relax with other gay men in gay clubs. Apart from noting how this looks at the world, and gay clubs, through male eyes only and totally fails to mention that even less exists for gay women, a number of other fascinating points may be culled from it.

The only social life possible is seen to centre on commercial club facilities. However, the idea that anybody can 'relax' in a commercial gay club is, for anyone who has ever been anywhere near one, ludicrous. Such clubs aren't friendly or relaxed places, and little conversation is possible in them. They are places in which men are frenetic, concerned with the physical impression they give to others; and most behaviour is oriented aroung getting drunk and/or getting off with someone. Frequently, this doesn't happen with anyone known to them outside of the context of their next meeting in that place and that time. Indeed, as this article goes on to say, many gay men find it impossible to have sexual relationships with people that they know. And such clubs provide them with a constant stream of strangers who, for as long as they remain young and 'attractive', will have sex with them. 'Needing the company of other gay men' basically means having sex with them. Apart from anything else, the level of noise in gay clubs isn't conducive to any other kind of interaction than picking up.

When divested of the phrases, what is said in this paragraph and in the rest of this article, I suggest, is that gay men go to gay clubs in order to find other gay men to fuck (and I use this word advisedly). They aren't willing to give up the opportunity to use gay clubs in order to do this, no matter what this might mean in terms of their overtly expressed political beliefs.

Running alongside this paper's analysis of men's behaviour in the clubs is an analysis of lesbian-feminists' reactions. It suggests that one of the reasons why men aren't nearly so active in opposing gay clubs as they ought to have been was because women weren't prepared to take the responsibility for organising such activity – that there was 'little enthusiasn from lesbians themselves to participate' (Shiers, 1978, p 13).

The idea that, if a person reaches a particular political ideology, then she or he ought to live in ways suggested as politically desirable by that ideology seems quite strange to many people. And particularly to 'revolutionary' men it would seem. I suggest that the *only* action which most lesbian-feminists in Manchester wanted was that the men who claimed to be their friends and who preached a feminist ideology should not then do sexist and oppressive behaviours. But by now we have come to accept that what we call the 'talking head syndrome'[7] is both a feature of everyday life and a hallmark of most male revolutionary analysis.

Most revolutionary analyses are 'structural' ones. They see oppression as lying outside the behaviours and relationships of everyday life, and so outside of and beyond their responsibility. Such analysis suggests that 'the revolution', if it ever comes, will come from outside the activities of ordinary people, ordinary gay men. To think otherwise, it states, is a bourgeois individualist trip. When the revolution occurs then everything will be changed. We don't have to change our lives – that has nothing to do with the revolution.

I and many other feminists of course don't see it like this. But it provides a very comforting ideology for those people who don't really wish to change. It tells them that personal change is irrelevant to any possible revolutionary change. Revolutionary change is structural, personal change is a cop-out from doing revolutionary work. In the context of gay men in Manchester, 'revolutionary work' involves fighting cases of discrimination, holding meetings, organising petitions. And it doesn't preclude participating in activities provided by people whose money-making depends upon the continuance of sexism, racism, capitalism and the oppression of gay people.

The second article continues the same arguments and themes. In discussing why gay men don't withdraw from situations and activities which are in direct confrontation with their expressed beliefs, it argues that:

> What may be true, however, is that however well individual men get on with individual women, we become misogynists at the point we begin to acknowledge and express our needs *as men*. It may also be that gay men are no exception to this. Why we are no exception is that our needs as gay men are conditioned by our maleness and these needs are, in many ways, very different from the needs of

lesbians whose oppression we partly share (as gay) but also partly sustain (as men). (Shiers, 1979, p 5)

Powerless to change the policies and attitudes of the men who run such establishments, these gay men refuse to act in ways which square with their expressed political beliefs for another set of reasons, it argues. Gay men are socialised within patriarchal society; and this includes their relationships with each other 'in the area of sexual relations'. This article goes on to state that any situation which is male-dominated numerically will also become male-dominated in other ways. However it seems to me that this statement conflicts with things argued in the previous article – for example, it suggests this of gay clubs: 'typical characteristics of gay male contexts: unfriendliness, high tension, cruisiness, nervous anxiety' (Shiers, 1979, p 5).

It goes on to argue that not only sexual behaviours and relationships are so affected by male-domination. In addition the fantasies of many gay men orientate around machismo ideas and values. More than this, they depend on the objectification of sexual partners, role-playing and other oppressive features. And each of these, and more, are provided for in the context of the gay club. Talking about the ambiguity of gay men's reactions to the commercial gay scene, this article suggests 'we need them because we can meet our fantasies there' (Shiers, 1979, p 5).

So then, the answer as to why gay men will not take individual action against such clubs may be unpacked from their written, verbal and other responses. It is because they have 'male needs', needs which are defined by their very 'maleness', and which can be provided for only in the gay club. This is because they are socialised into the ideas, attitudes, beliefs and values of patriarchal society. Therefore there is nothing that any gay man or group of men can do about this, because the answer to it lies outside of everyday action, if it lies anywhere. Who then must take the responsibility for stamping out such examples of sexism, insofar as this can be done outside of structural change? We have the answer in this second article: 'the discrimination will go on in the gay clubs until women put a stop to it . . . in all honesty I can't see that it will stop in any other way' (Shiers, 1979, p 5).

What we have here, then, is exactly the response of many other men to the existence of feminist women and the analysis that feminism makes of sexism. If sexism is to end, if patriarchal society is to be surplanted, then women have to do it. Men cannot, because men cannot take responsibility for their own actions – men are conditioned and controlled by a whole set of needs which stem from their 'maleness'.

What I suggest that this means, in relation to gay men, is quite simply this: if it cuts down the amount of time and opportunity they have for fucking each other, then gay men won't do it. In other words, I feel that the only possible interpretation of 'maleness', the 'needs of men', is purely and simply 'sex'. And sexual 'needs' of a very particular kind, as these articles stress. These are the needs to behave in sexist, objectifying, unemotional and entirely phallocentric ways. This, I also suggest, is exactly the attitude expressed by straight men in the obscene phone calls and other responses to lesbians.

But there is something else about this 'answer' to the problem that needs some further comment. The 'answer' envisaged is for women to do something so that they too can go into, become members of, commercial gay clubs. As I have previously argued, that the response of lesbian feminists might genuinely be one of total, outright, opposition is never even considered. The implication is we would really like to go into them if we could. That we actually meant exactly what we said isn't even considered because 'talking heads' don't live in a world where people live out their beliefs. Living out your beliefs is seen as extreme, eccentric, perverse; and hypocrisy rather than honesty is to be valued.

Gay Men and Straight Men are all Men

What I think is demonstrated in the discussion of 'male needs' in these two articles, in other responses from gay men, and in a comparison of these with responses from straight men to lesbianism and feminism, is that to all intents and purposes *all* sexist men behave, think and feel in similar ways. They see their sexism as absolutely no responsibility of theirs. They suggest if any change has to be made then it has to be made by other people, usually 'sympathetic' women who can lead them on to the paths of righteousness. They construe women as 'objects', and for gay men this objectification concerns women's use-value. The 'use' of lesbians in the gay movement is to salvage men from the consequences of their sexism, but to do this in such a way that nothing is disturbed, nothing changes. And the idea of male sexuality which is offered by both straight men and gay men is the same. This suggests that the cock, the penis, is the centre of men's being, and also the centre of the entire universe. Phallocentrism rules, perhaps not OK, but that's how it is and will remain.

This, then, is why I describe myself as a separatist; why I will no longer work with any men; why I argue that there are not different kinds of men; and why I know that the oppression of lesbians is quite different from that of gay men. What I have described are some of the events, minus the pain, anguish and anger that accompanied the experience of them, which led to my describing myself so. What I shall now do, briefly and finally, is to outline why I feel that the oppression of lesbians is quite different from the oppression of gay men.

The gay movement used to argue that the oppression of all gay people, both women and men, homosexual and bisexual, was rooted in the centrality of the nuclear family within patriarchal capitalism (GLF 1971, CHE 1973). Both argued that of crucial importance in this was the division of labour within the family and, more specifically, the construction of gender divisions. This is, in most respects, an argument very familiar to feminists. Commonsense ideas about femininity and masculinity, and their supposed innateness, therefore identify gay people as 'failed feminine' and 'failed masculine' people. These two oppressions were seen as the same oppression – as the two sides of one coin.

What I now feel about the oppression of lesbians is that it is quite different from the oppression of gay men. Sheila Rowbotham, in *Woman's Consciousness, Man's World*, has said that the only picture that we have of free women is in the fears and fantasies of threatened men (Rowbotham, 1973: p 34). I insist that the fears and fantasies of threatened men are full of lesbians, or rather their understanding of what it is to be a lesbian. Such fears and fantasies, I argue, are exemplified in the content of the obscene phone calls that I and many other lesbians have received. What the content of these calls tells us is this.

Many men are frightened by the mere existence of lesbianism because it says something which they feel undermines their entire being. What it says to them is that women's sexuality does not depend upon the penis. It says that women can live lives, and sexual lives, which are totally independent of men; and, more than this, which are totally independent of the phallus or any phallic substitute. Lesbianism demonsrates, in a very direct and threatening way, that the penis is essential to men and to men only. It may be a vehicle through which sperm can be used to fertilise zygotes, but it isn't *essential* in any sexual encounter between men and women or women and women where that sexual encounter is about pleasure rather than procreation.

This is the message which is shouted, screamed, spat at us through the reactions of straight and gay men to lesbianism. And this is why I will no longer work with gay men. There is no way, absolutely no way, in which our interests can be said to be the same. Gay men, perhaps more than any other men, ally themselves with the activities and products of sexism. More than any other men they choose to act and construe themselves, and each other, in ways dominated by phallocentric ideologies and activities. At the beginning of this paper I pointed out this is nothing innate, nothing which can't be changed. I also said that it might as well be all the hope of change there is. I want here to reiterate this. This is a deeply pessimistic paper, I don't see what else it can be. But I believe that such pessimism is necessary. The quality of everyday reality is such that the only sensible response to it is pessimism.

In effect, sexist society *is* a separatist society. It is a society in which it is extremely easy for men to live totally separate lives from women if they so wish. But a feminist society, even a non-sexist one, would be one in which the essentials of phallocentrism are challenged and dismantled. Its achievement would entail the end of the lifestyle of the average, sexist, phallocentric gay man. It would provide less opportunity for them to fuck each other, and fuck each other over. And so they resist it.

However, a feminist society is the only kind of society in which lesbians can be free, can achieve liberation, because the essence of the oppression of lesbians is sexism, this and nothing else. It is the reaction of all phallocentric and sexist men to women who, they fear, do not need 'them' as they define themselves – as phalluses on legs. And so in finishing this paper, I can find no better way of summarising what I feel than by repeating what Del Martin wrote when she left the 'mixed' gay movement:

> As I bid you adieu, I leave each of you to your own device. Take care of it, stroke it gently, mouth and fondle it.
> As the centre of your consciousness, it's really all you have. (Martin, 1972, p 46)

Notes

1 For many of the ideas in this paper, as for many other things, I am indebted to Sue Wise.

2 I should perhaps point out here that the activities of the WCC weren't carried out on and in a totally sexist stronghold. To imply this would be to give an erroneous impression. Whatever CHE may be like now, then we were supported by most of the other members of the EC and some men, as well as some women, within the local groups. Now, of course, it seems obvious that the WCC was used to do what all of CHE should have been concerned with, as the token feminist committee responsible for 'women's things'. But at that time, the WCC seemed an exciting advance.

3 It might be useful to point out that the kind of reactions described

weren't confined to me or other WCC members. In 1975, an international conference of people involved in mixed gay movements in Holland, Belguim, Norway and Britain was held in Holland for the specific purpose of discussing antagonistic reactions on the part of gay men towards lesbians (*Oegstgeest Papers*, 1975). There we found that our experiences were those of other women too. About the same time, an international gay conference in Edinburgh saw women denouncing the sexism of their male 'comrades', and many left the conference early. Prior to these events, women in the London GLF had already made their exit (as their sisters in the 'mixed' gay movement in the states had done earlier – Martin, 1972) for the same reasons – the sexism of gay men towards women and other men.

4 In the context of this paper, I have used 'gay' to refer to people who publicly identify themselves as homosexual or bisexual, regardless whether they are or are not sexually involved with people of the same sex. I have used the word 'straight' to refer to those people who may see themselves as homosexual, bisexual or heterosexual, but who behave as 'straight' – i.e. conventionally and stereotypically heterosexual.

5 I am not saying that there aren't men who resist this, who seek to become people rather than merely men. The point is that such a process is difficult and problematic for them – they have to resist rather than simply 'be'.

6 'Befriending', as the gay movement originally saw it, was about trying to help people with problems associated with their gayness. Befriending was undertaken by people who shared the gayness and also felt the necessity of working through feelings about this and about the reactions of other people to homosexuality. The 'problems' included: wanting to know where and how to meet other gay people; violent husbands; rejecting parents; job discrimination; fear of meeting other gay people; fear of 'eternal damnation'; having VD; and so on . . .

7 One of the most perceptive observers of this phenomenon, and the person who coined the term, is Bob Crossman.

BETSY ETTORRE

The 'Perks' of Male Power: Heterosexuality and the Oppression of Women

Editorial note

Betsy's paper attempts to explore the foundations of institutionalised heterosexuality, chiefly, the notion of a natural division between the two sexes through which women's reproductive capacity is controlled in the interests of male power. From Betsy's point of view is it possible (theoretically at least) to separate heterosexual behaviour from institutionalised heterosexuality. It follows that if women who are having sexual relations with men refuse to be consigned by men to their 'natural' role as reproducers within institutionalised heterosexual relationships organised in the interests of men, they may be in a position to undermine the foundations of institutionalised heterosexuality and male power. The option of 'autonomous' sexuality is, in this sense, available to heterosexual women, as it is, more immediately, to lesbian women who engage neither in heterosexual relations nor in institutionalised heterosexuality. Unlike Revolutionary Feminists, Betsy does not feel that conventional sex between a man and a woman is of itself a manifestation of male power (see Love Your Enemy, *1981, for discussion of the Revolutionary Feminist position). However, in approaching the issue solely from a theoretical viewpoint, she does not confront the problem of how a particular heterosexual act, and the surrounding relationship, may be separated from cultural and institutional forms in a patriarchal society, in practice. It is this area – concerning the practical options available to all women for some measure of self-determination in a patriarchal society in which it is impossible for any women (even Lesbian Separatists) to live completely outside male control – which demands urgent attention. Needless to say, the practical options available to women will vary according to race, ethnicity and class, as well as in relation to our sexuality (whether we view the latter as 'chosen' or not).*

Introduction

The purpose of this paper is to point out the various ways in which men benefit from institutionalised heterosexuality. I will discuss heterosexuality from the point of view of its structural or practical implications (the way sexuality is organised in society) as well as its ideological implications (how sexuality is viewed in society). In the final section I will draw some conclusions concerning future feminist strategies.

The argument of this paper rests on two central assumptions: first, that institutionalised heterosexuality is a social construction; and second, that men benefit from institutionalised heterosexuality.

Sexuality a Complex Social Issue

In order to understand sexuality fully, we should look at how it is organised in terms of both the structure and culture of society. By culture I mean the way of life of a particular society. By structure I mean those social forces which determine that way of life. We may view sexuality as a complex social issue. From a feminist standpoint or from the viewpoint of women's oppression, a critique of sexuality poses a threat to society. A feminist standpoint exposes contradictions in our beliefs about biology and culture, sex and ideology and women and femininity. The organisation of sexuality in society throws light on questions like: does the source of the vast social differences between men and women lie in biology or culture? how is biology defined in society? are women 'naturally' female and men 'naturally' male? what is 'natural'? does 'human nature' really exist? and are our beliefs about sexuality based on a false foundation? Whatever the answers to these questions, the fact still remains that sexuality is organised in a patriarchal society which is heterosexual and male-oriented and whose culture produces sexual ideas with those dominant interests in mind.

Culture and Sexuality

Sexual ideas develop in light of specific biological bases: the sex organs. However, these sexual ideas are also found within, and change through, concrete human experiences. Sex is viewed as a basic human need which must be satisfied. (Freud was keen on furthering this view and he predicted that individuals would have problems if their sex drive was left unfulfilled). Furthermore, the norms of society, the unwritten rules which govern social behaviour, tell us that this 'powerful instinct' should be satisfied not only socially, that is with others (preferably one 'other' of the opposite sex), but also according to certain characteristics such as age, race, class, etc. Normal sexual behaviour which reflects sexual norms usually becomes a way of achieving a certain amount of social status. When a dominant sexual viewpoint like heterosexuality is produced, it tends to be dependent upon the ways in which society organises, processes and structures social relationships. This process of organising sexuality appears directly related to power.

Many people experience culture as a way of life. However, it may also be experienced as a productive process which provides us with the tools to master the world around us. In the area of the 'sexual', or 'sex', culture further provides us with an unquestioning acceptance of a sexual instinct. Through socialisation, culture presents vivid images and ideas of the acceptable sexual behaviour: heterosexuality. Through culture, sex becomes institutionalised or ritualised and ultimately imprints on our minds a dominant sexual ideology. However, it is important to be aware that acceptable ways of satisfying a basic human need are based upon biology and moreover, culture's definition of this biology! Sex is structured or organised according to two sub-groupings, viewed as 'naturally distinct' from one another: men and women. These two groups are physically different from one another and develop socially on the basis of the biological differences between them. Yet, the entire physical or material world, of which human sexuality is supposed to appear only as a segment, becomes dominated by these differences. A fundamental biological tension exposes itself and our male culture thrives on it. Perhaps Freud was correct in suggesting that biology is destiny. For women, biology is the root of our subordination.

Culture perpetuates the idea that sex is a powerful drive as well as a physical need. Therefore, individuals should experience 'sex' not only as an irrational, uncontrollable desire but also as a basic impulse. As a result, sex is transformed from a physical or biological base to human want or from material reality to a type of necessary awareness. Nonetheless, sexual activity which is primarily heterosexually orientated remains a biologically discriminating process based on those who appear to reproduce, women, and those who do not appear to reproduce, men.

Power and Sexuality

Earlier I indicated that sexual relationships have to do with power. I would argue further that all social relationships in a patriarchal capitalist society are power relationships. Our society is capitalist, where a minority of people make money at the expense of others, and patriarchal, where women are subordinate to men for purposes of sex and ultimately to reproduce society. Simply, contemporary society has developed as a patriarchal capitalist society in which power lies in the hands of men and capitalists. Both of these groups reflect how power is established, organised, distributed, mobilised and perpetuated in relationships between people in society. Both capitalism and patriarchy compose society's structure and reflect how people in power so far have created society. Thus, the most fundamental way of making society is through power relationships: male-directed or money-related or both. Hierarchy becomes the order of the day.

Within the above social organisation of power, women lose out. They have less power and less social value. Society places higher premiums on men, male activities, production in the factories and waged labour than on women, female activities, reproduction in the home and domestic or 'wageless' labour. Women are viewed in the truest sense of the word as the 'weaker' sex. They have little value as workers, as *real* producers or as *real* money-makers. Women are members of a secondary workforce; men are members of the *primary* workforce. All of these ideas are embedded within our value system and become part of the dominant sexual ideology which is heterosexually orientated. Social value which is sex-based is measured by one's productive value (the apparent ability to make money), rather than on one's reproductive value (the apparent ability to make babies). More simply, social status which is directly related to social value is grounded in productive labour (men's work) and not in child or reproductive labour (women's work).

Ironically, however, women are essential for the continuation of any given society. As a social group, women are the *real* producers in society: the bearers of future generations. Why then does society deny women the social importance that is due to them? Perhaps, the answer lies within our understanding of women's biological vulnerability or periodical physical 'weakness', which in our society implies the need for protection: male protection and control. Observing this perplexing situation, Simone de Beauvoir suggests (in *The Second Sex*, 1974) that a woman is situated in the world through her body. She also suggests that a woman's body is not enough to define her as a woman. The implication here is that ideas about women have a great deal of social power. A woman, like a man, is her body. Yet, historically, she has been enslaved to it. Her reproductive function, which is (my term) her *species-producing power*, has resulted in a limitation of her social power as well as a denial of her social value.

During the course of history, the forces of production (both the instruments and human labour through which material goods are produced) were and are generated under different economic conditions (factors which determine how people produce goods in the range of societies whether primitive, ancient, feudal or capitalist). A particular society not only governs how people in general relate but also determines sexual relations between men and women. This is how history appears to develop and how the forces of production have operated. However, within this view an important element is missing: the forces of reproduction. Where does one locate women's species-producing power? Throughout the history of the Western World, these forces have been constant and women have remained subordinate. In this way, the category 'sex' and the organisation of heterosexuality have emerged only to divide the development of our material world and to split human history!

Social thinkers as well as feminist theorists speak of a 'sexual division of labour'. They describe this division as a part of the social labour process in which men are engaged in 'male' jobs and women function in 'female' tasks. This 'sexual division of labour' solidifies in the modern family structure.

Yet, I would argue that the above explanation is not thorough enough. The sexual division of labour does not take fully into account the persistence of the sexual dominance of men and the subordination of women. An explanation of sexual divisions in society must include an analysis of male power as well as the reasons for the subversion of women's species-producing power.

Power and the Sexual Division of Labour

The sexual division of labour maintains an unwavering social importance both ideologically and practically. Because of this presence, sexuality is given the power to define cultural value and social productivity. However, regardless of its power, sexuality is consistently made private or divorced from society. Sex/work; the private sphere of 'people'/the public sphere of 'things'; the family/society; work in the home/work in the factory; domestic labour/productive labour; reproduction/production; female/male are all socially constructed opposites which relate directly to ideas about the sexual division of labour. These opposites conflict with each other. They also indicate the existence of a dominant sexual ideology which is heterosexuality. Heterosexuality dictates that women should enact passive or subservient roles and be concerned with procreation or reproduction, while men should live our dominant social roles and concern themselves with protection, providing for others and production. These roles set up a hierarchy between the reproductive sphere of life and the productive one. Within this framework the productive sphere of life dominates, and perpetuates male interests.

Society tells us that the productive sphere of life is primary. Society also tells us that the respective roles of men and women are not only 'natural' on the individual level but also 'morally correct' on the social level. Thus, the 'goodness' of any society's sexual morality preserves itself in and through the continuance of the sexual division of labour and, ultimately, the perpetuation of heterosexual roles.

Human Nature and the Subtlety of Male Power

Men have a vested interest in maintaining the view that heterosexuality is the only natural and therefore correct form of sexual behaviour in society. Implicit within this view, is a fundamental acceptance of the existence of 'human nature'. I would contend that human nature is really a male concept. It seems that human nature is men's answer to the general question 'Why is society the way it is?' and the specific question 'Why do people act the way they do?' Although there is no evidence that human nature exists, patriarchal society accepts the real existence of human nature. With this acceptance, people learn to justify all forms of social hierarchy whether it appears in the form of sex, age, class, intelligence, race etc. If we accept human nature, we say that things, people, events are predetermined. Our social lives are fixed, static or unchanging. Regardless of our views about social change, we implicitly deny it. We become, in a very subtle way, dogmatic. Through human nature, we become fixed and inflexible in our ideas about a chaotic and ever-changing world. Ultimately we accept that individual people are born a particular way and we create social divisions. A patriarchal society is obsessed with order, social hierarchy, power and social divisions. A patriarchal society teaches us that people who hold the reins of power are 'born' more productive, more competitive, more intelligent, more aggressive, stronger, more rational and more creative than those who do not have power. If we slot a particular group of people into these 'predetermined', natural aspects of power, we find consistently that men rather than women appear to reflect them. Men have a vested interest in giving human nature a powerful place in society. Human nature provides order. In order to maintain inequalities in a patriarchal society, the powerholders (men) maintain that women are born the weaker sex, less productive, less competitive, more emotional, more irrational and more chaotic than men. Because of these views, and because society is supposed to be rational and ordered, women must be controlled. Male power is an effective way of establishing this necessary control. Since the presence of male power has a definite sexual basis, the organisation of sexuality is a key to understanding how male power operates.

Men's Creation of the Notion 'Reproduction'

In the foregoing discussion on the organisation of sexuality I outlined a general area covering the concepts of sexuality, social power and the sexual division of labour and the links between them. In the following sections of the paper, I will point out the specific notions from which the above concepts emerge. They are the 'root' notions of reproduction, male power and the sexual division of nature, respectively.

We have seen that the belief in human nature sets up social hierarchies. The contention here is that human nature is not only a concept which furthers male power or the interests of men, but also a false concept which cannot be justified. One of the most effective ways for a particular social group to oppress another social group is to claim natural superiority. It is obvious that men as a sex claim this type of superiority in relation to women. Patriarchal society as a direct result of men's claim, sets up the belief that it is natural for a woman to be a mother or simply to be reproductive. Furthermore, women are told that because of their species-producing power (ability to bear children) they are more reproductive than men. In a very well defined area, women appear to have more social power than men. The reproductive sphere of life appears to develop as the domain of women. However, if we look closely at the area of human reproduction, we see that women and men are equally reproductive. In other words, although women appear to have more species-producing power than men, both men and women are equally necessary for reproduction. Furthermore, although women appear to have more social power in relation to what their bodies do – make babies – their whole reproductive sphere of life is totally controlled by men in a variety of ways.

A patriarchal society accepts that reproduction is necessary. A society which is primarily concerned with male interests dictates that sexuality should have a primary procreative function. Men tell women that sex is necessary for the perpetuation of the human race and the continuation of the social world which men have created. It is in the interests of men to pass on their power to future generations. Men tell women not only that they should be mothers, but also that they have a natural instinct to be a mother. Again, the appeal to human nature raises its ugly head. For women to be mothers implies a physical vulnerability, child bearing. Men become the protectors of women's child-bearing function. Male protection of women's child-bearing function sets up a whole series of social divisions. Women as the primary reproducers are divided from men, the primary protectors and producers. Women are divided from each other in a private area of society, the 'home'. Women are divided within themselves. On the one hand they are sexual objects who provide pleasure for their protectors. On the other hand they are reproducers who provide future generations for society's primary producers. In effect, through the acceptance of the notion 'reproduction', a social hierarchy between men and women is created. Reproduction is also viewed as a social necessity. Reproduction is a social category or root notion which dictates that sex must be useful, have a procreative function and ultimately be beneficial to the future production of a male society.

Reproduction or making babies, although viewed as a root notion, remains subordinate to production: making things in a patriarchal capitalist society. It is consistent with male interests that reproduction should be seen in this way. If the notion of reproduction is viewed as equally important to the notion of production, various changes in society could occur. These changes could be perceived as a threat to our present male-directed society. Male power would be fundamentally questioned. Although attempts have been made to see men and women as equally productive, obvious imbalances exist in the social sphere of making things. However, the private sphere of making babies (reproduction) has never been questioned. Reproduction is for women and not seen in relation to men. If the apparent dominance of women in the area of reproduction shifts to include men, women will not make many social gains. As I stated earlier, the fact remains that the area of reproduction is totally controlled by men. Although women reproduce, their bodies, their reproductive function, and their reproductive lives are structured by men. If men would see themselves as they really are (equally reproductive in relation to women), they would perhaps have consciously to reorganise their power which oppresses women. Ultimately, men would have to give up and reject male power for themselves.

Male Power: A Source of Women's Structure

In contemporary society, male power structures women's lives in a variety of ways. Male power says: 'Women are naturally feminine, passive, inferior or subordinate' or 'Women should want to be reproductive mothers'. With the creation of these basic dicta, reproduction is given a form: heterosexuality. Society states that it is only through heterosexuality that these dicta can be realised.

The way a woman becomes heterosexual in a male society is uncritically to accept male expectations. A woman falls in love with a man; marries him; becomes his wife and his property; pledges to be faithful to him and to live as a monogamous partner for the rest of her life; has *his* children and organises the private sphere of his life: the family (which he protects). All of these ideas – romantic love, marriage, fidelity, monogamy, child bearing, child rearing and the family – are the reflections of a rigidly structured heterosexual society. Men structure women's lives. Women play a minimal part in defining their own lives, their own sexuality, their own bodies and their own ideas and experiences of their bodies. The structures which women slot into so easily are male creations, just as are the notion of reproduction and the concept 'human nature'. In our society women are not able to own their own chaotic experiences such as individual feelings of physical vulnerability, anger, rage, fear of violence, hate and social protest. Women are told to be strong, caring, nurturing, tender, loving and conciliatory. The structures of their own life experiences are removed from their hands through the patriarchal strategies of violence, containment, isolation and privatisation of women. Male power intrudes in all areas of women's lives and attempts to create structures, hierarchy and rationality. The justification for this power is that women are irrational, chaotic, unthinking, etc. Perhaps, women really feel these feelings. However, it is our bodies, our reproductive 'space', which make these feelings real for us. I would contend that the bodies of women are enough to define us in a hostile male world. Because a woman reproduces, her physical or bodily structure is set in an uncontrollable, chaotic, or 'hit or miss' mentality. She has the potential to disrupt the male world: to become pregnant. In turn, her chaos is structured by male power. The famous Cartesian statement, 'I think therefore I am' does not apply to women, only to men. For women the statement, 'I feel therefore, I'm told what I should feel', is more apt. Male power creates the 'oughts' and the 'shoulds' in a women's supposedly 'natural' feeling and chaotic world. Nature, Reproduction and Sexuality become rigidly structured ideas.

Patriarchy and the Sexual Division of Nature

As we have seen, an analysis of power and the sexual division of labour includes a critique of patriarchy. I would argue that a more fundamental division exists. This division is the sexual division of nature. If the current feminist analysis were to include this division, perhaps it would become a more expansive analysis. Simply by focusing on the root notions of 'human nature' and 'reproduction', feminist theory has the potential to see the issue of women's oppression in its totality. At present, much feminist analysis skirts the area of human reproduction and its full implications. When we focus on the productive sphere of the family where an analysis of the sexual division of labour originates (The Domestic Labour Debate), we ignore important elements of women's oppression: not only the area of human reproduction but also the areas of sexuality, heterosexuality and human nature. If one begins an analysis of women's oppression within the family structures the sexual division of nature is not seen to exist. It is my contention that this division exists, and furthermore that it is a root cause of women's oppression.

How do we explain the sexual division of nature? As far as the development of society is concerned there exist natural divisions between men and women as distinct human groups. Simply, women appear to have more species-producing power and to be reproductive, while men appear to have less species-producing power and to be less reproductive. This view accepts a fundamental division between men and women on a purely natural or biological level. From this natural division of nature emerges a whole series of assumptions concerning women as a weaker sex. These divisions of human nature help to create social divisions between men and women. Women as a social group emerge as females. Females are seen to be both naturally and socially more passive, weaker, submissive and subordinate in relation to men who represent 'males'. This social division of nature helps to maintain women in an oppressive situation in the world. Both the natural division of nature and the social division of nature make up the sexual division of nature. In other words, human nature, which doesn't exist, is said to exist. The acceptance of human nature becomes a way of setting up divisions between men and women on both the 'natural' and 'social' levels in society.

All of these ideas effect the organisation of sexuality in society. The organisation of sexuality into heterosexual roles, male and female, is believed to have a natural foundation. In reality, heterosexuality has no material foundation. It is primarily a way in which men harness women's reproductive power in order to further their own interests. Men deny their own species producing power. By doing so they are able to continue to coopt women into believing they are more reproductive than themselves. Heterosexual sex is organised as reproductive sex or procreative sex. It is most certainly an effective way of furthering male superiority and male power. Female sexuality appears less important than male sexuality within the total context of heterosexuality. Heterosexuality organised along patriarchal lines 'sanctifies' male pleasure. The effect of this sanctification is the blocking out of male's awareness of their species-producing power or reproductive function as being equal to that of females. Male sexuality revolves around the potent, erect life-giving penis. Male sexuality implies forceful penetration by the penis. As well as being reproductive, penetration gives pleasure. For male sexuality two elements coincide: pleasure and procreation. Regardless of the myth of the vaginal orgasm, these two elements do not coincide for female sexuality. The form of patriarchal sexuality, heterosexuality, places priority on the species-producing power of females. Although sexual pleasure for females may occur as a result of male penetration, traditionally the emphasis has been upon the sexual potency of the male. For females to experience sexual pleasure is a digression from their real experience, which is to reproduce children and to become mothers.

From the above discussion, we see that the organisation of patriarchal sexuality into heterosexual roles is based on false foundations. For men to hold the reins of social power, these foundations must not only be perpetuated but appear as natural for both groups of sexes in society: men and women. My contention is that the following foundations of heterosexuality serve male interests and are untrue:

Heterosexuality is natural sexuality;

Reproduction is the sphere of activity reserved for women or women's domain;

Women are more reproductive than men;

Women are inherently female, passive and have a mothering instinct;

Men are inherently male, dominant and have an instinct to protect or to be aggressive;

Human nature exists.

Conclusion: An Autonomous Sexuality for Women

If we agree with the above contention that the basic foundations of heterosexuality are false, we may begin to discover feminist strategies in the area of female sexuality. One strategy is to develop alternative forms of sexuality for ourselves as women. In developing these alternatives, women take power away from men. They make their own choices about what to do with their bodies. If women define their own sexuality as women, they create choices that contradict patriarchial methods which oppressed women. Whether women choose to be heterosexual, bisexual or lesbian orientated, is not the real issue. The real issue is that women develop a sexuality that is autonomous from men's interest. Obviously the results of this development would have far-reaching social effects. However, women would no longer collude with men in maintaining their own oppression. The choice of an autonomous sexuality is a step towards women's liberation.

Author's Afterword: The Workshop Discussion

Two major arguments are central to this paper. They are that heterosexuality is not *natural* sexuality, and reproduction, although the apparent domain of women in society, does not necessarily have to be their *primary* domain. Autonomous sexuality implies the choice of whether or not a woman decides to be a mother with or without a man's support; wants to be economically independent of a man or chooses to be sexually independent of men. The main direction of the paper is to see the possibilities that are open to *all* women for some measure of autonomy from male control.

The discussion after the paper was lively (to say the least), and stimulated a heated debate among the women who participated.

Some women argued that the paper was too academic and removed from the area of feminist practice. Others complained that the paper lacked a statement which upheld the lesbian position as the only possible way for women to express autonomous sexuality. Some women felt that the ideas which were presented did not relate to their feminist practice as lesbian mothers who had consciously chosen to separate from men and who held this position as a political strategy for themselves.

Throughout the debate, it was interesting to see that divisions rather than similarities among the women who were present became clear. The basic point of division was whether or not it was 'politically correct' to state that lesbianism is not only the best but also the *only* way for women to create an autonomous sexuality separate from male heterosexual values and from men themselves. The position of the paper on this point was clear: whether or not women chose to be heterosexual, bisexual or lesbian was not the real issue. The real issue was that women develop a sexuality autonomous from men's interests. The implication was that heterosexual feminists as well as bisexual and lesbian feminists had this option open to them. Perhaps if some of the central arguments of the paper had been developed in the discussion the various divisions which resulted from the above implication would not have been so extreme.

AMANDA SEBESTYEN

Sexual Assumptions in the Women's Movement

In the recent period there has been passionate debate around the politics of heterosexuality and lesbianism, not only in WIRES and the London *Women's Liberation Newsletter* but also in the American feminist magazine *Off Our Backs* and the French *Questions Féministes*. Reading the English arguments in the light of the much more sophisticated and perceptive American ones has made me think again about how many sexual assumptions the movement still takes for granted, both here and in the States (the difference is that over there the assumptions do at last seem to be under observation). Anyway, here's a list of those I've come across most often.

Sexual Assumptions in the Women's Movement

1 That relationships with men mean sexual relationships;

2 That the only feminists who have relationships with men are 'heterosexuals';

3 That 'heterosexuality', whether it's wilfully chosen or painfully stuck in, consists of the following – liking to fuck, liking someone taller and stronger, liking someone older and richer/more expert or clever, liking someone muscular and narrow hipped, being scared to go without eye makeup or with hairy legs, never fancying other girls when you were a teenager . . . etc;

4 That all heterosexuals fuck;

5 That only a penis can penetrate a vagina (i.e. that no woman can penetrate another or would wish to have anything in her vagina except a penis);

6 That the only men who mean anything to women are men they sleep with or have given birth to;
that the choice to leave a child is unthinkable;
therefore that separatism is about sexual choice for childless women or women with daughters;

7 That male friends, brothers, (even oddly fathers) are irrelevant – we can either leave them without a pang, or continue seeing them without compromising our feminism;

8 That 'the personal is political' means none of us can bear to separate our love life from our political life;
so that it's understandable, if despicable, for a feminist living with a man to argue for mixed events, incomprehensible in a lesbian;
so that it's OK to bring our female lovers to any and every women's group;
so that it's good for women to display physical affection anywhere any time (like two women at a recent feminist summer school who attended every meeting as a couple and took vocal part in the final plenary sitting on each other's knees);
so that heterosexuals won't have the same need for a social life with women;
so that women's culture is for and about lesbians;
so that heterosexual feminists will go on spending their free time with men unless they decide they prefer sleeping with women and there's no point in challenging one without the other;

9 That 'flirting' is OK;

10 That flirting isn't OK but we all do it anyway. ('Flirting' is another word like 'heterosexuality' which takes for granted as 'natural' – if 'unsound' – a whole bunch of different conciliating social behaviours. I haven't written them all down here but I'd certainly like to talk about them);

11 That Men Against Sexism consists of men in ongoing sexual relationships with women in the women's movement;

12 That gay men organise in the mixed gay movement, heterosexual men in 'men's groups';

13 That men inside men's groups and the gay movement are better;

14 That men inside men's groups and the gay movement are worse (advance guard of the counter-revolution . . .);

15 That radical feminists don't have relationships (cf. Assumption No. 1) with men;

16 That each radical feminist in a 'relationship' with a man is Doing It Her Way;

17 That the only women who wear eye makeup or shave their legs are 'heterosexuals';

18 That a bisexual is a woman who lives with a man and has sexual relationships with women on the side;

19 That being celibate is being on the way to another sexual relationship;

20 That being celibate is a consciously chosen state of total freedom to spend every scrap of your emotional energy on the movement;

21 That celibates are unhappy because everyone needs sex;

22 That celibates are special because they *don't* need sex (all the rest of us do, no matter what the compromises);

and last –

23 That all our sex lives were much easier before we joined the women's movement!!!

It probably goes without saying that all these assumptions are highly conservative and have no place in a movement that's aiming to transform human relationships. They are also making a lot of women really uncomfortable whether they stay inside the movement, leave or keep away altogether.

My own sexual life looks something like this:

celibacy	80%
men	15%
women	5%

My social life is spent something like this:

women	45%
men/mixed	35%
going places with myself	20%

My political activities go like this:

women	95%
mixed	5%

My sex life is an absolute mess! (With the exception of about half the celibacy time, which passes very happily – the other half is bad, though). It's not just that my sexual relationships are full of contradictions in themselves, but that they're completely marginal to the rest of my life and politics. It sounds impossible doesn't it? Well, here's how.

I've become certain, after some years of separatism and many more in my present compromise position, that I do want some relationships with men, sexual and otherwise. But I still want to transform my life in the way that separatism is aiming for. I'm a radical feminist which means I see men as my political enemies. But I don't want to kill them, that's too conservative a solution! I want men to *stop being men* any more. And I don't want to wait till after the revolution for them to stop being men, I need the personal satisfaction of making something happen NOW.

Within a foreseeable future I can see that separatism makes more obvious sense, but it's not what I want at this time. In fact it's my experience of separatism that's the bedrock of any confidence I feel in being able to take men on at all. And it's as I get closer again to mixed-sex situations that I see more and more clearly how 'heterosexuality' as it's presently constituted is a – if not the – foundation of men's power. Every single little bit of the institution has to be taken apart. Going away and leaving it (separatism) is only the best line of attack feminists have worked out so far; and I hope I've shown in the list of Assumptions how many aspects of this 'heterosexuality' are taken for granted and not challenged either by separatists or anyone else in the movement.

I feel a great need to pool my personal experiences of sex. When I joined the movement in 1969, heterosexuality was taken for granted and any lesbian feminists were deep in the closet. There seemed to be a lot of women around more or less like me, who had lived sort of heterosexual lives but who found their relationships with men unbearable. Some of these women came out of their crisis into an improved relationship with a man, more started living with women which gave a chance of bigger changes. But the majority just drifted away from the movement altogether. From time to time I meet them, and they seem something like me still – men on and mostly off, lots of antagonism – and the main part of their lives spent with women. But I don't come across anyone like that *inside* the movement any more. Are you all really as sorted out as you seem?

I think the coherence of separatism has driven those radical feminists who do have any dealings with men into unsatisfying directions:

1) The closet. Much the biggest category – I'm always being amazed to find how many apparent separatists aren't at all. We seem to have no language to express engagement with brothers, sons, lovers and male friends or workmates that doesn't also express compromise with their power. And so uncompromising feminists will tend to stick to a separatist rhetoric which leaves out whole areas of their lives but at least declares 'no surrender'.

2) Forced confidence, bravado, individualism, '*I Do It My Way*'. This is the one I fall into most often myself, and I can recognise the tone in some of the letters that heterosexual feminists have written to WIRES newsletter, and even more in their contributions to the 'off our backs' debate. Take, for example, Vickie Leonard in *Off Our Backs*, October 1979: 'I call myself heterosexual, not straight. Straights are uptight sexual conservatives who support the status quo. I am heterosexual.'

3) Radical-humanism. In the *London Women's Liberation Newsletter* internal debates on transsexuals, and more recently boy babies, I've been in agreement with the 'humanitarians', but worried by the way some of their writing seemed to be calling a halt to the sex war altogether. I feel it should be possible to work out a human radical feminist position without dropping into the libertarianism of *Beyond the Fragments* (Rowbotham, Segal and Wainwright, 1980) where divisions between men and women are seen as a social (capitalist) tragedy or a 'problem of hierarchy' and not the fault of men at all. Or into the maternalism of the *Scarlet Woman* group who concentrate the struggle between men and women into a struggle over reproduction where 'the vagina has belonged to men ever since the defeat of mother right', and even pornography is seen as a 'desecration of the birth canal'. This analysis highlights men's power as sexual partners and fathers but says little about their power as children, colleagues or friends.

I think we'll only get out of these binds by *speaking out* about the contradictions of taking men on personally in any way whatever, about all the bad experiences and all the sexist norms we are unwillingly upholding. It will be a disaster if all the risks and daring of the separatists only provoke a face-saving response from the rest of us.

Having spoken out, what next? This is where my separatist past starts an inner shout of *waste of time*, but I think we have to sort out as a movement what we want men to do; and what we want each other to do with men. Our 'private' lives are private still. Isolation is still making me compromise where I don't want to; and still making me disorientated for weeks when I see another feminist putting up with something from a man that I would fight over. Because we still haven't created *political* terms to discuss these situations and change them, any confrontation enters the realm of therapy (personality differences) or moralism (that kind of lifestyle imperative that devalues a lot of what the separatists have to say).

How many years since *The Politics of Housework* was written? (no prizes for guessing – look up MAINARDI in the refs.) At the start of the American movement women were writing contracts and lists of demands on men, strategies for women to employ with them, all over the place. It never happened here – the British fear of 'regimentation' (euphemism for taking politics seriously) held us back. But do-your-own-thingism can be just as reactionary.

The recent upset in the 'Men's Movement' over a proposed set of anti-sexist Commitments has made me see this with horrendous clarity. The Commitments basically suggested that men's groups should be doing more than just express the male experience, but should unite around detailed written undertakings to support the women's liberation movement and devolve male power. The response of most men seems to have been horror – and interestingly the criticism made most often and taken most seriously and answered at the most length was simply this: the idea of making *any* organised political commitments was 'heavy'. By the time even five men had been found to consider signing the commitments, they'd reworked them so that in the place where the first drafted has stated 'Support the Women's Movement' the second had managed to insert 'Importance of Therapy'! And even after that the signatories all apologised and said they weren't necessarily going to stick to all the commitments, they just wanted to think about them . . . All the opponents of the commitments claimed it was the form they objected to, not the ideas. But looking through the *Men Against Sexism Newsletter* and the journal *Achilles Heel*, I see ideas which could never possibly be contained within a set of anti-sexist commitments, not because they're too complex, freeflowing and poetic but because they're naked expressions of male power:

> a man asks for support in his custody battle, and receives warm wishes for success from the brothers;
> a therapy group gets together over the grain coffee 'to reassert the ancient man-bond';
> a man who's always feared and hated other men goes to a men's conference and finds out how brilliant and beautiful they are;
> a long article questions the existence of patriarchy;
> another reproves feminists for making men feel *too guilty to change* (think about that one, sisters);
> several men talk about how unfair it is that women have more contact with babies;
> several applaud their own prowess at nappy changing and say what marvellous fathers they are;
> a beautiful long-haired guy is described singing a song called 'Manpower'.

OK. The point I'm trying to make is not that men will never change or even that men's *groups* are inherently reactionary, though both could be argued from the evidence. What I feel is that men will consolidate their power any way they can – in the pub or the boardroom or the local men's centre – *if women let them*. If we as a movement sorted out the demands we want to make on men as a whole, then men's groups as we know them would be forced to make a definite anti-sexist commitment too. The struggle between those who want a 'Men's Movement' and those who want a Men Against Sexism movement is of direct interest to me, even though I have no personal connections with any of the men involved.

Anyway, most men aren't in any political group and lots of women want them to stay that way. A set of agreed movement demands on men in general would be a way of getting *ourselves* together too. I'll give an example of the kind of dilemma that comes up in my life – how do I express my own personal feminism in an uncompromised way to men, without in practice putting other women down? The problem comes at me several ways:

1 Do I admit criticisms of Margaret Thatcher when a man is around?
2 Do I admit to disagreement with any feminist position that differs from mine in a pro-male direction? With feminists who attack other women's actions in public (at events like the TUC abortion rally)? Or with books discussing the women's movement clearly aimed at a male readership?
3 Do I confront a woman whose stated position I totally agree with, but who cancels out her words by flirting or dressing in ways I have stopped doing for political reasons?
4 Do I admit to disagreement with a revolutionary feminist paper on transsexuals, or any other feminist position that differs from mine in an anti-male direction?

When I joined the movement I was in no doubt – I would defend any woman against any man and no man could criticise any woman in my hearing. But over the years I've lost my certainty, partly through other feminists making me feel my position was rather absurd. I mean, why favour a woman who may have been dismissing your politics totally over a man who might be a very old friend? (Not that old friends never dismiss your politics.) The separatist answer to the dilemma is clear – stop having male friends. The socialist-feminist answer is clear too – some men are comrades, some women are enemies. But for a radical feminist who's not a separatist it's just bravado to pretend that crises of loyalty don't occur even over small and almost forgotten things. For myself, I know I've definitely slid over into doing 1) and 2) on occasions – things I would never have dreamed of once. The reason I don't throw stones at woman No. 3 is that I live in a glass house: I'm still very uncertain how far – and why – my own dress and manner really have changed. The reason I haven't done 4 is that I've been protected from doing so by the movement itself. If a paper is for internal distribution, reproduced in a newsletter for women only, there is literally no way I can take public sides with men against it. This seems to me an excellent example of the importance of movement discipline. If only we could extend it to cover not only situations where we're carving out all-female territory, but those where feminists are interacting with men too – whether that interaction be friendly or hostile (and we all know those vanguard feminists who'd sooner be confronting a man than talking to 'his' woman – that's male orientation too).

It's interesting that the list of movement demands does *not* so far contain a demand for an equal division of housework, childcare and care of older, disabled or sick people. To both the cultural separatist and the socialist feminist it's a demand that probably seems liberal (and that certainly could be put forward in a liberal framework). But to radical feminists it should be essential. It would be a demand made by women on men directly, without the mediation of the state, and without any payback in the form of personal or sexual servicing. We also need to think about ways that women can get at least half the money men are now 'earning' – also without having to pay in the usual ways. These demands are in my immediate interest even though I have no intention of sharing a household with a man. They would be victories in the sex war. Even more in my interest would be demands that would attack the hierarchy of the couple over the single person, or stop competition between women. Sexual caste works in so many ways: youth, political seniority, children, childlessness, looks (what you do with them), blondeness (race is part of sexual hierarchy too), sexual experience/confidence, sexual innocence/challenge, education, intellectual confidence, fame even. They all affect our position in the slave market, and you just need to look around a women's disco to see those hierarchies operating without any men physically present at all. It seems like some of these divisions are too hot for us to handle: I've only heard them mentioned by the Right, who turn them against us with 'You'll never make everyone the same, some people will always be prettier than others, or cleverer'. To which of course our answer is that women will be far *less* the same when we stop having to conform to established ideas of what is 'clever' or 'pretty'. But in practice our movement still seems to be divided very much along caste lines – and any onlooker can pick up on it. Take for example an article about *Spare Rib* in *Time Out*, an article not only intended to be sympathetic but *experienced* as sympathetic by plenty of feminists, an attempt to defend us against the *Daily Star's* allegations that we were a bunch of arrogant puritans. *Time Out*'s defence rested on the fact that some of us did wear bras, and that the pregnant one among us was actually living with the prospective father, and on a story about my lipstick! Something I'd hoped was my personal frivolous choice was being used to set me up against other women. 'Normal', 'pretty', or at least trying hard, not one of those *ghastly* combat-booted libber types . . . delighted letters from male *Time Out* readers made me sure I hadn't mis-judged the article's effect. Well, I've stopped wearing lipstick again. But that's not a solution if I'm just conforming to another hierarchy of correct feminist style. Similarly, if a woman writes in her own name she will often be rated over other women; the solution may not be to stop writing. It might be to write anonymously (but what about accountability?), or as part of a group (but we need feminist writers to risk laying their own individual experience on the line), or to force publishers to include the replies of other women in her work (I think this is the best idea so far, but you don't always know ahead of publication who'll want to answer, so you end up favouring those on the grapevine). These are just a few of the areas where we need to get to some agreed position or we end up cutting each other's throats.

Sexuality is the crucial area for me at the moment. If you are involved in a multiple relationship should the 'other woman' (it seems the other person is usually a woman whether your partner is male or female) always know about you? Is monogamy the only way to avoid competing with another woman? If it's *serial* monogamy some other woman will have been ditched altogether, won't she? And then what should feminists do in bed? To presume to answer this question seems to be seen by much of the movement as the ultimate fascism, judging by the response to the Revolutionary Feminist's paper on political lesbianism (Onlywomen Press, 1981).

I can't afford to agree with the idea that judging sexual technique politically is either laughable or an invasion of privacy, because for several years of my life I was raped. I was penetrated against my will because I didn't dare insist on any other kind of sex. And I *still* have a fight any time I start a sexual relationship with a man. I do realise that not every woman feels the same about penetration, whether she is a lesbian or bisexual or heterosexual or celibate. But I believe that most do – 20 years of information-gathering from Masters and Johnson and Anne Koedt and Shere Hite may not be 'proof' but they're certainly strong support for the hypothesis.

So why am I still feeling alone? I suggest because a combination of embarrassments have kept women silent whose sexual lives with men are nonconforming. There's embarrassment inside the movement at seeming to excuse oneself in the face of separatism ('He's not really a man, he doesn't put it in'. Rubbish, obviously). And embarrassment in the outside world because a 'proper fuck' still has much higher status (and that seems to go for some of the more heterosexual circles of the women's movement too, we don't escape the ruling ideology as long as men are still in power). One of the contributions to the 'off our backs' debate that I liked best was a list of ways by which women and men who are sleeping with each other can undermine the institution of heterosexuality. The first of these is to make it clear if they are not fucking!

> Intercourse is the institutionalised expression of sexuality. Individuals, lesbian or not, do not have to accept that. Just as cuddling, snuggling, oral and manual stimulation are satisfying for lesbians, they are also satisfying and rewarding experiences for some female-male partners. Because of heterosexism, we have no way of knowing to what extent mixed-sex partners, past and present, have chosen activities other than intercourse as the 'pinnacle' of sexuality. Just as same-sex sexual activity has always existed, female-male alternatives to intercourse have always existed. Just as many lesbians have hidden their expression of sexuality for fear of being labeled and punished, female-male partners may have hidden and continue to hide their expression of sexuality. One way for mixed-sex partners to put pressure on heterosexism is to identify the forms of sexuality they find more gratifying than intercourse. (Martha Thompson, *Off Our Backs*, December 1979)

Other strategies follow:

> With the help of other feminists, the individual feminist who has a male partner must assess her own situation. Is she economically, politically, socially or sexually dependent upon him? If so, what are the steps necessary to eliminate that dependence? If she is not dependent on her male partner, then how can she most effectively violate people's assumptions that she is dependent? Through verbal and nonverbal communication, a feminist living with a man must continually make people aware that she is not dependent on him. No behaviour is too small to consider. Handling money, touching behaviour, public decision-making are only a few of the areas in which feminists and men with whom they have a relationship can consciously violate the assumptions of others . . . We should avoid presenting ourselves as attached to men, unless absolutely necessary. The language of many women living with men, including

> feminists, is littered with references to a male partner. Since people may misunderstand the meaning of our connection with a man, we must eliminate unnecessary references to men from our language and from our appearance (for example, wedding bands, clothing specifically designed to be attractive to the 'opposite' sex).

I'd like to end by closing the circle and repeating that my own sexual relationships are a mess. Not the sex itself any more, I've got that more or less sorted out by now though I could do with more public support, but everything else that goes on between me and the person I have sexual feelings for. Sometimes it feels like there's nothing but antagonisms and contradictions and nonrequitals (cf. celibacy!) and ripping or being ripped off . . . I can only say that the same things have happened with women and with men, and that neither separatism nor therapy has altered them. In fact both in different ways have helped me push the problem back out of the public arena. It's getting so I'm using the movement as a compensation for my 'private' life – what I want is to change! And I certainly can't do it on my own.

ANGELA HAMBLIN

What Can One Do with a Son? Feminist Politics and Male Children

I say:
you shall be a child of the mother
as of old, and your face will not
be turned from me . . .
Robin Morgan (1976)

This summer my son will be ten years old. In 1971, when I joined my first women's group, he was just ten months old. What impact, if any, has my feminism had upon his development and awareness during this past decade?

Does he know, for instance, that as a woman living under patriarchy I am oppressed every day of my life by the power which men hold over me? Does he yet have any glimmering of the future role which patriarchy has allotted to him in this scheme of things? Does he yet understand that to succeed as 'a man' in this male supremacist culture he will have to turn his back upon me and everything I have tried to teach him since infancy? Can he yet grasp the complexity of the choices he will be forced to make?

Can I bear to witness his struggle during the next ten crucial years when patriarchy will redouble its efforts to lure him from me with promises of power and male privilege? Will I find him anxious only to rid himself of these bonds with the mother so that he may take up his allotted place in the 'world of men'? Or will he resist patriarchy's tempting inducements and choose instead to identify with me, with my struggle, with my politics? Dare I hope that I may see a 'different' kind of male emerge from this boy-child whom I have nurtured with my feminism?

And how long must I go on waging this battle, against the patriarchal culture, for the heart and mind of my son? And will I be able to bear the pain if I lose? And have I yet discovered the tools which would make it possible for me to win?

New Ways of Being Men?

In her book *Of Woman Born* Adrienne Rich asks 'What do we want for our sons? Women who have begun to challenge the values of patriarchy' she says, 'are haunted by this question. We want them to remain, in the deepest sense, sons of the mother, yet also grow into themselves, to discover new ways of being men even as we are discovering new ways of being women'. (1977) But, if, as Adrienne Rich suggests, we are to encourage our sons to develop 'new ways of being men' then we need to work out for ourselves exactly what we would like these 'new ways' to be.

Do we, for instance, have any positive image, however tentative, of what we think a 'non-oppressive' adult male might be like? Or are we only clear about all those things which we *don't* want our sons to become? We have plenty of negative images of maleness, but very few, if any, positive ones. And this can create a number of problems both for us and our children. How, for instance, can we communicate to them that they have any real choices in developing their male identity if there are no positive alternative models of maleness with which they can identify? And yet this issue of choice, and the existence of valid alternatives, is a crucial one.

Is Change Possible?

Do men oppress us because they are *biologically* programmed to do so or because in patriarchal cultures, like ours, males are given *power* over females? This is a central question because the balance of power within a society can be *changed* by political action – biology cannot.

If male oppressiveness is seen as being biologically determined, then since it is impossible to change biology it can seem impossible to change the system by which women are oppressed by men. Male oppression of women can come to be seen as inevitable, unchangeable and irreversible.

This is, in many ways, a fatalistic view because it rules out from the start the possibility that feminist political action might be used as a means of forcing change. Instead, the biological argument is taken through to its logical conclusion: if the cause of women's oppression is male biology, which by definition cannot be changed, then the only way that women can rid themselves of their oppression is by ridding themselves of men.

It is perfectly logical to argue from this viewpoint, as some women have done, that one way of ridding ourselves of men would be for feminist mothers to abort male foetuses – thereby reducing the number of oppressors who are born. It is also argued that feminists should separate totally from those males who already exist, whether as children or as adults, because since it is impossible for them to change, any energy we expend upon them can only be wasted and debilitating for us.

My own son was just a year old when, in spring 1972, I first came face to face with these arguments. They were put to me very powerfully by women whose personal courage and political commitment filled me with admiration, and I took what they said very seriously indeed.

For months, thereafter, I sat beside the cot, watching my baby sleep, tormenting myself with questions I would have preferred to evade. Was my baby already an oppressor? If the biological arguments were true – then he was. Is this what I had given birth to? Was it already too late?

I didn't know what to do. If I was a committed feminist did this mean I should leave him? Give him to his father? Sever my connection with him now: completely? Never see him again?

How would he grow up then? What would he become without my influence and my love? Would he ever understand or would he grow up hating me for abandoning him?

Is there really no hope for him? Is it all so inevitable? Is change *so* impossible? He hasn't even learnt how to walk or talk yet – surely there must still be time? Is it anti-feminist of me even to think these things?

I struggled with my feelings for many months – trying hard to face up to the terrible agony of having to choose between my feminist politics and my male child. I knew it was a decision that only *I* could make and it was one of the hardest of my life.

Eventually, I came to realise that the choice itself was a false one. I just refused to believe that there was nothing I could do to alter the course of events in my own and my son's life. And it was this rebellion against my own feelings of powerlessness which finally led me to question the whole way in which I had been approaching this issue.

I began to re-examine the biological determinist arguments which I had previously accepted without question. For years I had been rejecting these 'biological' explanations when they were used to tell me that I, as a woman, was naturally passive, intellectually inferior and temperamentally suited only to menial tasks. I wasn't about to go back on all this now and accept that in relation to my son 'biology was destiny' – because, it seemed to me ultimately biology had to determine the behaviour of both sexes or of neither.

If biology is not destiny, then change has to be *possible*. It may not be likely. It won't be easy. It most certainly will not happen of its own accord. But if it is *possible* then it means that, if enough of us want it, we can make it happen.

I don't know how to force these changes. But what I do know is that once you believe change is possible, you start to ask yourself different questions. For instance, why do men oppress us? How can male power most effectively be challenged? How can I use my position and influence as a feminist mother positively to further feminism and weaken patriarchy?

I believe that the reason why men oppress us is not that their biology has endowed them with innate superiority or made them inherently more powerful than us, but that our society is run by men, in the interests of men and therefore men are given the *power* to oppress and exploit us. It is male power which I define as the enemy and which I want to see eradicated. The power which men hold over us has to be prised away from them. Men and their power have to be separated. And this can only be achieved through collective feminist action.

Separation or Confrontation?

It has been my experience that in Britain the belief that change is possible, and therefore worth pursuing, is a minority view within radical feminist circles. Over the years it has seemed to me that the arguments which insist on total separation from men and the abandonment of male children as the only solution to women's oppression, have tended to eclipse the earlier radical feminist ideas which focussed on forcing political change.

Barbara Leon, one of the Redstockings Collective, describes how this development occurred in the US. 'The current *insistence*,' she writes, 'in some parts of the Movement that women prove their feminism by leaving their men, while viewed by some as more "radical", really represents a limitation of tactics and a kind of accommodation. To those who accept the idea that male supremacy is incurable and therefore permanent, there can be only two alternatives – living with it or withdrawing from it. They will then pressure women to accept that analysis and resign themselves to one choice or the other'. (Leon, 1978, pp 139-144)

This certainly seems to be what has happened to radical feminism in Britain. Total separation has been put forward not as one possibility but as the *only* valid solution. Feminists who are trying to bring about change in their relationships with individual men, or attempting to influence the development of their male children, are seen then as squandering vital female energy, and have even, on occasion, been denounced as 'collaborators with the enemy'.

One of the most damaging effects of all this on radical feminists, like myself, who have made a political choice to stay and struggle within a relationship and attempt to influence the development of our sons, is that it seriously and constantly undermines both us and our politics. Many of us have found that we do not openly admit the fact, within the Movement, that we relate to men. If we have to declare ourselves, we mumble about it and quickly change the subject. Our relationship with a man, or a male child, is the shameful secret which we prefer to conceal. But what does this do to us personally and what are the consequences for our politics?

One of the consequences of this 'silencing' of political discussion around the issue of men is that a kind of Movement taboo has grown up around the subject. Women who talk about men are often seen as 'putting their energy into men instead of into women' as though the two were, of necessity, in opposition and as though this were a self-evident anti-feminist activity.

Obviously, if total separation is seen as the *only* politically viable solution, talking about men or discussing male children must seem completely irrelevant. But to those women who are seeking to change male supremacy in their personal relationships, as well as outside of them, discussing ways of confronting individual men/male institutions or influencing male children, can be very relevant indeed.

The original radical feminist goal set in the 1960s, says Barbara Leon, was 'to build a power base of women from which to attack the powerful and segregated bastions of male supremacy. Women were fighting for a new society that guaranteed full integration on a basis of equality'. And organising and building a separate and autonomous Women's Liberation Movement was to be the power base from which that attack would be launched, it was never intended to be solely a base for 'alternative female lifestyles'. As the Redstockings Collective puts it:

> *The original formulation for separate organisation was as a political base for militant confrontation with male supremacy not as a means of avoiding confrontation with men.* (Leon, 1978, pp 139-144)

Letting Men off the Hook?

One of the things which the taboo on 'talking about men' and the emphasis on total withdrawal from men has led to, according to

Redstockings, is a lowering of the demands we make upon them. In this respect they see a similarity between the socialist feminist position on men and the separatist position on men.

> Both, claim that men are irrelevant and suggest that we can and must talk about women without talking about men. They then attack feminists for talking about, worrying about and making public demands on men and the man's world. In fact what they are doing is denying that male supremacy is the problem, and while their refusal to even talk about men, much less deal with them, might seem to some a militant expression of contempt for men and very radical indeed, in fact what it represents is a lowering of demands on men, if not letting them off the hook completely. (Redstockings, 1978, pp 189-194)

If, as radical feminists, we are to reclaim the original goals and engage in 'militant confrontation with male supremacy' both collectively and individually, in our own lives, then we have to be able to talk about men and male children. We have to be able to discuss, for instance, which tactics are likely to be the most effective. We need to develop new theories and work out new strategies to bring about change, but we cannot possibly do this while the subject remains a forbidden area of discussion. The time has come when we have to break this taboo.

There are many ways of putting our feminist politics into practice. For some women total separation from men and male children will be the best and perhaps, in many circumstances, the only valid political choice. For others it will not. We have to build a strong Women's Liberation Movement which can encompass many different, but equally valid, political choices. And making demands on men, confronting male supremacy and attempting to influence the development of our male children must be allowed as part of a genuinely pluralistic approach.

What can one do with a son?

Well, I guess what I've been trying to say in this paper is that what you can do with a son depends on how you view the problem and what your politics are. If you see your son, from the moment of his birth, as 'doomed to be an oppressor' of women by virtue of his male biology, then quite frankly there's probably very little that you can do. If, on the other hand, you do not accept that male babies are born oppressors but gradually become oppressors by the time they reach adulthood, then obviously you are going to be very concerned to identify, and if possible sabotage, what it is that happens to them in between the time they are born and the time they are adult which produces this result.

Our small sons are tomorrow's adult male oppressors. If we want to change that, if we do not accept that this is inevitable, then we have to begin interfering in some way *now* with the process which brings this about. Patriarchy depends, for its continuation, on our sons. It needs them to become the next generation of adult male oppressors of women in order to continue to reproduce this system of male supremacy. But what would happen to the patriarchal system if our sons did not carry out this allotted task? If they did not identify their own interests as being the same as those of male supremacy? If, in other words, they refused to be used as front-line patriarchal troops against their mothers and, by extension, all other women?

How can we, to paraphrase Robin Morgan, ensure that our male children remain 'children of the mother' and that their faces are not turned from us? How can we devise feminist strategies which would successfully sabotage the social and political process by which our sons are turned into adult male oppressors? How can we subvert the male identification process so that our sons grow up to identify their own interests with ours, instead of defining them, as at present, in opposition to us? This I believe to be a much greater threat to patriarchy than handing over male children to their fathers; a prospect which would seem to make their subsequent adult oppressiveness inevitable.

Although I made a political, as well as a personal, decision not to abandon my son all those years ago, I discovered that when it came to the problems involved I, like many other feminist mothers of sons, had to struggle with them alone and unsupported. Because although I was able to share many other areas of my life with my sisters, the specific area of 'what to do with my son' was regarded as some kind of personal problem for me. It was never defined as a legitimate area of political discussion. I think that the time has now come when we have to change these definitions and recognise that as feminist mothers of sons there is important political work for us to do.

ASTRA

Poems on my Sons

Introduction

During the past decade, the process of becoming a conscious and active feminist has made me think a great deal about how my two sons, now teenagers, could be part of my politics and my daily life. It still does.

My poems have grown out of this concern; also out of numerous conversations – of both a practical and theoretical nature – with Angela Hamblin on the subject of our male children.

Some of my writings have been prompted by particular events involving my boys, some by specific feelings towards them, some by an attempt to analyse motherhood as a patriarchal institution.

My sons haven't wanted to read most of these poems (or other pieces of mine, for that matter) yet. I hope they will some day.

I've wanted to write down these feelings for many years but couldn't do so till last year, to my enormous relief.

single parent

it's almost seventeen years
since i fed the baby
in a chilled and silent room
after twelve days in hospital
where i longed to leave
yet dreaded coming home
being on my own
with him

i fed this child
and closed my eyes
and shivered
noiselessly:
i didn't want to waken daddy
sleeping in another room

i fed my son
and thought
is this what i waited thirty-six years for?
and quickly killed
that thought
though ten months later
i wrote two poems
which i hid away
till i came upon them recently
and knew that they were
suicidal poems

these feelings i could finally face
nine years after this baby's birth
but when i tried to share them
with his father
he wouldn't have me say
i hated motherhood
and why and how and when
not the children
but the role the isolation the loss of self

he turned away from me
when i needed him the most
leaving me desolate
with a double sense of betrayal
first by the world then by him:
i'd been a single parent
all this time
but couldn't bear to know it

it is this that even now
emptied my head of other thoughts sometimes
making me less able than i'd like
to work out
my future my past my present

it's time i grasped
how much single motherhood
has benefitted me and my sons
lately
anyway

This was written to my younger boy who's always been affectionate and open with me, and 'female oriented' as well, since he was tiny.

small son

small son's
in love with mum

does that bode well for his feminist future?

on the subject of sons

should mothers of sons

disown them at birth?
or put them up for adoption at a later date?
(not too late)
or have then undergo gender change surgery?
or attempt to counteract the kulture
by talking to them truthfully about
patriarchy
my oppression
their conditioning
the possibilities of
de-conditioning
themselves and myself?
or call on my sisters for ideas and support
and babysitting?

there is of course
no single right answer
or instant cure
or simplistic solution
only many many many questions

who will help me/us
and when?
it'll be too late in a year or three
when the darling baby boys
are full grown patriarchs
unless we interfere with
male conditioning
in some way
straight away

who will help me/us?

don't all rush at once

This came out of me a year after my elder boy had been away from home, at a progressive boarding school, and had begun to recover from the depression and hostility family life had created in him.

rescue for an eleven-year-old

i've saved my son from dying
by removing him from his
nuclear family nest:
will he thank me in years to come
or have i got it
all wrong?

will he ever know how much
he's come alive
blossomed forth
reached out
run free
into his own humanity?

will he ever heed
the obstacles i overcame
for his well being?
can he ever care enough
to peel away his maleness
and face me
as a woman?

This was composed after a conversation with my elder son when he was thirteen years old.

decision: future tense

my son talks to me of his new interest
reading
adventure/espionage/mystery/space fiction/war
stuff which little boys' and big boys' worlds
are made of
and where women have no place
though i don't tell him this yet
instead i watch him entering
faster and faster
this world (he can't wait till he's eighteen)
the man's world
which circumscribes/denigrates/exploits/obscures/omits
me
and i weep inside myself

i watch his agility his confidence his knowledge
expanding
and i wonder what we can share if anything
this boy and i
my first born
when our life styles interests desires
collide
and i weep inside myself

he's modelling himself on
daddy/uncle/headmaster/friends/cinema/TV/
his reading
and i know i stand small chance
(if i'm feeling optimistic)
and no chance at all
(if i'm not)
of countering that kulture
corroding those values
channelling that adolescent energy
replacing assumptions that only men
are inventive original memorable worthy
repairing the rifts that they create
between us

in a few years he'll be ready to read
my thoughts my feelings my politics
if he wants to
and if he does will he misconstrue pervert reject
my reality and me?
or attempt to understand accept believe
my reality and me?

the choice is his

if he cares

friends

how do i   will i   can i
be friends with
my still small sons
potential
actual
oppressors:
white
male
not christian
but jews too are patriarchal
having anticipated st paul
by a few thousand years

how will i cope
when these two boys
(how i wanted girls)
say
        you're only a woman
                mum

how will i not
                disown
                dismember
                destroy them?

can they become
ashamed of male power
                so i can love them?

(published in Spare Rib, *September 1980)*

golden boy

my little boy wants to be a man
and charm girls like his daddy does
still

and other men in films and books
who collect dominate conquer
women

my little boy hasn't done this
yet
but time's drawing near
when he'll want to be the lover
like any other
man

who hides his feelings his thoughts his hopes
from me from himself
who seeks out TV programs
where violence is commonplace
cowboys space travellers cops
and women hardly visible
who laughs at jokes on
ugly women spinsters mothers-in-law
who suddenly wants to read about anarchism
but doesn't link feminism
with the world of politics

yet his friends are girls
as well as boys
he shares some housework and shopping
with his brother
talks to other kids about
contraception pornography racism
went on an abortion march
hears what i say on
rape marriage battering

with future women in his life
will he believe they're lesser
necessary temptations
but really they don't matter?
or can he admire
able independent active women?
and will his sense of fair play
prevent him turning away
from them from me?

can i carry on
reaching out to him
again and again?
will other women do the same
with their sons and their friends' sons?
will my caring gestures words deeds
be enough soon enough
to ensure he'll want to be
more
than just another patriarch
with a heart
of gold?

to my sons

alas i fear
for my generation's men
it's too late
to relate
to feminism

maybe for my sons
there is still
a little time
if they're willing
to know the choices
open to them
between the world's values
and mine
in time
for my lifetime

common cause

six years past
when i was single again
i might've abandoned my sons
to their dad
and lived on my own again

six years on
i still think of what might've been
if my two had gone with their dad:
they'd now be halfway or more
towards the
competitive conforming insensitive materialist
non-questioning repressed unloving
little men
he could be proud of

six years back
i didn't i couldnt i wouldn't
hand over my kids
to any adult male:
i believed then
i believe now
it can be possible to have
two less oppressors
on the face of the earth

so i've hung in there
with my boys
despite apathy perplexity antipathy
from a few of my friends
uncertainty isolation upstream battling
for me

i often think
how much easier it would be
not to confront their dad their relatives their mates
not to challenge the values of an entire kulture
simply to say yes
to everything

but if other feminist mothers
could make common cause with me
what an impact we might make
shoulder to shoulder
on our sons with our daughters
on male power
within a generation

revolting kids

too soon
i have two teenage sons:
what can they rebel against
that has to do with me
my lifestyle my friends my feminist politics?
or have they been having their revolts
for the past many years
so that our future time together
may be
more relaxed more equal more supportive
all around?

they might even visit me at my flat
after they've moved out
on their own
or at the country cottage
i want to have some day
they might even settle in with me
for a while anyway
and talk about
their hopes their friends their work
their loves their woes their dad
each other
me

how soon will my kids
be my friends?
the sooner the better

References to Part Two

Achilles Heel Collective. Collective Editorial. *Achilles Heel,* 1. 1978.

Adams, Parveen. A Note on Sexual Division and Sexual Differences. *M/F,* 1979.

Adams, Parveen and Jeff Minson,. The Subject of Feminism. *M/F.* 2. 1978.

Alexander, Sally and Anna Davin. Feminist History (editorial). *History Workshop*, 1 (Spring). 1976.

Alexander, Sally, Davin, Anna and Even Hostettler. Labouring Women: A reply to Eric Hobsbawm. *History Workshop*, 8 (Autumn). 1979.

Alzon, Claude. *La Femme Potiche et la Femme Bonniche* (The Ornamental woman and the Useful Woman). Maspero, Paris.

Bauer, Carol and Lawrence Ritt (eds.) *Free and Ennobled: Source Readings in the development of Victorian Feminism.* Pergamon Press, Oxford. 1979.

de Beauvoir, Simone. *The Second Sex*. Penguin, Harmondsworth. 1974.

Beechey, Veronica. On Patriarchy. *Feminist Review*, 3. 1979.

Beechey, Veronica and Barbara Taylor. Women in the Labour Process. in *Papers on Patriarchy*, proceedings of the Patriarchy conference, London, 1976. Women's Publishing Collective, Brighton. 1978.

Branca, Patricia. *Silent Sisterhood: the Middle Class Woman in the Victorian Home.* Croom Helm, London, 1977.

Brownmiller, Susan. *Against Our Will. Men, Women and Rape.* Penguin, Harmondsworth. 1977.

Campaign for Homosexual Equality. *Introducing* CHE. CHE, Manchester. 1973.

Clements, Jan. Feminist's View of Anti-sexist Men. *Anti-sexist Men's Newsletter*, 9. 1980.

Cohen, Danny. 'Men Against Sexism' or 'Men's Liberation'. *Men Against Sexism National Conference*, 2nd Newsletter. 1978.

Conway, Jill. Stereotypes of Femininity in the Theory of Sexual Evolution. In Vicinus, Martha (ed.), *Suffer and Be Still: Women in the Victorian Age*. Methuen, London. 1980.

Coward, Ros, Lipshitz, Sue and Elizabeth Cowie. Psychoanalysis and Patriarchal Structures. In *Papers on Patriarchy,* op. cit. 1978.

Croll, Elizabeth. *Feminism and Socialism in CHina*. Routledge and Kegan Paul, London. 1978.

Dansky, Steven, Knoebel, John and Kenneth Pitchford. The Effeminist Manifesto. In Snodgrass, Jon (ed.), *A Book of Readings for Men Against Sexism*. Times Change Press, New York. 1977.

Davin, Anna. Women and History. In Wandor, Michelene (ed.), *The Body Politic: Women's Liberation in Britain, 1969-1972*. Stage One Press, London. 1972.

Davin, Anna. The London Feminist History Group. *History Workshop*, 9 (Spring). 1980.

Delamont, Sara and Lorna Duffin (eds.), *The Nineteenth Century Woman: Her Cultural and Physical World*. Croom Helm, London, 1978.

Delphy, Christine. Our Friends and Ourselves: the hidden foundations of various pseudo-feminist accounts. *Questions Feministes*, 1. 1977. Translated by Diana Leonard and Linnie Price.

Duffin, Laura. Prisoners of Progress: Women and Evolution. In Delamont, Sara and Lorna Duffin (eds.), op. cit. 1978.

Ehrlich, Carol. The Reluctant Patriarchs: a review of Men and Masculinity. In Snodgrass, Jon (ed.), op. cit. 1977.

Eisenstein, Zillah. *Capitalist Patriarchy and the Case for Socialist Feminism*. Monthly Review Press, London and New York. 1979.

Gay Liberation Front. *GLF Manifesto*. GLF, London. 1971.

Goldsbury, Mike. Notes about some Men Against Sexism/Patriarchy commitments. *Anti-Sexist Men's Newsletter*, 6. 1979a.

Goldbury, Mike. Huddersfield and other meetings. *Anti-Sexist Men's Newsletter*, 7. 1979b.

Grimstad, Kirsten and Susan Rennie. Men. In Snodgrass, Jon (ed.), op. cit. 1977.

Hollis, Patricia (ed.). *Women in Public, 1850-1900: Documents of the Victorian Women's Movement*. Allen and Unwin, London, 1979.

Hornacek, Paul Carlo. Anti-sexist Consciousness-raising Groups for Men. In Snodgrass, Jon (ed.), op. cit. 1977.

Huddersfield Commitments Group. Anti-sexist Commitments for Men, draft 3. *Anti-Sexist Men's Newsletter,* 9. 1980.

Jeffreys, Sheila. (forthcoming). Women's Campaigns against Male Sexuality in the Nineteenth and early Twentieth Century (provisional title). *Women's Studies International Forum,* 5 (5). 1982.

Kamm, Josephine. *Rapiers and Battleaxes: The Women's Movement and its Aftermath.* Allen and Unwin, London. 1966.

Lamm, Bob. Men's Movement hype. In Snodgrass, Jon (ed.) op. cit. 1977.

Leon, Barbara. Separate to Integrate. In Redstockings, *Feminist Revolution*. Random House, New York. 1978.

Letter. *Anti-Sexist Men's Newsletter*, 4. 1979.

Liddington, Jill. Rediscovering Suffrage History. *History Workshop*, 4 (Autumn). 1977.

Liddington, Jill and Jill Norris. *One Hand Tied Behind Us: the rise of the Women's Suffrage Movement*. Virago, London. 1978.

Mainardi, Pat. The Politics of Housework. In Morgan, Robin (ed.), *Sisterhood is Powerful*. Vintage Books (Random House), New York.

Margolis, Karen. The Long and Winding Roads (reflections on Beyond the Fragments). *Feminist Review*, 5. 1980.

Martin, D. If that's all there is. *Motive*, 32: 45-46, California. 1972.

Marquis, D. *Archy and Mehitabel*. Faber and Faber, London. 1958.

Men Against Sexism. *National Conference*. 2nd Newsletter. 1978.

Morgan, Robin. *Lady of the Beasts*. Random House, New York. 1976.

Morrison, Paul. *Pregnant Fatherhood*. Men's Free Press, London. 1977.

Morrison, Paul. Letter. *Anti-Sexist Men's Newsletter*, 5. 1979.

Motherson, Keith. Devolving our power. *Anti-Sexist Men's Newsletter*, 5. 1979.

Oegst Geest Papers. *International Conference on Women in Mixed Gay Organisations*. COC, Holland. 1975.

Onlywomen Press (eds.) *Love Your Enemy. The debate between heterosexual feminism and Political Lesbianism*. Onlywomen Press, London. 1981.

Pankhurst, Christabel. *The Great Scourge and How to End it. Women's Press, London. (Available from the Fawcett Library, London). 1913.*

Pankhurst, Emmeline. *My Own Story*. Virago, London. 1979. First published in 1914 by Eveleigh Nash, London.

Pankhurst, Sylvia. *The Suffragette Movement: an intimate account of persons and ideals*. Virago, London. 1977. First published in 1931 by Longman, London.

Peterson, Jeanne, M. The Victorian Governess; Status Incongruence in Family and Society. In Vicinus, Martha (ed.), op.cit. 1980.

Pickering, Bobby. Feelings Gay. *Anti-Sexist Men's Newsletter*, 9. 1980.

Pinchbeck, Ivy. *Women Workers and the Industrial Revolution*, 1750-1850. Virago, London. 1981. First published in 1930 by Frank Cass, London.

Pleck, Joseph and Jack, Sawyer (eds.). *Men and Masculinity*. Prentice Hall, Englewood Cliffs, New Jersey. 1974.

Raeburn, Antonia. *The Militant Suffragettes*. New English Library, London. 1974.

Ramelson, Marion. *The Petticoat Rebellion: A Century of Struggle for Women's Rights*. Lawrence and Wishart, London. 1976.

Redstockings. *Feminist Revolution*. Random House, New York. 1978.

Rich, Adrienne. *Of Woman Born. Motherhood as Experience and Institution*. Virago, London. 1977.

Rover, Constance. *Women's Suffrage and Party Politics in Britain, 1866-1914*. Routledge and Kegan Paul, London. 1967.

Rowbotham, Sheila. *Woman's Consciousness, Man's World*. Penguin, Harmondsworth. 1973.

Rowbotham, Sheila. *Hidden From History. Three hundred years of women's oppression and the fight against it*. Pluto Press, London. 1981 (1974).

Rowbotham, Sheila, Segal, Lynn and Hilary Wainwright. *Beyond the Fragments: Feminism and the Making of Socialism*. Merlin Press, London. 1980.

Sarah, Elizabeth. Reclaiming Christabel Pankhurst. In Spender, Dale (ed.) *Feminist Theorists*. The Women's Press, London. 1982 (forthcoming).

Schein, Leonard. Dangers with Men's Consciousness-raising Groups. In Snodgrass, Jon (ed.) op.cit. 1977.

Scott, Alan. Letter. *Anti-Sexist Men's Newsletter*, 9. 1980.

Scott, Hilda. *Women and Socialism: Experiences from Eastern Europe*. Alison and Busby, London. 1976.

Shiers, J. Two steps forward, one step back. *Gay Left*, 6: 10-13. 1978.

Shiers, J. Gay male sexism – confronting the gay scene in our heads. *Manchunian Gay*, 7: 4-5. 1979.

Sigsworth, E.M. and T.J. Wyke. A Study of Victorian Prostitution and Venereal Disease. In Vicinus, Martha (ed.) op.cit. 1980.

Smith, Chris. Letter. *Anti-Sexist Men's Newsletter*, 9. 1980.

Snodgrass, Jon (ed.) *A Book of Readings for Men Against Sexism*. Times Change Press, New York. 1977.

Spender, Dale (ed.) *Feminist Theorists*. The Women's Press, London. 1982 (forthcoming).

Stanley, Liz. Obscene telephone calls. *BSA Sexuality Study Group* paper. 1976a.

Stanley, Liz. On the receiving end. *Out*, 1: 6-7. 1976b.

Stanley, Liz and Sue Wise. Feminist research, feminist consciousness and experiences of sexism. *Women's Studies International Quarterly*, 2 (3): 359-374. 1979.

Stanley, Liz and Sue Wise. *Breaking out: Feminist Research and Feminist Consciousness*. 1982 (forthcoming).

Strachey, Ray. *The Cause: A Short History of the women's Movement in Britain*. Virago, London. 1979. First published in 1928 by Bell and Sons, London.

Vicinus, Martha (ed.) *Suffer and Be Still: Women in the Victorian Age*. Methuen, London. 1980.

Weeks, Jeffrey. *Coming Out: Homosexual Politics in Britain*. Quartet, London. 1977a.

Weeks, Jeffrey. Come all you gay women, come all you gay men. *Gay Left*, 4. 1977b.

Wilson, Elizabeth. Beyond the Ghetto: thoughts on 'Beyond the Fragments: Feminism and the Making of Socialism' by Hilary Wainwright, Sheila Rowbotham and Lynn Segal. *Feminist Review*, 4. 1980.

Contributors' Notes

Astra entered the women's liberation movement in 1971, since when her lifestyle and politics have irrevocably altered. In 1972 she joined the Women's Literature Collective, where she began taking herself seriously as a poet, and is currently working on a collection of poems about her mother. She has published two collections of her own poems to date: *Fighting Words* (1978) and *Battle Cries* (1981).

Jan Bradshaw is a lesbian feminist mother of a three-and-a-half-year old hyperactive male child. She works for the Women's Research and Resources Centre and has guest-edited a recent special issue of *Women's Studies International Quarterly* on 'The Women's Liberation Movement – Europe and North America' (Winter 1981). She is a dilettante writer, needleworker and piano player when she gets the chance.

Betsy Ettore was born in the USA and came to London in 1971. She has written a variety of articles on lesbianism, and a book, *Lesbians, Women and Society* (1980). Currently she has an interest in feminist mythology and lesbian relationships. This interest has evolved from a critical lesbian feminist reading of Jung's *Collected Works* over the past two years. Her article in this collection represents the very beginning of this interest.

Annabel Faraday worked with a project on male sexual variations at the University of Essex, where she was employed as a research officer. Her investigations and her participation in organising Reclaim-the-Night activities caused her to look more closely at pornography and its effects upon women. More recently she has been researching into 'lesbian identity in the 1920s and 1930s'.

Scarlet Friedman's involvement in women's self-help health groups provided the impetus for her research into 'Women, sexuality and contraception'. Her concern with the inadequacies of existing social explanations of women and sexuality, and the need further to develop feminist theory, led to her theoretical explorations and her participation in organising the WRRC Feminist Summer School.

Hilary Graham is currently a lecturer in Social Policy at the University of Bradford. The empirical work described in her paper on 'Coping' was carried out when she was a Research Fellow at the University of York, working with Lorna McKee. Her main research interest is in the impact of sexual divisions on the health, and health-care roles, of women.

Angela Hamblin has been a member of the women's liberation movement since 1971. She has written articles for *Women's Liberation Review*, *Shrew*, and *Spare Rib*, and her work has appeared in three feminist anthologies. She is a former member of the London Rape Crisis Centre Collective and a current member of a Feminist Theory Group and a Fiction-Writing Group.

Tina Hill has been active in Women's Aid for seven years, working with both women and children who have experienced male violence. Her analysis is based on this experience and a research project she conducted with 146 battered women. She has an M Sc in Social Psychology from the London School of Economics.

Stevi Jackson lives in Cardiff and teaches at the Polytechnic of Wales. She has done research on adolescent girls' views of their own sexuality, and is the author of *Childhood and Sexuality* (Blackwell, 1982). She is active in Cardiff Women's Centre and South Wales Rape Crisis Centre.

Sheila Jeffreys is a revolutionary feminist involved in Women Against Violence Against Women and has been active for several years in the campaign against male violence. She is currently engaged in research on 'Feminism, sexuality and sex reform, 1880-1930'.

Diana Leonard is a feminist sociologist who lives in London with her three children and some friends. She is a member of the WRRC Publications Collective, and is also currently involved in the planning of a Women's Studies course at the Open University (to be launched 1983) and in co-writing a book with Christine Delphy.

Jill Lewis is co-author of *Common Differences: Conflicts in Black and White Feminist Perspectives* (Doubleday, 1981). She holds a marxist feminist position in Humanist and Arts at Hampshire College, Amherst, USA, where she lectures each spring. The rest of the year she lives in Brighton, working on research on Paul Eluard, French surrealist and communist writer, and on a book on feminism and reproduction. Her son Jake is three years old.

London Rape Crisis Centre Group: Started off as a group of women who were angry about sexual harassment and rape. 'We talked a lot about things that had happened to us and to other women, and this paper came out of these conversations.'

Sandra McNeill is a member of a Leeds revolutionary feminist group and Leeds Women Against Violence Against Women.

Kathy Overfield's interest in science and scientific thought led her into the Brighton Women and Science Group in 1977, and thence to co-edit *Alice Through the Microscope: The Power of Science Over Women's Lives* (Virago,

1980). She lives in rural Wales, helps bring up children, and is researching into post-natal depression.

Elizabeth Sarah is a Jewish Lesbian feminist keen to reclaim all forms of creative activity as women's domain – including the intellectual. Currently her feminist commitments include: living with her lover; participating in a Jewish-lesbian consciousness-raising group and in the WRRC Publications Collective; doing a Ph D on the politics of the early feminist movement in England; and editing a feminist journal (*Women's Studies International Forum*) with some women friends.

Amanda Sebestyen has had a long involvement with the women's liberation movement and was a member of the *Spare Rib* Collective from November 1977 to December 1980.

Liz Stanley is a lesbian feminist who lives in Manchester and is just about to become 'an older woman' (hoping that when she does, sophistication, charm and poise will at last be hers!) At the moment she is pursuing the problem of men with research into the Yorkshire Ripper, and has a book in press with Virago on the diary of a working-class servant called Hannah Chadwick.

Jo Sutton was the first national co-ordinator of the Women's Aid Federations and worked alongside battered women for eight years, maintaining the position that women should work closely with other women in the movement against male violence. She is currently employed in Applied Social Studies at the University of Bradford, where she is teaching and researching into child abuse. She is also engaged in writing a book on feminism and social work.